RING OUT FREEDOM!

RING OUT FREEDOM!

THE VOICE OF
MARTIN LUTHER KING, JR.
AND THE MAKING
OF THE CIVIL RIGHTS
MOVEMENT

FREDRIK SUNNEMARK

Indiana University Press
BLOOMINGTON AND INDIANAPOLIS

Publication of this book is made possible in part with the assistance of a Challenge Grant from the National Endowment for the Humanities, a federal agency that supports research, education, and public programming in the humanities.

This book is a publication of

Indiana University Press
601 North Morton Street
Bloomington, IN 47404-3797 USA

http://iupress.indiana.edu

Telephone orders   800-842-6796
Fax orders   812-855-7931
Orders by e-mail   iuporder@indiana.edu

Manufactured in the United States of America

Library of Congress Cataloging-in-Publication Data

Sunnemark, Fredrik.
   Ring out freedom! : the voice of Martin Luther King, Jr. and the making of the civil rights movement / Fredrik Sunnemark.
      p. cm.
   Includes bibliographical references and index.
   ISBN 0-253-34376-3 (cloth : alk. paper)—ISBN 0-253-21659-1 (pbk. : alk. paper)
   1. King, Martin Luther, Jr., 1929–1968—Language. 2. King, Martin Luther, Jr., 1929–1968—Oratory. 3. King, Martin Luther, Jr., 1929–1968—Political and social views. 4. Rhetoric—Political aspects—United States—History—20th century. 5. English language—Discourse analysis. 6. English language—United States—Rhetoric. 7. Speeches, addresses, etc., American—History and criticism. 8. Civil rights movements—United States—History—20th century. 9. African Americans—Civil rights—United States—History—20th century. I. Title.
   E185.97.K5S866 2004
   323'.092—dc21   2003012813

1 2 3 4 5 09 08 07 06 05 04

To Ludvig and Viktor

Contents

Acknowledgments

This work would never have been completed without help and support from many individuals and institutions. For reading drafts of different parts of the manuscript at different stages of the process and forcing me to sharpen my arguments and pointing me in directions that proved to be creative, I would like to thank Eva-Lena Dahl, Bryan Errington, Klas Grinell, Maria Johansen, Johan Kärnfelt (whose computer wizardry also has been greatly appreciated), Kaj Johansson, Sven-Eric Liedman, Mikela Lundahl, Daniel Nordin, Ingemar Nilsson, Lennart Olausson and Amanda Peralta at Gothenburg University; Magnus Berg and Martin Åberg at University Trollhättan-Uddevalla; Mattias Gardell at Stockholm University; Keith D. Miller at Arizona State University; Richard H. King at Nottingham University; and Kate Babbitt and Robert J. Sloan at Indiana University Press.

For helping a bewildered Swedish researcher I would like to thank Diane Ware and the other staff at the King Library and Archives at the Martin Luther King, Jr. Center for Nonviolent Social Change in Atlanta and John H. Noël at Special Collections, Mugar Library, Boston University.

For financial aid I would like to thank Adlerbertska forskningsfonden, Jubileumsfonden, Paul och Marie Berghaus fond, Stiftelsen Anna Ahrenbergs fond för vetenskapliga mf.l. ändamål, Wilhelm och Martina Lundgrens vetenskapsfond, Överskottsfonden, and the Department of Work, Economics and Health at University Trollhättan-Uddevalla.

finally, my deepest sense of gratitude goes to my family. To my mother, Ann-Christin, my father, Per, and my brother,

Johan, who have given me everything a son and a brother can ask for and much more; to my wife, Petra, whose love and support have made this project possible; and above all to our two children, Ludvig and Viktor, to whom this book is dedicated. You make life beautiful.

FREDRIK SUNNEMARK
Lidköping, Sweden, February 2003

RING OUT
FREEDOM!

INTRODUCTION: "THERE MUST BE SOMEBODY TO COMMUNICATE . . ."

Between Cultures

The name Martin Luther King, Jr. (1929–1968) is recognized around the world. Many millions have heard his baritone voice cry out "Let freedom ring from Stone Mountain of Georgia. Let freedom ring from Lookout Mountain of Tennessee. Let freedom ring from every hill and every molehill of Mississippi. From every mountainside, let freedom ring" in his "I Have a Dream" speech.[1] This voice, in its many different aspects and in the widest possible sense, is what this book is about.

The period 1955 to 1968 has been called "the King years" of American history.[2] From the Montgomery bus boycott to the garbage workers' strike in Memphis, King and his words occupied a central place in American society and awareness during these years. This public figure and his position(s) are my focus, since I believe that they illuminate a set of specific and interrelated problems that have yet not been fully investigated. How is his rhetoric constructed? What meanings are embedded in this construction? In which ways are these meanings related to the creation of a certain understanding of the struggle and ultimately the world, in short that which can be called the civil rights movement discourse? And finally, what happens to the ideas embedded in King's rhetoric when they are uttered? What ideological meaning do they come to have in and due to the contemporary situation?

We all know King the brilliant orator and activist who preached nonviolence, who willingly (albeit filled with anxiety) went to jail, and who, until at least 1965–1966, had the rhetorical ability to make America listen, to take note of a problem, to understand that something was happening and that something needed to happen. I want to arrive at a deeper and new understanding of this rhetoric. King was a part of and in certain ways also a product of several historical traditions, the specific historical contexts of the 1950s and 1960s in the United States and the international climate of those decades. His relationship to those contexts is essential to our understanding of him. As one of his associates said, "The movement made Martin rather than Martin making the movement."[3]

Obviously, there is a relationship between these contexts and the rhetoric King produced in both spoken and written forms—in sermons; in books; and in speeches at movement mass meetings in Montgomery, Birmingham, Selma, and Chicago; before labor unions; at fund-raising events, to the whole nation, and—ultimately—to the whole world. This rhetoric, this voice, was a focal point of the civil rights movement and it deserves attention both in and of itself and in social and historical context.

In this study, I survey King's rhetoric from a different angle than many other studies do. I am not primarily focused on discovering its building blocks or on constructing a fully rational and coherent political or, as some have tried to do, philosophical project from these words. Instead, I view King's rhetoric as a whole both in itself and from the outset.

I will argue that King created a specific civil rights movement discourse through a process in which he named and ordered the world, the civil rights struggle, and the "us" inside particular frames. In a sense, we can view King's rhetoric as a painting, a work of art. The frame around the painting both demarcates the area of the painting and is part of what determines its meaning. If you change the frame, something also happens to the way you view the objects on the canvas. King used politics, religion, science, psychology, and history to frame the images he drew on the canvas of his civil rights rhetoric. Each time he changed the frame, we are able to see those images in a new way. Through this framing discourse, he created layers of meaning. He established an understanding of the civil rights movement that is discursively situated within a context of particular rules of speaking, thinking, and acting. I will argue that this has *ideological* effects; it is not a process that is an end unto itself but one that has several meanings in and for the society within which it is created. This means that I will analyze King's rhetoric *as it is expressed* and as *creating meaning* through its *effectuation* in a social and political situation. What happens when the rhetorical messages are expressed? What meaning do they come to constitute in themselves? And what functions do they come to fulfill when they are expressed in the contemporary context? Through these questions one is able to not only find how King's rhetoric names and orders the world but also to understand how this naming process is ideological; how its definitions of humanity, society, history and so on consciously or unconsciously comes to serve particular political interests.

In a specific way, King positioned himself between different cultures; not only between white and African-American cultures but also between political, social, religious, and academic cultures; between African-American religion and white Protestantism; between faith and theology; between middle classes, working classes, and underclasses; between the South and the North; between the spoken and written word; between the pulpit and the picket line, and so on.[4] King's rhetorical project and the discursive process it forms was one in which he tried to synthesize these many contexts, to bring traditions together and, in certain instances, combine them, to be able both to speak different languages in different situations and to *create one language*, a single and whole discourse. Since this process was situated in a specific historical and political context, it was also always interacting with this context, an interaction that is creative in the sense that it creates meanings and relations that can be called ideological.

I will analyze the rhetoric of the public figure Martin Luther King, Jr. to see how this position between cultures and traditions was constructed, to see how his civil rights movement discourse was constructed, and to see what ideological effects it has had. What does a process that aims to reach "all" groups in American society include? There is a duality here: At the same time as King acted in the space between cultures and traditions, he strove to make this border area as general and common as possible so that as many as possible could hear him. He always tried to make one from many, and he was involved in a continual process of communication which he attempted to control in order to keep the discourse intact.

Even if King did not speak of his rhetorical project in these terms, he was acutely aware of this set of problems. In the public turmoil that followed the many controversies around the slogan "Black Power" in 1966, King once said: "You just can't communicate with the ghetto dweller and at the same time not frighten many whites to death. I don't know what the answer to that is. My role perhaps is to interpret to the white world. There must be somebody to communicate to two worlds."[5] I would add between many worlds, cultures, traditions, and even individual lives. Even though this statement must be understood in its specific context—the internal conflict within the movement and the white backlash of the late 1960s—King put his finger on a general problem that was present throughout his public career. King not only had to interpret the black world to the white world; the opposite was also true. This was more than a need for someone to communicate to two worlds; there was a need for someone to create particular frames for a process of communication inside which individuals from many different worlds could find room for and be involved in an ongoing exchange of meanings. But how is this possible; how does it takes place and what are the consequences?

The Material

King published four books during his lifetime: *Stride toward Freedom: The Montgomery Story* (1958), which narrates the circumstances and events of the bus boycott; the collection of sermons called *Strength to Love* (1963); *Why We Can't Wait* (1964), which is mainly concerned with the Birmingham campaign, and *Where Do We Go from Here: Chaos or Community?* (1967), which discusses the Chicago campaign, the emergence of Black Power, and the situation after the legislative changes in the mid-1960s. *The Trumpet of Conscience* (1968), a collection of later speeches and a sermon that was originally broadcast over the Canadian Broadcasting Corporation in November and December 1967, was published posthumously.[6] The bulk of the King material consists of his many speeches and sermons. Two large collections have been published: *A Testament of Hope: The Essential Writings and Speeches of Martin Luther King, Jr.*, which includes speeches, articles, parts of books and interviews; and *I Have a Dream: Writings and Speeches That Changed the World*, both edited by James Melvin Washington.[7] A Herculean effort is also being undertaken by The Martin Luther King Papers Project based at Stanford University, led by Clayborne Carson. At the time of writing, four of the planned fourteen volumes have been published (the fourth volume ends in December 1958); they include school and university papers, letters and internal memos, and many previously unpublished speeches and sermons.[8] The project has also published a collection of (with one exception) previously unpublished sermons, *A Knock at Midnight: Inspiration from the Great Sermons of Reverend Martin Luther King, Jr.*, and a collection of King's most famous speeches, *A Call to Conscience: The Landmark Speeches of Dr. Martin Luther King, Jr.*[9]

But, despite these collections, there is still much unpublished material in both The Martin Luther King, Jr. Papers at Boston University and The Martin Luther King, Jr. Papers at King Library and Archives in Atlanta, Georgia. I have conducted research at both archives, and some of the material used in this study can still be found only in those archives.[10]

There are generally two ways of viewing the King material. On the one side stand those who argue that to understand King you have to, to a large extent, disregard his published material because it was ghostwritten in parts and the content was frequently adapted for a northern white liberal audience. Instead, they claim, it is in the unpublished material that you can find the "real" King, in the sermons held before the Dexter Avenue Baptist Church and Ebenezer Baptist Church congregations and in the speeches at mass meetings. On the other side stand those who argue that there is no fundamental difference between King's published and unpublished material; the same thoughts and arguments are expressed, many identical and similar wordings and metaphors are employed, and there are no major contradictions in the two bodies of work.[11]

I find myself somewhere between the two sides in this debate because I believe that there is truth in both assertions. Parts of some of King's books were ghostwritten, as were several articles, and many speeches in fund-raising contexts were specifically pitched to a liberal white audience. When studying him biographically—both historically and intellectually—the largely unpublished sermons and speeches therefore provide a better base from which to understand his rhetoric than the published books and articles. But at the same time, I too have trouble finding exact dividing lines, ideological differences, and essential contradictions between the two types of material. The books do not contain anything that would have been impossible for King to say at a mass meeting, and the unpublished sermons do not contain chunks of beliefs and argumentation that he systematically refrained from using before northern white audiences. But there are often differences in tone, minor differences in choices of words, and different positions in regard to the fundamental problem of racial discrimination. These differences are a focus of this study.

This also means that I position myself and the Martin Luther King, Jr. of my study outside this controversy. I will analyze King's rhetoric as it manifested itself in his public messages between 1955 and 1968—in his books and articles as well as in his speeches and sermons. My object is not to find the "real" or "true" King that hides behind or inside these messages; my object is the King that is manifested *through* them. The "Martin Luther King, Jr." of my study is the public persona King projects with his words.

All messages, published or unpublished, ghostwritten or not, written or spoken, plagiarized or original, de facto represented King as a (or *the*) leader of the civil rights movement. I argue that it is this King, manifested in his rhetoric, who creates a specific discourse that has particular ideological effects. Instead of beginning with the attempt to find the "real" King, instead of trying to distinguish between what material can be said to convey his "real" beliefs and "real" voice and what material can be said to be unrepresentative, hollow, and of lesser or no importance, I will use the whole body of work as a starting point in itself and instead point out the different functions of different aspects of his rhetoric. If you ignore large parts of the King material with the thought that "that is not the real Martin," you also ignore the possibility of seeing, understanding, and analyzing its potential meaning and functions. At the same time, if you categorically state that all the King material is a coherent unity and downplay or even ignore the different shadings that do exist, you will miss the opportunity to find the aspects of these shadings that have significance.

The Martin Luther King, Jr. of my study is that persona which is manifested in the (ghost)written books and articles, the sermons preached in the churches of Montgomery and Atlanta and many other places, and speeches delivered in many different contexts all over the United States. That is the Martin Luther King, Jr. who was active in the American public arena between 1955 and 1968.

Another controversy regarding the King material concerns the location of the roots of his ideas and rhetoric. Once again two general tendencies can be found. On the one side stand the older works on King with their focus on the theology and philosophy he encountered in graduate school and their attempts to understand his ideas within these realms. On the other side stands the newer trend of emphasizing his African-American heritage and arguing that any real understanding of King must involve a kind of bypassing of his own references to a white theological and philosophical tradition and look beneath certain phrases to see a worldview that clearly and fundamentally evolved from the black church.

In the older works, to be able to understand King in depth you had to be familiar with the major twentieth-century American and European theological and philosophical positions and debates. To understand King was to present him in terms of this debate and outline his thought in the language he himself used when he discussed his theoretical background.[12]

In the newer works, to be able to understand King, you must begin in the African-American tradition and in the black church. This will lead you to see that the philosophical and theological standpoints King often confessed to were not due to knowledge and insights brought to him from the outside during his education. If you scratch the surface you will, for example, discover that the "personalistic" God King spoke of in "white" theological terms was the same God that he had heard and met in his father's sermon's throughout his childhood.[13]

Generally, my position is compatible with the latter view. Faced with the question of where King's central faith, ideas, and central values ultimately stemmed from, I would stress the black tradition as the necessary foundation for both his thinking and speaking. King was a Baptist preacher, he was the son of a Baptist preacher, he was brought up in the segregated South, and the black church was the central institution not just during his childhood and adolescence but throughout the whole of his life. To that extent, he was a product of southern African-American culture, and this was bound to be reflected in everything he did up until that day when the shots rang out over Memphis.

Having that said, how then can one explain the frequent use of academic philosophy and theology, for example, in his writings, speeches, and sermons? As I will argue, this practice has distinctive discursive and ideological meanings that are fundamental in King's rhetoric and it had effects that cannot be neglected when we try to understand his ability to communicate in the American 1950s and 1960s. In my study I will not try to

separate a "real" content in King's thinking, writing, and speaking from the form in which he presents it. It is rather the in-
triguing surface in itself that is the actual object of this study.
This represents a new way of approaching a material that has
been most often approached with the purpose of finding its
essence.

Disposition

The five chapters of this book are both interconnected steps
in the analysis of King's civil rights movement discourse as a
whole and attempts to individually address specific areas within
this discourse creation. Different aspects of the King material
will be highlighted in different chapters, but the purpose of
analyzing the discourse as an interacting whole is a recurring
theme.

This organizational structure corresponds to the way that
King's practice of signification[14] is constructed and structured
through different levels of determination: The first chapter is
primarily concerned with problems related to the presence and
functions of religion and religious determination in King's
rhetoric and what I call the religious level in the civil rights
movement discourse, the three following chapters deals with different instances of what I call the idealistic level of the discourse,
while the fifth and last chapter analyzes this discourse structure
as a whole in relationship to King's gradual radicalization.

The chapter "A Discourse of Faith" is the longest in the study
and serves as a ground for the further analyses that follow.
Here I outline the basic structure and different levels of the
discourse. I present and discuss the function of religious faith
and more specifically Christianity in the discourse through an
analysis of the concepts of God and Jesus as nodal points. I also
closely examine the position and meaning of the church as the
central institution of faith. Finally, I discuss the direct relationship between religion and ideology in the civil rights movement discourse through an analysis of King's term "the beloved community." It is in this chapter that I outline the basic

framework of the discourse. The themes discussed in the following chapters take place within this structure because they are inextricably bound to and limited by the centrality of religion in a dialectical relationship of meaning.

The chapter "Western Intellectualism and American Ideals" deals with King's use of allusions. He regularly used many philosophers, theologians, and authors as well as the American political tradition in his writings, speeches, and sermons, and I discuss in what ways this technique has specific meanings and the part it plays in the formation of a civil rights movement discourse. I also examine the question of whether this technique is an ideological practice.

The chapter "The Problem of Race" is concerned with finding the specific and different meanings of "us" and "we" in King's public messages and his use and understanding of the concept of "race." I describe the different ways the notion of "the Negro" is used and situated in King's rhetoric and the discursive functions this use has.

The chapter "Third World, Cold War, and Vietnam" discusses the recurring appearance of international situations in King's rhetoric. I argue that this can be a key to understanding how King's discourse is constructed and that it also illuminates our understanding of how such situations are related to different ideological positions and circumstances.

The last chapter, "Radicalization," has a slightly different aim. Unlike the three preceding chapters, it is not primarily focused on a specific theme in King's rhetoric, but is concerned with the differences between King's "early" and "late" rhetoric. I discuss how and why King's rhetoric changed during the years. The chapter also summarizes and develops several of the themes presented earlier.

1. A Discourse of Faith

When he was doing research for his study *Martin Luther King, Jr.: The Making of a Mind,* John Ansbro asked Wyatt Tee Walker, chief of staff of the Southern Christian Leadership Conference (SCLC) during several of the movement years, which writings most influenced King. Walker simply answered "Matthew, Mark, Luke and John." Walker added that "[t]he basis of Martin Luther King's ministry and mission was the ethics and morality of the Crucified Carpenter from Galilee. . . . [F]irst and foremost he was an unapologetic proclaimer of the Gospel of Jesus of Nazareth."[1] These statements illustrate the centrality of religion in the activities of King.

But this centrality also provokes questions as much as it provides answers and it merits a careful examination if one wants to understand how King's rhetoric works. The basic influence of the gospel and the ultimate grounding in Jesus Christ cannot be viewed alone. King's faith was part of a public and societal struggle that had many different dimensions, and his rendition and "use" of his faith must be viewed within the realms that this context constitutes.

This first chapter is therefore concerned with this the most fundamental element of King's rhetoric: How does he use religion and faith to signify, define, and understand? What are the consequences of using religion and faith in this way? How is his use of his religious faith related to the movement's self-understanding and place on the American political scene and to King's position between cultures?

For these questions to be answered, the basic structure of the civil rights movement discourse as a whole must be analyzed and its fundamental workings must be mapped out.

The Structure of the Discourse

The classic dichotomy of *idealism* and *materialism* is a fruitful tool with which to explore King's religious rhetoric. *Idealism* can be defined as the notion that reality is ultimately constituted by ideas, thoughts, and knowledge and that any change or progress in this world ultimately depends on these factors. *Materialism* can be defined as the notion that reality is ultimately constituted by the practical activities of man[2] and that any change or progress in this world is finally dependent on material factors.[3]

These notions can help to formulate a question that make visible the construction of King's discourse of faith: In what ways does King let idealistic values determine his description of practical reality and what position does that practical reality—or materialism—have in relation to these values by which it is described? The question becomes even more helpful if the qualifications of the notions are enlarged with the caveat that it is meaningless to speak of objects or facts as existing independent from the concepts and terms by which we describe them, but it is also at least as problematic to, as idealism does, view these concepts and terms as reality in themselves. The dichotomy between idealism and materialism as here defined points to a deep ambiguity in King's rhetoric, but the caveats can help us to understand how this ambiguity in itself is creative.

To further understand this ambiguity, let us turn to King's speech "The Church on the Frontier of Racial Tension," given before the Southern Baptist Theological Seminary in Louisville, Kentucky, in April 1961. The speech is both thematically and rhetorically quite typical of King's public speaking before this type of audience.[4] Its main theme is the place of the civil rights movement in relation to the responsibilities of the church, and its goal is to challenge the audience to realize that the church is and must be the central institution of the struggle. The criticism the speech offers is aimed mainly at the passive attitude still persisting within some quarters and the failure of some to realize the important part the church has to play as a vehicle for political and social change.

After an initial mention of how the civil rights movement is a part of a worldwide uprising against oppression in the forms of imperialism, colonialism, and segregation and how the world stands on the threshold of something "new," King presents a historical survey explaining why the American civil rights movement was born at its particular point in time and what this moment consists of and will lead to. It is this explanation that provides an entry into the questions of this chapter.

At one point King states that

> living with the conditions of slavery and later segregation, many Negroes lost faith in themselves, many came to feel that perhaps they were less than human, perhaps they were inferior. But then something happened to the Negro. Circumstances made it necessary for him to travel more: the coming of the automobile, the upheaval of two world wars, the great depression. And so his rural plantation life background gave way to urban industrial life, his economic life was gradually rising through the growth of industry and the influence of organized labor and other agencies, and even his cultural life was rising through the steady decline of crippling illiteracy. All of these forces conjoined to cause the Negro to take a new look at himself.[5]

The history behind the civil rights movement is thus explained in *materialistic* terms. But when King turns to the contemporary struggle, his definition of how change comes about is different. He then turns to the wisdom of the academic world:

> Professor Sorokin of Harvard University wrote a book some years ago entitled *The Crisis of Our Age*, and his basic thesis was that a crisis develops in a society when an old idea exhausts itself and society seeks to reorientate itself around a new idea. This is what we see today, the old idea of paternalism, the old idea that [sic] segregation has exhausted itself; and American society is seeking to reorientate itself around the new idea of integration, of person to person relations. This is something of the crisis we see.[6]

Here it is the death of an old and the birth of a new *idea* that stands at the center of change, an idea that will create and develop the new society. But it will not come to life on its own. Its birth involves a struggle, and when, in the speech, we reach this struggle and the future it will bring about, King adds yet another dimension. He says:

> [L]et me say that we must have faith in the future, the faith to believe that we can solve this problem, the faith to believe that as we struggle to solve this problem we do not struggle alone. But we have cosmic companionship. Oh, before the victory is won, some people may have to get scarred up. . . . Who will be part of that creative minority that will stand firm on an issue will help us bring into being the Kingdom of God, knowing that in the process, God struggles with us. The God that we worship is not some Aristotelian Unmoved Mover who merely contemplates upon himself. The God that we worship is not merely a self-knowing God, but he is an ever-loving God, working through history for the salvation of man. So with this faith we can move on.[7]

There is no denying that King's worldview is at base idealistic. Ultimately the universe is moral; it is created and upheld by the almighty God. This basic assumption is always present in his sermons, speeches, and writings. But how should we then regard his often-recurring materialistic explanations, of which the above is one of many examples? The contradiction is perhaps not too bewildering. Any ideology contains contradictions of different kinds, as does any thought and speech of a human being; who goes through life without contradicting him or herself? That both idealistic and materialistic explanations can be found in King's rhetoric does not mean that they hold an equal position or that they create meaning at the same level. It is exactly this point that provides a way into the structure of King's civil rights movement discourse.

If we formalize the three passages above we see the past as materialistic, the present as idealistic, and the future as religious. These three philosophies represent different layers of King's civil rights discourse; they form a hierarchy that orders his system of belief. King's rhetoric orders and understands the world through this hierarchy of values.

In the first quote, King states that the Negro's changing self-evaluation had its main origins in the changing historical and material realities of the first half of the twentieth century. In the second quote, he continues the story by stating that this led to a struggle between two systems of ideas. His story ends in the third quote with the guarantee that this struggle will be won since the universe is upheld by an active God. This is a typical example of what may be called an actualization of a religious superstructure through a *ladder of signification,* a central feature of the civil rights movement discourse as a discourse of faith. The signification structure of the discourse has three different levels: the religious, the idealistic, and the materialistic. Each of these three modes of explanation is used in King's rhetoric. But these three modes of explanation are also interconnected, and they are interconnected according to a certain order. In this sense, they can be understood as three rungs on a ladder, connected with each other by the sidepieces of the ladder. This order means that the modes of explanation have different definitional powers. The religious mode is the most powerful and therefore the highest rung of the ladder. It is there that the ultimate definition is always anchored. Thereafter come the idealistic mode, and lastly the materialistic. But, and this is what is central to the functioning of the discourse, since the modes are interconnected in the form of a ladder, the power of the ultimate definition also becomes a part of the other modes, which means that materialistic explanations become vested with the authority of God and his universe of idealism.

In this speech, King wants to describe the background of the civil rights movement, its current struggle, and the consequences of its coming victory. In that sense, the speech is highly representative of King's project in general. In these three segments he explains the "whats," the "whys," and the "hows" of what he is doing and aiming for; these general positions are present throughout his entire public career.[8] But there are still some interesting discrepancies to note that highlight the differences between materialism, idealism, and religious idealism: The material and historical explanation of how the civil rights movement came about is broad in scope; it describes the society in general in which the new Negro emerges. The idealistic definition of contemporary society takes a much more narrow view; the idea of segregation stands opposed to the idea of integration. Finally, the religious definition of the struggle provides a context to both the earlier explanations. It positions them inside its own frames of meaning and understanding. Such positioning is a defining characteristic of the discourse of faith.

The three levels of materialism, idealism, and faith are interconnected. They form a hierarchy in which each new level contains a further element of truth that posits the earlier definition. And on the highest rung of this ladder of signification stands faith (or, if one wishes to personalize it, God). In brief: Religion determines the ideals that determine the material reality; once this process has taken place, it is possible for religion to explain both ideals and material reality within its own sphere.

This is the function of the religious superstructure and the basic building block of the construction of the civil rights movement discourse as a discourse of faith. King's concrete historical reality takes place within the framework of religious reality. A discourse of faith means that meaning is always given from above. A concrete situation is always determined by ideals that have their home and final end in faith.

This reveals how closely connected the discourse of faith is with the project of creating an discourse of inclusion, a process by which the discourse of faith is able to incorporate a totality, as opposed to separate parts, through its monopolistic claims that it is grounded in truth. Through its naming process, a discourse of faith can create frames around a content that is vastly diverse. But despite this diversity, when the discourse of faith is used successfully as it was, generally speaking, in King's pre-1965 rhetoric, it gives the speaker and also—and this is important—the ideologue almost the same power as Adam, who was given the power to name the earth's inhabitants.

In King's rhetoric, an always-present religious superstructure determines the discourse of faith. What finally gives meaning, and indeed, what finally *is*, is the ultimate truth and tangible presence of (ontologically) God and (epistemologically) faith. Religion broadly defined is what gives humankind a structure and context in which it can be fully defined and explained. It gives humans meaning. There are always several ways of describing one thing, but the religious definition is always the ultimate, and it is always necessary if the full meaning of something/everything is to be understood. This is the retrogression of the religious superstructure: Even when the most earthly demand is made or when the most materialistic explanation is given, it already inhabits the meaning that it is given through the religious interpretation.

When discussing the discourse of faith in its more specialized relationship with the rhetoric and activities of the civil rights movement, it is also necessary to remember that a discourse not only creates the frames inside which speaking and understanding are possible. This position also implies an outside location. You can stand on two sides of every boundary.

This means that the discourse of faith cannot be viewed as separate from the world and society it names and defines. The interaction with this world and this society produces something that goes beyond the initial scope of the religious definitions. But what does King's civil rights movement discourse as a discourse of faith produce? Four areas are discernable.

REALITY

The first area is that which states that reality is a religious manifestation. The universe is moral. Knowledge and truth is what is needed to, from the viewpoint of God, uphold and, from the viewpoint of man, comprehend the universe. This basic religious-idealistic outlook also forms a scale—the ladder of signification—and a relationship: The frames of the discourse determine its internal content.

It is easy to say that King uses grandiose words to describe the little things in order to make them important, to motivate the masses of civil rights activists and to interpret the struggle in such a way that it can and will be accessible to as many as possible. This is more than a style of speaking. In speaking this way, King establishes that reality is constituted in this way. This is not a surface below which we can find a "real" understanding or a "reality." King's rhetoric rests on and expresses a logic that in a comprehensive way defines reality in all its aspects.

So when King states that reality is moral and idealistic, when he states that the struggle against segregation is not a struggle between white and black or between individuals but is a struggle between the forces of good/light and the forces of evil/darkness, the way he expresses the struggle itself reveals what the struggle is, how it should be fought, who should fight it, and what it will lead to.[9]

The struggle is ultimately about values. A change of values precedes a change of the concrete relations. The struggle must therefore be fought in a way that produces these values, and the agents of the struggle are all those who want new values infused into society (this is a core inclusive value of the civil rights movement's discourse), and the goal of the struggle is what King later in his career dubbed "a revolution of values."[10]

King's oft-repeated version of the course of events of the Montgomery bus boycott illustrates this point. As he explained, the boycott was precipitated by the Negro's new self-evaluation and the values produced by the Supreme Court through their *Brown v Board of Education* decision in 1954. Together this produced the zeitgeist that influenced Rosa Parks's decision to remain seated on the bus. The boycott itself was a symbolic action to force a change in white attitudes and it was led by clergymen, representing the church and, ultimately, God.[11] The core of King's notion of nonviolence indeed contains and creates this idealistic effect. The goal is to reach the conscience of the evildoer and thereby change him/her and his/her activities. Changing the conscience of the evildoer is also a metaphor for what social change is as expressed in King's notion of reality. You change the world by changing man's perception of it and attitudes toward it.

The ideological effects of this notion of reality have also another component that is based on the same notion of change. From the beginning of his public career King spoke of economic equality, but the potential radicalness of this demand was largely defused. It was embedded in and to a degree shielded by the fact that the movement was perceived as "radical" in itself. In the 1950s South, the different aspects of this radicalness did not need to be pointed out. Another reason for the defusing is more directly linked with the idealistic notion of reality and the characterization of the struggle as a struggle to change values that then in their turn would change society. The demand for economic equality becomes a part of a discourse where the demand for racial equality is the defining demand and in this discourse, ultimately determined by the truths of the moral universe of God, a change of values, a change in the way man comprehends the world, precedes, in a temporal sense, a change in the "material" world. Economic equality therefore becomes a value issue. It is part of the demand for racial equality, a demand that is sanctioned by God and the Bible. If African Americans were to achieve economic equality, the thinking and attitudes of man must first be changed. Once that was done, a material change would follow.

This partially explains why the "acceptance" of the demand for economic equality was much greater before 1965 than afterward. The radicalization of the demand was a change of degree, not of kind. But during the early struggle the demand for change could, through the unified discursive process it was then a part of, accede to hegemonic notions. It attacked not the actual structure of wealth but man's perception and acceptance of that structure. King argued that if the values were changed, the structure would change, not the other way around. This logic was partly transformed when the discursive process changed after the legal victories and the move to the North. The result of the unified discourse of faith was a set of ideological demands that would have been perceived differently out of their discursive context, but as expressed within that frame, they fitted well within the dominating ideological notions of the day.

MAN AND SOCIETY

The second area of the ideological effects of King's discourse is that it is connected with particular notions of what man and society are. Here we can find strongly normative ideological effects of King's rhetoric, and here we can also find the importance of the ladder of signification discussed in relation to reality.

In one sense it is quite easy to comprehend what man and society are in King's rhetoric (even if the emphasis varies slightly during his career). Man has both a material and a spiritual side. The former must not be neglected, but it is in the latter that the point of contact with God can be reached through the divinity within man's personality, that which causes him to be made in the image of God.[12] In a similar way, society is quite simply the general form for how man organizes his collective life. Ideally it should involve democracy, equality, and justice.[13]

But what happens when material ideals and spiritual ideals meet? Are there any specialized norms involved in this relationship, or does the generality of the divine righteousness mean that it becomes a rhetorical construction that harbors little more than a slight adjustment to mainstream U.S. values? And what is the role of the "Kingdom of God" and "the beloved community" here? These questions are so central in King's religious faith and ideology that they need to be discussed in close association with the messages in which he spoke of a new and ideal society created by and for a new man who had learned to view reality in a different way, one that corresponded to the ultimate truth and knowledge of God. The last part of this chapter is devoted to a more detailed discussion of this "beloved community."

HISTORY

The third area of ideological effects of King's rhetoric is that his discourse contains definitions of what history is. As can be seen in the passages from "The Church on the Frontier of Racial Tension," history and historical change are closely associated with progress, which King ties to a sense of the rationality of history—the notion that history unfolds according to a certain plan. This is contained both in his guarantee that the struggle will be victorious and in his discussions of the material changes in the first half of twentieth-century America. But it is important to note that values and ideals lead this progress. This interpretation is also tied to King's version of what reality is. Since ultimately reality is truth, knowledge, values, and so forth, any rational progress in this reality must be initiated in and through those areas. History unfolds, but it does so according to a particular pattern. This is true of all three ideal understandings of history that are present in King's rhetoric. Whether history is endowed with a force in itself (zeitgeist), understood typologically, or depicted as neutral and dependent on the activity of humankind, it is still a journey toward liberation in one sense or another.[14] Man must therefore put as much effort as possible into the institutions that promotes this righteous path of history, which is mainly religious and educational. Again, progress is determined by the values of humanity.

MORALITY

The fourth area of ideological effects of King's rhetoric is that the discourse is constructed and upheld by the assumption that right and wrong (good and evil) are real entities.[15] The dichotomy does not mean that man cannot move between them, but it means that in the reality of man on earth, there always must be someone who can define the dichotomy and be in the position where his or her words will be taken as God's words and his or her judgment will be taken as God's judgment.

There is an interesting gap in King's assertions of faith relative to this problem. On one side stands the belief that man and God share the same reality and, to some extent, even an identity which is connected with the fact that God is an active participant in the reality of man and therefore exists as a norm in Himself. On the other side stands the freedom of man, who can act according to his own will but must be aware that his actions are constantly measured by an absolute right and an absolute wrong. But for this judgment to have relevance for an otherworldly existence, there must be some way to claim the authority of God in the this-worldly existence. Man (or some men or even *a* man) must be able to define this absolute morality of the universe he exists in.

The ideological effects of proclaiming a moral universe in this sense are far-reaching, and the preacher and the church are crucial. Man and the institutions of man can and do have the right to act with the authority of God. Through interpretation the word of God becomes the word of man, and these words are used as a model against which the present reality is understood and judged. This formula states that the notion of an absolute morality carries with it a hierarchy of individuals. So although the notion of equality is central in several ways in King's civil rights movement discourse, there is a gradation inside this equality in relation to absolute moral values. In a this-worldly situation in which morality must be manifested and brought into society by humanity, some people are subjects and others are objects, depending on one's relationship with the interpretation of and access to the absolute moral values of God as expressed in the language and culture of humanity.[16]

So far we have concerned ourselves with the functioning of the discourse of faith as a whole, but to fully understand it and to see more directly how it is created both in and by King's rhetoric we need also to move from the structure of the discourse to its construction. The first two notions we come across are, quite naturally, those of God and Jesus. It is through an analysis of their function in King's rhetoric that we can begin to understand how meaning is ultimately fixed in the discourse and how King defines the identity of the movement and its struggle.

God as a Nodal Point in King's Rhetoric

Even at an early age King tried in various ways to define what and who God was, and in the different essays and exams of his education we can follow a development where he was always testing various theological proposals against the religious beliefs he had inherited from his father and grandfather.[17] This youthful and curious approach to the possibility of defining the God that was part of the young King's life and faith later had its counterpart in a constant real-world practice where in a particular social environment and struggle God became a firm backbone in a rhetoric that thereby became a continual attempt to define what and who He was.

The same can naturally be said of Jesus, whose meaning and function within Christianity were transferred into King's civil rights movement discourse. In addition to grounding the struggle in the supreme morals of God and the universe that was His creation, it was also grounded, and its righteousness guaranteed, through several aspects of the Jesus figure.

Originally conceived by French psychoanalyst Jacques Lacan, the idea of nodal points is a theoretical concept that has been further developed as a tool to use in the analysis of discourse by Ernesto Laclau and Chantal Mouffe.[18] They argue that there is always a lack, something missing, in the construction of society. It is due to and in this gap that articulatory practices take place, practices that establish, position, and change identity. The social structures that are established through this totality are what they call discourse. Discourse is therefore, in this sense, to be understood as closely resembling a set of rules that determine the meaning of activities that take place in the social world. It is what makes material reality into what it "is" as it tries to fix the meaning of praxis.

Nodal points are the instances of a discourse that attempt

"to arrest the flow of differences, to construct a centre."[19] It is through these nodal points that meaning is fixed; it is there that the frames of understanding that the discourse constitutes are ultimately locked since they determine the other articulatory practices of the discursive structure. The floating signifiers, signifiers with no preordained discursive function or ideological meaning, are positioned by these nodal points, since they constitute the center from which the floating signifiers are to be understood.

God and Jesus are very much directly used in this way in King's rhetoric, and the structure of the discourse, with the specific logic it evokes, is both determined by and emerges from these fixed positions. It is through God and Jesus, and their positions as fixed points that always structure meaning, that other central terms become integral parts of the discourse. They are secured and given a home through the functioning of the nodal points.

It is from this angle that the central questions may be approached: How are God and Jesus related to some of the central understandings of the discourse and what is their role in the solidifying of the highest level in the ladder of signification? How do "God" and "Jesus" encapsulate the meaning of some of the discourse's central articulations and make of this a structure inside which the struggle of the civil rights movement becomes firmly posited? "Love" and "justice," "righteousness" and "judgment," "eternal law" and "morality," as well as man, all stand at the core of this process.

Another important component of this analysis is the relationship between God and Jesus in the discourse. While God is the overarching structure, the ultimate guarantee or the final trial we all must face, Jesus walks among men, delivering his message of hope and helping man in his daily struggles and being the example man can both follow and strive to become. While King uses God to create the structure in which the meaning of the struggle is established by the struggles between good and evil, Jesus is what makes this structure into an actual and active process in itself. This relationship is a both creative and solidifying aspect of King's discursive formation since for every social change it establishes the necessary link between rhetoric and action, argumentation and organization, life and faith.

LOVE AND JUSTICE

King's discourse is built up around the undeniable truth that at the heart of a universe there is a God of love that guarantees that history is a forward movement toward liberation, freedom, and harmony. This all-encompassing love, the strongest force in the universe (for which King so often used the notion of "agape"), is throughout King's career what God himself is.[20] All other aspects of him rest upon this foundation; if it was not there, King's entire religious cosmos would fall apart. God cannot be just, moral, or judgmental if at the same time he does not love. This is a continual theme in King's rhetoric.

Essentially this can be said to be a general and broad Christian belief; few preachers, theologians, and, for that matter, Christians would argue with the general belief that God is love. In terms of faith, this is a rather straightforward manifestation of one of the central tenets of Christianity.

But what is the more direct meaning of this union of God and love in King's rhetoric?

The first thing to note is the generality of the theme "God is love" as a Christian belief. Its breadth is important for the arguments and beliefs of the civil rights movement. To emphasize love is to emphasize common humanity, and to emphasize love as the prime argument against segregation is to emphasize the importance of every individual who participates in the movement. And it should not be forgotten that this is a rather oblique confrontational tool even if King frequently points out that the love he speaks of is a love far removed from sentimental emotionalism. Love is a force that can transform in the same manner as God can create.

But the breadth of this idea is important in another sense,

and it is primarily here that the importance of God as the prime signifier can be seen. The discourse of Christianity is transferred into the arena of the civil rights movement, and the two come to share meaning and legitimacy; they are both discourses of faith. The civil rights movement discourse is stabilized and always confirmed whenever the association between God and love is actualized in the rhetoric, since it evokes a specific reality where the movement is situated and thereby understood. It situates the movement's identity within the identity of God.

The central position of love in King's rhetoric and its often-repeated significance for the concrete activities of the movement—nonviolence is a prime example—means that it is a central definer of the struggle itself.

But love does not stand on its own in the discourse. Since it is determined by the nodal point God, love becomes part of the highest rung in the ladder of signification. Love is absorbed into the identity of God. This relationship must be remembered even when formulations such as "God is love" or the concept of Christian love that stands at the core of the movement are individually found in King's rhetoric. The meaning of the movement becomes fixed by the meaning of love, whose meaning in turn is fixed by God. In this sense, it is possible to speak of a multiple encapsulation of legitimacy and identity that has its cornerstone—its nodal point—in God. Love, and thereafter the movement, is caught in a network of specific meaning that is ultimately signified by the incontestability of God Himself. The rhetorical power as well as the creative and inclusive discursiveness of this process should not be underestimated.

But even aside from the fact that it is signified by God and thereby defined according to this process, love is seldom left to stand on its own in the civil rights movement discourse. It is fixed in a discourse that defines the identity of the struggle through its association and shared meaning with God, but it is also inevitably linked with another concept that is also grounded in the guaranteed truth of this God: justice. King explained the relationship between love and justice in the very first speech of

the Montgomery bus boycott, delivered at Holt Street Baptist
Church on December 5, 1955:

> I want to tell you this evening that it is not enough for us to talk
> about love, love is one of the pivotal points of Christian face, faith.
> There is another side called justice. And justice is really love in
> calculation. Justice is love correcting that which revolts against
> love.
>   The Almighty God himself is not the only [sic], not the God
> just standing out saying through Hosea, "I Love You Israel." He's
> also the God that stands up before nations and said: "Be still and
> know that I'm God, that if you don't obey me I will break the
> backbone of your power and slap you out of the orbits of your
> international and national relationships." Standing beside love is
> always justice. Not only are we using the tools of persuasion, but
> we've come to see that we've got to use the tools of coercion.[21]

The creative force of love in the reality of humanity is always
threatened by that which works against it. What love creates
in this battle, what it strives for, can be defined as justice. In
other words, when love and its creative possibilities are triumphant, justice is the end result—it is "love in calculation." Both
are also grounded in the God who, as King says, not only loves
but also issues a serious warning by constantly implying his
power to brush aside that which opposes his will. The duality
of righteousness presented here indicates something that is a
central feature of King's rhetoric throughout his career: It is
inclusive not just in the sense of being inviting and making
room for as many as possible inside the understanding it offers, it is also inclusive in the sense of constantly attempting to
include a "whole," an argument from which there is no escape.
This is clearly the aim of any rhetorical construction; its defining purpose is to use as skillfully as possible the available means
of persuasion. But it is still important to note how King does it
here.

"God is love"—that statement endows a particular kind of
righteousness to the movement, whose identity is linked to
this God, and provides it with an obliquely confrontational tool.
But God is also justice—and this fact guarantees that the reality in which the movement is situated squares with the will

and intent of God. This use of God as the prime signifier not only posits love and justice in a determining relationship with himself but also posits them in a determining relationship with each other. Neither of these signifiers can be fully understood without the other, since on their own they are "floating"; they do not have any fixed meaning without each other. But through the grounding in God they become discursively creative since they come to take part in offering a complete understanding of reality to the individual. We can begin to discern the structure of the discourse.

But what is justice? What does it include? These may seem to be legitimate questions, but it may also be argued that this line of thinking only illustrates King's own general affirmations and fails to reach the deeper and more specialized meanings of justice. This observation is in a sense correct, but it is also the actual point here. Since I am interested in the discourse King creates and develops, his rhetoric must be must be understood on its own terms and with the understanding that it creates an inclusive generality inside which other and more specialized claims can be made. The breadth of "justice" when it is situated in King's system of signification is what creates the possibility of a particular definition. To understand this, we must acknowledge the broad generality inside which the signifiers work— the ways in which they link justice with love to form an inclusive rhetorical tool and the ways in which they posit both love and justice as crucial signifiers in the discourse through their grounding in the nodal point "God." In this way meaning can be contained within the discourse and guide a constant flow of differences into a reality that King's rhetoric has already constructed and made completely accessible.

"Justice" is therefore in one sense the very sweeping term described here, working beside love to guarantee that history is working toward freedom. That is not to say that it does not come to have a specific or ideological meaning in the historical situation of the movement. But if we want to understand how this meaning is created, established, and upheld, we must accept its wide boundaries and its rather nebulous content. Justice is needed in the discourse order to set the stage, to posit the movement within particular frameworks and to endow it with a particular identity. What more could one ask for than a struggle that is about "love" and "justice"?[22]

One specific characteristic of justice is pivotal for the determining level of the discourse. To seal the guarantee that the struggle will be victorious and to make justice as powerful a signifier as possible, the term is also defined by the God who says, "If you don't obey me I will break the backbone of your power." Here the intervening omnipotence of God does more than limit justice to an eschatological promise related to the general development of history. Justice comes also to include and signify the consequences of man's sinfulness, both individually and collectively. Just as the meaning of justice is determined by a God who loves, it is also determined by a God who speaks of the consequences of injustice, a God with the power of apocalypse in his hand, a God who upholds the old truth that you will reap what you sow.[23] King's rhetoric comes to include the warning of a prophet while at the same time retaining the soothing, welcoming, and embracing meaning of love. Thereby, the signifiers "righteousness" and "judgment" are established at the highest level of the discourse's network of meaning.

ABSOLUTE MORALITY AND ETERNAL LAW

Another relationship between love and justice in King's rhetoric forms a bridge between the two and thereby stabilizes the structure of the discourse. Two concepts are fundamental for both King's rhetoric and the civil rights movement discourse; they mediate and are a manifestations of love and justice: absolute morality and eternal law.

Let us turn to a short passage from the sermon "Our God Is Able" as printed in *Strength to Love:*

In our sometimes difficult and often lonesome walk up freedoms's [sic] road, we do not walk alone. God walks with us. He has placed within the very structure of the universe certain absolute moral laws. We can never defy nor break them. If we disobey them, they will break us. The forces of evil may temporarily conquer the truth, but truth will ultimately conquer its conqueror.[24]

This passage can be coupled with a passage that reappears in many of King's speeches, sermons, and writings. This particular example comes from the speech "Love, Law and Civil Disobedience," which was presented in Atlanta before the annual meeting of the Fellowship of the Concerned in November 1961:

> Well, a just law is a law that squares with a moral law. It is a law that squares with that which is right, so that any law that uplifts human personality is a just law. Whereas that law which is out of harmony with the moral is a law which does not square with the moral law of the universe. It does not square with the law of God, so for that reason it is unjust and any law that degrades human personality is an unjust law.[25]

As we can see in these passages, King legitimizes the existence of this morality and these laws by directly linking them to God. The civil rights struggle becomes a way of revealing and actualizing these laws.

The notion of the eternal laws also comes to have powerful signifying qualities. In the passage from "Our God Is Able" where King says that what stands opposed to evil is not only love and justice but also truth, this truth is posited by eternal laws and absolute morality since they are, in a sense, what the universe of God is—ultimate reality. In this reality absolute morality and eternal laws are inextricably linked with the other fundamental concepts of love and justice. And the common denominator, that which unifies the three and makes them into a discourse-structuring network, is God.

The result is that the civil rights movement has right on its side since its actions are launched in connection with the moral laws of the universe and God is those laws, this morality, and this truth within the logic of the discourse. Through its actions the movement actually reveals God and his power, it establishes him, makes his immanence obvious.

Again one may ask: What are these moral laws? How is such a powerful absolute truth formulated? I think it is crucial to note the manifestations of faith in themselves. The moral truth is the truth that makes the civil rights movement and the struggle against segregation righteous. It legitimizes the legitimization, so to speak. It is within this frame that particular and more specialized arguments can be found.

In King's faith, God is present in a reality that is structured around particular moral principles, which in this case are not possible to identify in more detail than the expression "moral principle" indicates. "Moral truth" and "moral law" carry particular meanings within the discourse. They are important elements in the strategy of creating a wholeness, signifiers that reveal to every listener what King speaks of and how the struggle they are involved in shall be understood. But the signifying element is still loosely defined; it states an inclusive generality rather than a more particular definition. Together with love and justice, God posits moral principles to form a level of religious truth in a discourse in which ultimate legitimacy can always be found. This group of ideas forms the basic religious quality of the civil rights movement's identity, an identity that King creates through his rhetoric.

Absolute morality and eternal law also point to another part of God's activity as a nodal point of the discourse. While love and justice are what may be called divine qualities that organize the universe that the discourse actualizes, absolute morality and eternal law have a slightly different character in that that they, when understood as parts of this specific organization of the universe, do not represent directly intervening powers. Instead, laws and morality must be activated by the individuals that exist in this universe. Absolute morality and eternal law are what must ultimately regulate the lives of man.

Man

The identity of man is another central feature of King's civil rights movement discourse. His rhetoric frequently refers to the attributes as well as the responsibilities of man. But how does he posit man inside the network of significations he uses? It is naturally of paramount importance when constructing an inclusive discourse of meaning to have control over the definition of man; to stabilize its floating character. As the view of man often stands at the center of what makes ideologies different from each other and thereby in conflict with each other, the possibility of integrating and legitimizing ideologies often hinges on the ability to formulate this identity and make it definitive. And in King's rhetoric we find an almost constant attempt to formulate and stabilize the identity of man; a meaning of "man" that is fixed so that it becomes an integral element in the identity and purpose of the struggle.

Man as a floating signifier in civil rights movement discourse is determined and stabilized through association with certain fixed nodal points in this discourse. One of these is God and the intricate network of meaning that is centered on him in King's rhetoric. But in King's rhetoric, there is another nodal point: The signifying activity of the figure of Jesus becomes evident when we begin to view how the fixing of the identity of man takes place. It is an activity that is central for the discourse as a whole.

But let us first consider the structuring function of the relationship between man and God. Two typical sermon passages in this context provide good starting points. The first example comes from "What Is Man?" as printed in *Strength to Love*. Here King says:

> This brings us to a second point that must be included in any Christian doctrine of man. [The first point was that man is a biological being.] Man is a being of spirit. He moves up "the stairs of his concepts" into a wonder world of thought. Conscience speaks to him, and he is reminded of things divine. This is what the Psalmist means when he says that man has been crowned with glory and honor.
>
> This spiritual quality gives him the unique capacity to live on two levels. He is in nature, yet above nature; he is in time and space, yet above them. . . . By his ability to reason, his power of

memory, and his gift of imagination, man transcends time and space. As marvelous as are the stars is the mind of the man that studies them.

This is what the Bible means when it affirms that man is made in the image of God. The *imago dei* has been interpreted by different thinkers in terms of fellowship, responsiveness, reason, and conscience. An abiding expression of man's higher spiritual nature is his freedom. Man is man because he is free to operate within the framework of his destiny. He is free to deliberate, to make decisions, and to choose between alternatives.[26]

The second example, which is more directly related to a social struggle, comes from "The American Dream," as delivered at Ebenezer Baptist Church in July 1965:

You see, the founding fathers were really influenced by the Bible. The whole concept of the *imago dei*, as it is expressed in Latin, the "image of God," is the idea that all men have something within them that God has injected. Not that they have any substantial unity with God, but that every man has a capacity to have a fellowship with God. And that gives him a uniqueness, it gives him worth, it gives him dignity. And we must never forget this as a nation: There are no gradations in the image of God. Every man from treble white to bass black is significant on God's keyboard, precisely because every man is made in the image of God. One day we will learn that.[27]

In almost all the sermons and speeches where King discusses the nature of man he speaks of the need to acknowledge the duality that is manifested in these two passages—to see that man has the capacity for love, creativity, and change as well as for evil, destruction, and violence—and that this duality must always be understood in the light of man's relationship with God. This idea and reasoning is illustrated in a typical way in this passage from "What Is Man?": Man has free will, "he is free to operate within the framework of his destiny," and this is what creates a particular relationship with God. Man is made in God's image and thus has the ability to use the divine qualities within him. But to do so he has to activate those qualities. Even though every man has value because he is loved by God and is endowed with a personality, he has to take action to become a part of God's being. The divine worth of every person is always acknowledged by God since he loves unconditionally, but man's divine qualities are connected with his free will, with his active and conscious participation in the Supreme Being of God.

But as we can see in these sermon passages, the relationship between man and God involves several problems. At one moment to love is to participate in the being of God, at the next man has no "substantial unity" with God. At one moment man and God are related through their personalities and to that extent they are linked through their sameness, but at another moment, man can never reach the level of God—man loves; God *is* love. At one moment man's ability to do good, *his* moral actions, is what reveals God's immanence; at another, man has experiences of God where the link between him and God, especially during times of suffering or insecurity, is created or withheld by *God's* actions. When the strength of the divinity inside man fades, a God of the outside intervenes.[28]

For our purposes it is more interesting to note this apparent contradiction and strict duality in itself rather than attempt to solve it. To understand how man is defined in King's rhetoric, the dual relationship between man and God manifested in the two passages quoted above is important as just that, as a duality or even a contradiction. King gave man a stable identity through man's similarities *and* dissimilarities to God. The privilege of God as a nodal point in the discourse creates this opportunity; man is signified through and by him and it is therefore in this *relationship* that we can begin to discover how man is constructed in King's discursive process.

IDENTITY

King defines man's identity through relation—man's similarities and dissimilarities—to the identity of God. God is a constant reference point in the definitions of man that are present in King's rhetoric, either through himself, as "God," or through the concepts that in the discourse are features of his stability and definitiveness—love, justice, absolute morality. The understanding of man and his identity are accomplished in this way through an understanding of God. Put in another way, it is through the signifying activities of "God" that the meaning of man is established.

From his black Baptist background and milieu King brought a notion of a fatherly, loving, and personal God. God is never an abstract and incomprehensible force. He is concretely a personality, manifested in the universe. This basic self-evident truth of King's faith was then reinforced and formulated in theological language during his education, and this amalgamation was something he used in different ways.[29] But when noting this process we must also remember what its constant was: the idea of God as a personality and thus directly related to man who also, ultimately, is a personality. God relates directly to man through that which connects them with him. Humans can never be entirely God, and God is not entirely human, but God is always utterly recognizable for humanity. That which they both in essence are—a personality—is what connects them. As King says in the passage from "The American Dream," even though man has no "substantial unity" with God, what gives him "uniqueness," "worth" and "dignity" is his "capacity to have fellowship with God." And man is made in the *image* of God, something that is also mirrored in the way "man" is determined by God as a nodal point of the discourse.

This insistence on the divine value of personality provided King with many ways to use it in several aspects of the civil rights movement discourse, the most typical being the strong link between evil and segregation since it deprived the individual of his or her worth as a person. King's argument—that personality is what is most real in the universe and that it is what unites man and God—enabled him to attack segregation not only morally but also in a religious sense that went beyond the daily life experiences of whites as well as blacks. Through the complication of explaining the equality of all people in terms of personality and thereby associating this with a system not directly following from (or being the same as) the overarching demand—racial equality—it became a way of cementing the faith of the protesters. It became a proof of the righteousness of their cause. This principle made it more complicated for the proponents of segregation to refute since their arguments did not meet King's on the same moral level. They were left outside the discourse, a discourse that was much more accessible to liberal northerners, who were much more comfortable with theological systems such as Personalism, for example. It is in this sense that King's discourse was inclusive—its nodal points created a breadth that drew in many potential supporters. How do you dispute the argument that segregation is wrong because it opposes the ultimate reality in the universe—personality—with arguments such as the one that "the Negro must remain in his place"?

ACTION AND DIVINITY

In King's rhetoric, the abilities and actions of man are fixed by their similarities and dissimilarities to the abilities and actions of God. If the relationship and similarity between man and God regarding the essence of their being—personality—is something that gives man worth and definite identity and thereby makes oppression of him/her a defiance of God, this second relationship reveals how man has inside him qualities, such as the capacity for goodness, that gives him the power to do God's will and work in the reality of this world.

King often stresses the possibility of positive change and speaks of the creative ability of humanity to give birth to something new. As endowed with this ability, humanity is identified through a relationship with God and the strong signifying concepts that are parts of him as a supreme signifier: love, justice, and the eternal law.[30]

Man has the ability to love because he can use nonviolence to create a new harmonious whole, he is the tool of the God who in the end guarantees a victory for justice, he can recognize and actualize the eternal laws and thereby bring them into the struggle, and he is able to incorporate within himself the very structures of the universe that God has created and manifests himself through.

It is these possibilities and qualities that King ascribes to man when he emphasizes his goodness and it is therefore through these qualities, and their status as the "home" of the discourse, that man further becomes what he is in King's rhetoric and in the meaning this rhetoric creates as a part of a public dialogue.

When man actualizes those qualities, which in themselves are divine because of the status of love, justice, and moral law in the discourse, he actualizes the sameness between his identity and God's identity. This corresponds to some crucial elements in the civil rights movement discourse. Segregation is wrong since it degrades human personality, that which represents a divine streak within humanity. To actively struggle against oppression, against that which opposes love, justice, and moral law, is a necessity for the actualization of the relationship. The identity of humanity and the divine streak that stands at its center only exist when they are confirmed by the actions of human beings. This gives the struggle a religious quality that is essential for the civil rights movement discourse as a discourse of faith.

This is also the anchoring of meaning that is the prerequisite for—in a sense what makes possible—the view of man that is manifested in the passage from "What Is Man?" that we began this discussion with. Man has a spiritual side that can transgress nature, and that stands above the actual reality in which he must exist. Through this he has the ability to infuse divine meaning into the situation itself, and man's moral abilities give him the power to judge situations with the authority of a divinity as long as he activates the parts of himself that are divine or are in touch with divinity.

But if the relationship between God and man is crucial for the construction of the discourse, what upholds this relationship, what establishes it as a possibility and as a definite reality, is Jesus.

Jesus as a Nodal Point in King's Rhetoric

If man is determined to be in a constant relationship with God, Jesus is what mediates this relationship within the discourse. And just as he determines the meaning of man through his constant presence as an ethical example in King's rhetoric, Jesus also mediates the signifying powers of love, justice, and morality. In King's rhetoric, Jesus personifies these powers. He is what every person must strive to be.

This theme is present in several practices in King's rhetoric. The most straightforward process is when Jesus is held up as an ethical example through his acts as told in the Bible. This is given specialized meaning within the movement discourse when ethical perfectibility is directly related to the strategy of nonviolence and the admonition never to be silent in the face of injustice. Another type of rhetorical process where the Jesus ethic comes to determine the movement and its participants is when he is used within a typological framework. Finally there is a third process, often combined with or present within a typological logic, where the definitions of humanity, love, justice, and morality take a detour through the words and parables of Jesus and are then posited within the structure of King's rhetoric.

The Ethical Norm

The many examples of King's straightforward use of Jesus as an ethical example use one basic strategy. King simply tells one of the biblical stories of Jesus' acts and then places it before the congregation, audience, or reader as an example of how a truly righteous life should be lived.[31] This strategy is very simple. It works both as an incitement to act and as a confirmation that the means of the struggle and the struggle itself are righteous. It is not even necessary to tell an actual story, it is often enough to refer to the name "Jesus" for this ethical righteousness to be invoked. But the strategy is more complex when it is placed in the context of the more overarching position that Jesus occupies as a fixed point of meaning in the larger discursive framework.

In the sermon "Loving Your Enemies," delivered at Dexter Avenue Baptist Church in November 1957, several different aspects of Jesus as an ethical example and perfect man can be found:

> Certainly these are great words ["love your enemies"], words lifted to cosmic proportions. And over the centuries, many persons have argued that this is an extremely difficult command. Many would go so far as to say that it just isn't possible to move out into the actual practice of this glorious command. They would go on to say that this is just additional proof that Jesus was an impractical idealist who never quite came down to earth. So the arguments abound. But far from being the impractical idealist, Jesus has become the practical realist. The words of the text glitter in our eyes with new urgency. Far from being the pious injunction of a utopian dreamer, this command is an absolute necessity for the survival of our civilization. Yes, it is love that will save our world and our civilization, love even for our enemies.
>
> Now, let me hasten to say that Jesus was very serious when he gave this command; he wasn't playing. He realized that it's hard to love your enemies. He realized that it's difficult to love those persons who seek to destroy you, those persons who seek to defeat you, those persons who say evil things about you. He realized that it was painfully hard, pressingly hard. But he wasn't playing. And we cannot dismiss this passage as just another example of Oriental hyperbole, just a sort of exaggeration to get over the point. This is a basic philosophy of all that we hear coming from the lips of our Master. Because Jesus wasn't playing; because he was serious. We have the Christian and moral responsibility to discover the meaning of these words, and to discover how we can live out this command, and why we should live by this command.[32]

There is a certain discrepancy in this passage. In one sense, "Jesus" is the name for the ethical argument in itself and the principle that states that loving your enemies is the highest good. In another sense, and what really is the gist of King's argument, Jesus also *embodies* this ethical argument in his earthly and human existence. He brought this ideal into the world of humanity not only as words but as a concrete actuality. He did come down to earth. It is thus far possible to quite openly accept King's line of argumentation. But as *what* did Jesus come down to earth?

To survive, our world and our civilization need the wisdom of the Sermon on the Mount, and such survival hinges on our ability to transform it from words to action in our everyday existence. Therefore, Jesus the "impractical idealist" needs to be the "practical realist." But we should not neglect the importance of the wisdom, the "text" in itself, in this process. Jesus as an ethical example, which determines the identity of humanity and the meaning of the civil rights struggle, inhabits both these worlds. Jesus represents a man who walks among men, showing them how to reach the level of divinity by activating the goodness that God has planted in their personalities. But Jesus as an example of ethical perfection also represents something that points beyond the perfect man, beyond the man who existed. This is what gives Jesus his specific position in King's rhetoric.

What King says in the above passage is not that Jesus is solely a practical realist; he criticizes the argument that loving your enemies is a utopian dream that is not possible in the world of man. King argues that this position is based on the belief that Jesus *never quite came down to earth.* If loving your enemies is impossible, Jesus cannot have been a man who walked among us. Jesus' form of revelation as a man is therefore of the highest importance; it symbolizes the possibility of transforming ideals into reality.

Jesus is closely connected with the central notion of hope. He, as the Son of God, personifies and, as a nodal point in the civil rights movement discourse, fulfills the guarantee that change is possible, that what may seem to be impossible dreams can become reality if they as ideals become truly integrated with the way man acts. For this to occur, it is necessary to make an actual reality of a textual reality. Jesus, understood this way, is the guarantee that positive change is not only possible but also sacred.

"Jesus" as a name for an ethical argument and Jesus the concrete man therefore depend on each other for meaning in the same way that the "practical realist" needs to have an ideal that lies beyond the practical reality. Those who do not accept loving your enemies as a practical possibility have neglected the fact that Jesus came all the way down to earth.

As in so many other areas of King's rhetoric, it is the relationship in itself that gives meaning to the two poles that it combines. That Jesus did come to this world, that he is the perfect man and thus unites divinity and humanity, is the proof that divine morality is not only possible in this world but also the only feasible path if humanity wants to develop the world in harmony with God's will. It is hard, it is a struggle, but it is not an impractical ideal. The life and concrete acts of Jesus are the ultimate proof that ideals are always within our reach. Our spiritual side can determine our material being. Practical reality is never something that is divorced from the moral universe in which it unfolds. Through his acts Jesus the man signifies the Jesus the ethical argument. He is an earthly material revelation of the biblical principles, the actual cluster of words that give meaning to his name within the framework of the Bible.

TYPOLOGY

But the life of Jesus does not have a meaning solely in relation to a divine ethical principle. His humanity has also another function in King's rhetoric and is related to one of its specific techniques: typology. This use of Jesus is a variation of the Jesus of the African-American religious tradition expressed within the framework of the civil rights movement.

In the famous sermon "Drum Major Instinct," delivered at Ebenezer Baptist Church in February 1968, where King speaks of his own funeral, he also includes a passage that he had used before but that becomes even more laden with meaning through the context of the sermon:

> I know a man—and I just want to talk about him a minute, and maybe you will discover who I'm talking about as I go down the way because he was a great one. And he just went about serving. He was born in an obscure village, the child of a poor peasant

woman. And then he grew up in still another obscure village, where he worked as a carpenter until he was thirty years old. Then for three years, he just got on his feet, and he was an itinerant preacher. And he went about doing some things. He didn't have much. He never wrote a book. He never held an office. He never had a family. He never owned a house. He never went to college. He never visited a big city. He never went two hundred miles from where he was born. He did none of the usual things that the world would associate with greatness. He had no credentials but himself.

He was only thirty-three when the tide of public opinion turned against him. They called him a rabble-rouser. They called him a troublemaker. They said he was an agitator. He practiced civil disobedience; he broke injunctions. And so he was turned over to his enemies and went through the mockery of a trial. And the irony of it all is that his friends turned him over to them. One of his closest friends denied him. Another of his friends turned him over to his enemies. And while he was dying, the people who killed him gambled for his clothing, the only possession he had in the world. When he was dead he was buried in a tomb, through the pity of a friend.

Nineteen centuries have come and gone and today he stands as the most influential figure that ever entered human history. All of the armies that ever marched, all the navies that ever sailed, all the parliaments that ever sat, and all the kings that ever reigned put together have not affected the life of man on this earth as much as that solitary life. His name may be a familiar one. But today I can hear them talking about him. Every now and then somebody says, "He's King of Kings." And again I can hear somebody saying, "He's Lord of Lords." Somewhere else I can hear somebody saying "In Christ there is no East nor West." And then they go on and talk about, "In him there's no North and South, but one great Fellowship of Love throughout the whole wide world." He didn't have anything. He just went around serving and doing good.[33]

Technically this segment is built around the tension between the earthly existence of Jesus and the power his activities came to have. But again, it is in the connection between the two that we can see an ethical norm beginning to establish itself: service to others.

Two further typologically laden meanings can be found in

this passage. First, it places Jesus in direct relation to the congregation. An important part of the story as it is told here is that Jesus' name is not mentioned. By presenting the story in this way King offers a double opportunity of identification, one reinforcing the other. When the obvious riddle the story forms is answered with the name "Jesus," it makes an important point. Since Jesus is this man, he is definitely present in the congregation. He is typologically extended over time, signifying an attitude toward life that stands at the center of the ideal civil rights ethos.

The greatness of Jesus lies in something that everybody can achieve. King offers comfort in the tradition of black religion that should not primarily be understood as a "soft" comfort, as someone weeping away the tears of sorrow, but as a comfort based on hope, as a comfort based on the promise of liberation from the hardships of life.[34] The one who guides the struggle against oppression was a man born in a shed and brought up by a poor peasant woman, a situation that members of the black congregation can clearly identify with. Jesus was a man like them, born in a situation similar to theirs, and still he is the most important man in the history of the world. The redeemer from injustice and the friend giving meaning to their daily struggles meet here. His abstract and metaphysical qualities are deemphasized in favor of his earthly troubles, but in the latter part of the story this is turned around to form a presentation of the rewards given for an ethical life, for a life that has recognized what is important in human existence: to act in accordance with the divine morality that is present in one's spirit. In this Jesus defines the redemption from sin that the civil rights movement offers America. He is a part of the contemporary struggle.

Second, the passage places Jesus in direct relation to King himself. There is a definite identification between the two. Even if Jesus' background, as King describes it, is not compatible with his own, the combination of the "what" regarding the life of Jesus and the man King wants to be remembered as establishes the relationship. The ethical example Jesus symbolizes in the story is the same ethical example King wants to be remembered in terms of after his death. There are some concrete points of this identification in the text: the accusations that both men were troublemakers and agitators, the highly contemporary expression "the tide of the public opinion turned against him," and the use of civil disobedience. All these are "model" typological expressions by which Jesus becomes not only someone who is alive in 1960s America but also someone who is closely connected with the role of King himself. Even the description of how Jesus was betrayed by his friends and forced to live through a mockery of a trial can be viewed as description of what happened to King after his public stand against the Vietnam War when some of the civil rights establishment turned their backs on him and he had to suffer an array of accusations in the media.

This emerges as an ethical norm of how King wants to be perceived and as a norm for the congregation to follow. King merges himself and Jesus into one to form a picture of a moral leader. Jesus is intimately intertwined with the public persona King.[35] The role he designates for himself as the leader of the civil rights movement is the same role as that he designates for Jesus as the leader of humanity. Both their actions stem from the absolute righteousness of the moral universe of God. Jesus showed this in his earthly existence and the task of the civil rights movement is to develop his legacy.

TEXTUALITY

The "textuality" of Jesus has another side that involves further complexity: King spoke not only of a Jesus who exemplified ethical perfection through his actions but also of the Jesus who told stories in the form of parables that exemplified the norms of how human beings should live.

The three parables King most commonly uses in his sermons and speeches are "The Good Samaritan," "The Return of the Prodigal Son" and "Lazarus and Dives." Some sermons are entirely built up around these stories, but sometimes they also appear inside sermons.[36] The following passage is one such example. It comes from "Remaining Awake Through a Great Revolution" as delivered in the National Cathedral in Washington, D.C., in March 1968.

Jesus told a parable one day, and he reminded us that a man went to hell because he didn't see the poor. His name was Dives. He was a rich man. And there was a man by the name of Lazarus who was a poor man, but not only was he poor, he was sick. Sores were all over his body, and he was so weak that he could hardly move. But he managed to get to the gate of Dives every day, wanting just to have the crumbs that would fall from his table. And Dives did nothing about it. And the parable ends saying, "Dives went to hell, and there was a fixed gulf now between Lazarus and Dives."[37]

After a passage in which King explains that this should not be understood as "a universal indictment against all wealth," that Dives was not doomed to hell because he was rich (even if Jesus once advised a rich ruler to "sell all," which King calls "individual surgery" rather than a "universal diagnosis") and that the parable also included a conversation between Dives in hell and Abraham in heaven, he continues:

Now, Abraham was a very rich man. If you go back to the Old Testament, you see that he was the richest man of his day, so it was not a rich man in hell talking to a poor man in heaven; it was a little millionaire in hell talking with a multimillionaire in heaven. Dives didn't go to hell because he was rich; Dives didn't realize that his wealth was his opportunity. It was his opportunity to bridge the gulf that separated him from his brother Lazarus. Dives went to hell because he passed by Lazarus every day and never really saw him. He went to hell because he allowed his brother to become invisible. Dives went to hell because he maximized the minimum and minimized the maximum. Indeed, Dives went to hell because he sought to be a conscientious objector in the war against poverty.[38]

How is Jesus involved in this sermon passage? It is Jesus who starts the story, but it is King who ends it. It is also King who fills the story with contemporary meaning and through this he gives contemporary arguments the force and truth of the biblical argument in retelling the parable Jesus tells.[39] Jesus is the eternal wisdom that is always applicable. The problems he addresses in his stories are of a universal kind and can therefore be told in a universal language. The universal truth then transmits its wisdom to a particular situation. As a metaphor it points beyond itself.

What King does in his rhetoric when employing Jesus as a storyteller is to move the parable out of the direct field it exists in as related to Jesus and the ethical norms he stands for. When King tells the story in the third stage (first Jesus tells the story, then the Bible tells the story of Jesus telling the story), he in a sense multiplies the technique of Jesus himself as he uses the absorbed meaning the story comes to gain in this process. This also solidifies the civil rights movement discourse; how can eternal wisdom be questioned? This means that there is a great deal of comparability between what King does in this passage and the civil rights movement discourse as such.

The discourse is built up around universal terms and norms in a highly particularized situation. This is also how Jesus as a storyteller appears and functions. The parables of Jesus both are and symbolize an eternal divine wisdom that serves to explain the ethical norms man must abide by. By retelling, and in parts also coopting, the parable Jesus told of Lazarus and Dives, King connects his project with this general universality. It provides an excellent opportunity, in a way that is accessible to all, to show how the moral universe of God is related to poverty and discrimination on earth.

But Jesus is also involved in other ways in this sermon passage. Jesus still is the revealed God. This highlights an incongruity in the understanding of history present in this sermon as in many of King's public messages.

On the one side stands the history that is directly linked to justice, a forward-moving process which promises that liberation, freedom, and salvation will come at its end. History is a movement from one point to another during which a creative change takes place and is as such rational. On the other side stands the notion of typological time and the comprehension of history it introduces. Here history is a constant recurrence of biblical themes. But typology does not necessarily mean that history "repeats itself." It is rather a special way of understanding and using the Bible. It is not a truth that is concealed within the pages of a book. The Bible *is* reality. It is constantly actualized both *in* and *as* history.

Both of these understandings exist side by side and simultaneously in the rhetoric and faith of King. And it is *together* that they combine to create the specific power in King's rhetoric. For the liberation to have divine qualities, for the struggle in this world and in a concrete social situation to be based on faith, it must be a liberation that can be explained and defined through the patterns of a sacred universe. It is quite possible to imagine a history that is a movement from oppression to freedom through a creative activity that is at the same time a recurrence of a biblical archetype. The Bible *can* give us the prototype of history as it unfolds. Without this relationship history would not have any larger meaning than the meaning of its events themselves and would be unable to guarantee freedom. It would lose its idealistic qualities, and social struggle and religious faith would be more difficult to combine.

Instead, King argues through his rhetoric, history and religious faith are impossible without each other. They fill each other with meaning. Faith is history and history is faith. The content of liberation comes in the form of biblical archetypal stories which are free to move in and above this linear progress. It is the connection in itself that is important.

It is through being this connection that Jesus as a storyteller takes his place in the rhetoric of King. The wisdom in the parable is typological, but it is embedded in a process where the abolishment of oppression and the gaining of freedom stand at a point in history that will one day be reached. This means that as storyteller, Jesus functions more through being the revealed God than through being the perfect man. He stands in the text, both in the Bible and in King's sermon, as someone who not only represents God and the ethical norms he wants every man to realize through his actions but also as someone who gives meaning to history by pointing beyond his own actions to the universal truths that are embedded in God's moral universe. While Jesus as the ethical example signifies a model for man's activities, the use of Jesus as a storyteller signifies divine wisdom, the higher understanding of and ground for this model of actions. It shows that the ethical norm is not tied exclusively to Jesus but is in itself a part of God.

Since God is always present in history as both the promise of liberation and as love, and since the Bible is always happening in historical time, the parables are always relevant in history. The parables of Jesus represent the wisdom of God and by incorporating them through the figure of Jesus who tells them, King defines his aim and its righteousness by being what Jesus is in the Bible in this respect: the medium through which the will of God is presented to man. One further step of interpretation is necessary between Jesus and King—the parable—but that is only of secondary importance. King, like any preacher, implements and thereby interprets the story in a contemporary situation, but here he does it typologically. He is not saying that "the story of Lazarus and Dives means this to us" or that "we must compare this to our situation." He is saying that Lazarus and Dives is *what is happening right now*. Its relevance lies in itself as a signifier of God's will.

Naturally, the Lazarus and Dives story has the function of clarifying something—the ethical demand to share wealth. This immediate function of Jesus' parable should not be neglected, either in relation to the biblical figure Jesus or in relationship to King's rhetoric. Because in addition to being God's way of manifesting himself through Jesus and a way for King to connect himself with this and so assert a typological truth, it also serves to provide meaning within the structure of a specific text—in Jesus' case the gospel and in King's case the sermon "Remaining Awake Through a Great Revolution." As such the story is linked with some fundamental issues in black preaching.

To be clear and to always tell a good story are two crucial imperatives in the black preaching tradition.[40] King's use of the parable of Lazarus and Dives can be seen as answers to both these demands. King uses the parable to criticize the economic structure of America in a way "to make it plain" in a double sense. It makes it real in relation to the lived experience of the listeners and it makes a complex situation understandable through the use of familiar story that represents a familiar structure of righteousness.

King's and Jesus' use of the story in this context merge. They both want to reveal and explain something. In King's case this reminds us of the centrality of "the story" in the black preaching tradition. To make a sermon interesting for the congregation, it was necessary to relate the faith to their real-life experience. Abstract reasoning had to come second to the truths and emotions that emerged from the biblical stories that came to life through the words of the preacher. The task of the preacher was to take a structure or parts of a structure from a biblical story and add contemporary flesh to it. Just as the faith must be directly relevant to the believers, so the stories must manifest this relevance. King's use of Jesus as a storyteller and the stories in themselves can be viewed as a renewal of this practice. Not only does King insert the meaning of the story into a contemporary situation, not only does he evoke its typological qualities, but he also he puts words and expressions such as "surgery," "diagnosis," "long-distance call," "millionaire," "multimillionaire," "conscientious objector" and "war against poverty" into the mouth of Jesus. He lets Jesus tell the story with and through the words and experience of the congregation. And King the preacher is the central link in this transfer.

finally, there is the most fundamental aspect of Jesus in any Christian faith: In addition to divine ethics and divine wisdom, he also represents divine salvation. As Christ, he is what gives man the possibility to reach eternity. Obviously, this is a feature of King's rhetoric as well.[41]

While the ethical, typological, and storytelling functions and meanings of Jesus give King the opportunity to define how the struggle should be fought and to define the struggle as a mediation of God's will and moral principles, Jesus as Christ simply states that he who believes will be saved.[42] King's use of the specialized functions of "Jesus" is consistently tied to this cornerstone of Christianity. This simultaneity is central for endowing concrete civil rights arguments with the same weight as the absolute truth "Jesus as Christ and Savior for every Christian individual." And it need not be pointed out how powerful this could be in the religious environment of American society in the 1950s and 1960s.

In this environment we can also find another constitutive element of King's rhetoric and the civil rights movement discourse: the church. And as we will see when we examine the meaning and function of this institution, which was central not only to his rhetoric and the discourse but also in his life, it becomes even harder to discern a difference between the building and its building blocks or, to put it another way, between the map and the landscape itself.

Ideal and Utopia I: The Church

As in the African-American tradition, the church is as much a social institution as it is a religious one and it therefore holds a special place in King's rhetoric and in civil rights movement discourse.[43] The church is the inevitable bridge between faith and society, both in material terms—it is from within the realms of the church that the message of the civil rights movement is disseminated in society—and in his rhetoric; the church is in many ways the medium in which religious faith is transformed into a societal struggle. These intricately intertwined issues will be dealt with here. In what ways is the church a part of the civil rights movement discourse?

To explore this question I will mainly use King's speech "The

Church on the Frontier of Racial Tension" of April 1961 and the sermon "Guidelines for a Constructive Church," delivered at Ebenezer Baptist Church in June 1966.[44] In both of these examples, King's focus is the responsibility of the church for the moral guidance and development of the individual, the church as a political agent, and the church as the conscience of society.

MORAL PROGRESS AND THE TRANSFORMATION OF THE INDIVIDUAL

In a passage in "The Church on the Frontier of Racial Tension," King says:

> Now whenever the crisis emerges in society, the church has a significant role to play. And certainly the church has a significant role to play because the issue is not merely the political issue; it is a moral issue. Since the church has a moral responsibility of being the moral guardian of society, then it cannot evade its responsibility in this very tense period of transition.[45]

This is a theme King varied in different ways throughout his career, but the essential argument was always the same: The church is the institution which is responsible for upholding the morality of a community and society.

five areas of responsibility are indicated in the speech: The church has the responsibility to instill a "world perspective" in its congregation.[46] It must state firmly that segregation and Christianity are incompatible.[47] It must examine critically the "ideational roots of racial prejudice" and base an educational project on the results of this examination.[48] It also has a responsibility to be active outside its walls and participate actively in "social reform."[49] Finally, King states, the church "must urge all their men to enter the new age with understanding, creative good will in their hearts."[50]

The speech is designed to give the church a particular place within the struggle. This is very much the case with regard to the "world perspective." The church must reflect the geographical unity of the world by constantly speaking of the interrelatedness of all life, another recurring theme in King's rhetoric.

But beneath the rather general demand made here—the reality of the church must answer to the reality of humanity—two other demands are firmly established. First, the church is to moral progress what science is to material or technical progress. Second, the church has an important educational role to fill.

Let us first consider the demand that the church must be the guardian of moral progress. What does it mean? In the speech, King says "the world we live in today is a world that is geographically one. And in order to solve the problems in the days ahead we must make it spiritually one."[51] He further defines this project thus:

> Through our scientific and technological genius, we have made of this world a neighborhood. It is urgently true that now we are challenged through our spiritual and moral commitments to make of this world a brotherhood. In a real sense we must all live together as brothers or we will all perish together as fools. We must see this sense of dependence, this sense of interdependence. No individual can live alone, no nation can live alone; we are made to live together.[52]

It is the responsibility of the church to turn the neighborhood into brotherhood. To do so it is necessary that the church produce values. That is the first amplification of this statement. King's ideal is presented as a world where everyone knows and understands that his life is intertwined with every other life. This may not seem to be intimately tied in with the civil rights struggle within the world in which the speech is given, but this is how King's rhetoric often functions. It is generally applicable and answers to a universal truth, but since it is universal it also has meaning for the civil rights struggle. Who would argue with the idea that it is a generally positive thing—as an abstract formulation—that the world should become a brotherhood? King's more specialized arguments are then determined by this general norm. The key is that if you refute the special arguments you also collide with the general argument. In this process King comes to symbolize rationality and coherence, the opponents the opposites of those qualities.

The transformation of a neighborhood into a brotherhood implies that morality is something that can be spoken of in terms of progress in the same way as science and enlightenment. The transformation of an old world into a new involves a process of refinement. The abolition of segregation and the movement toward integration is a moral progress that evolves from the struggle to give birth to a new society. Several things can be said of this.

first, King's use of the language of material and scientific progress functions in one sense as a metaphor in his rhetoric. The discussion of progress forms a challenge similar to one that King often formulated in relation to the realities of the Cold War: How can we speak of the United States as a modern and advanced nation when segregation and prejudice persist? (Here all one needs to do is exchange "modern and advanced nation" with "defender of the free world" to apply the moral question to the context of the Cold War.) Second, the discussion of progress is related to King's view of humanity and its relation to God through its spiritual qualities. As the church is the arm of God in a world that exists in a moral universe, its prime responsibility must be to harmonize society and the will of God through the channels human beings have at their disposal.

Third, the discussion of progress speaks of the church's educational and enlightening mission. The church has the responsibility to produce truths that can challenge the false truths of segregation. King describes this responsibility in the following way:

> The church also has the responsibility of getting to the ideational roots of racial prejudice. Racial prejudice is always based on fears, and suspicions and misunderstandings that are usually groundless. The church can do a great deal to direct the popular mind at this point, and to clear up these misunderstandings and these false ideas. Many of these ideas are disseminated by politicians who merely use the issue to arouse the fears and to perpetuate themselves in office. The church can make it clear that these things are not true. The church can rise up and through its channels of religious education tell the truth on this issue.[53]

And a bit farther on:

> So there are many false ideas that are constantly disseminated
> that the church can do a great deal to refute. And then the church
> can do a great deal to open channels of communication between
> the races. I am absolutely convinced that men hate each other be-
> cause they fear each other. They don't know each other because
> they are separated from each other. No greater tragedy can befall
> society than the attempt to live in monologue rather than dia-
> logue. The church has the responsibility to open the channels of
> communication.[54]

Here we can see how King views the church as an educational
and communicative institution and urges it to act as such. The
church is an institution that can influence the individual and
give him the necessary tools to both fight to change society
and actually change it in the long run. Not only does it have
the ultimate truth of religious faith at its side in this mission,
King also says that the church must use the truths of modern
science to dismantle what he calls the "ideational roots of racial prejudice." This creates a special relationship between the
church and the individual worshiper (and the individual civil
rights activist). The church must be something that produces
and mediates knowledge that the individual can use to build a
new identity, an identity that then becomes a base for the project
of the civil rights movement. The transformation of society is
therefore to be carried out by this individual who, through the
church's body of knowledge, has broken free from what almost
can be described as a false consciousness.[55]

But it must also be remembered that the individual who becomes transformed in this manner influences society in primarily the same way as the church transformed him and broke
down his old identity. We are still at the level of morality; it is
through the transformation of values and the transformation
of the individual mentality that the new society will be born.

There is further complexity regarding the church's social
role (and it gets even more complicated when the religious function of the church is added to the mix). But that does not mean

that the pattern of change presented here and linked with the church's educational and enlightening role can be diminished in any way. It is one of the processes that the church is involved in and it also leads to a certain ideal; a community of brotherhood where the central notion is the equality between its members and where truth and knowledge create the possibilities for a moral authority in society.

THE POLITICAL AGENT

Another responsibility of the church is put forth in "The Church on the Frontier of Racial Tension," one that can be said to be a further consequence of the incompatibility between segregation and Christianity. If the first responsibility is to change the minds of the individuals that together exist in a community where communication and truth are possible, this second responsibility makes the church itself the active agent, not through giving the individual the possibilities and tools to act, but through itself participating in a social struggle as a powerful institution. This is what King names as the responsibility to participate actively in social reform.

King says that "the church must not only clarify the ideas, but it must move out in the realm of social reform. The church must develop an action program. Wherever there is injustice in society, the church must take a stand."[56] He then goes on to point out two of these injustices; economic injustice and the persistence of segregation within American churches. Regarding the first issue, he ends a passage where he points to the differences in wages for blacks and whites with the conclusion that "the church must make it clear that if we are to solve the problem and to create better conditions in society these economic conditions must be equalized."[57] Regarding the second issue, King says:

> Where there is segregation in any area the church must be willing to stand up with an action program. One of the best ways that the church can do this to remove the yoke of segregation from its own body. Oh, it has been said many times, and I am forced to repeat it,

it is tragic indeed that the church is the most segregated major institution in America. It is tragic indeed that on Sunday morning at 11 o'clock when we stand to sing "In Christ There is No East or West," we stand in the most segregated hour of Christian America. So often in the church we've had a high blood pressure of creeds and an anemia of deeds. But thank God we are beginning now to shake the lethargy from our souls, and we are coming to see that if we are to be true followers of Jesus Christ we must stand up and solve this problem.[58]

Here the church is a political institution. It must develop action programs to get rid of certain injustices that exist as a reality in present society, a society that the church is a substantial part of.

The key here is the type of change the church must enforce. It is not a change for which the church educates the transforming entities (individuals free from false consciousness); it is a change in which the church itself must be the transforming means.

The role the church plays vis-à-vis the individual worshiper is different from the role it plays as educator. In this respect it is necessary that the individual believers become a collective that is represented by the church as an institution. When the church then acts, it does so by incorporating all the individuals that are given a group identity through the process of the church, a process by which it comes to speak as a power bloc in society, representing both a corpus of religious faith through which it can give meaning to its actions and the worshipers who become associated with the activity of the church through their participation. The uniting force between these two sides is the implicit assumption that the church is the voice of Christianity in society and as such it is a force for righteousness. While the church's role as an educator stipulated that it had to help the individual gain an identity outside the alleged truths of segregation, this role stipulates that these individuals constitute a collective with a group identity which is represented by the church as a social agent. Here the church itself must act, whereas in its former role it was what gave the individuals the potential to act.

This difference is significant. Where the church in the former role was what established truth in a false reality and could thereby help the new world to cast off the shackles of the old, the church as a political agent goes a step beyond this since as a church it represents and incorporates truth. The transformation demanded is more specialized since the general change is already taken for granted. Truth is already established. But what must the church do with this truth in a society that still tries to hold it back? This conflict is of a different order.

The responsibility to work against economic injustice is a prime example. When King makes this claim, no religious legitimization is necessary. He simply states the economic facts of the differences between Negroes and whites in hard numbers and he concludes that "to create better conditions in society these economic conditions must be equalized." Several things can be noted in the self-evident way King discusses this as a responsibility of the church.

King's speech begins with the uncontestable premise that this-world responsibilities are inextricably intertwined with religious, or "other-world" responsibilities.

As an institution in society, the church is a constitutive part of this society. It does not stand above or outside society, since by definition it is an institution that takes an active part in social processes and conflicts. Therefore economic injustice is a responsibility of the church. The strong identification of the black church with the civil rights movement establishes a similar bond that reinforces further demands based on this relationship. It all rests on the assumption that the church is an institution that not only has a relationship with individuals but also has a relationship with society as a whole. Because the church offers a possibility for individuals to relate to society's institutions through a structure that interacts at the macrosocial level, other issues can be raised and other changes can be demanded.

In this the church of the African-American religious tradition can be recognized. From the beginning it was a simultaneously social and religious institution representing the identity of the black community—its past, present, and future. Religion and life were never separated; all experiences and aspects of life found a home and were molded into a cultural identity through the institution of the church. When King speaks of the responsibilities of the church, he is alluding to the understandings created in this tradition over the centuries. This also gives King room to maneuver and put forth demands while not stepping outside the movement discourse, since the church and the movement are two faces of the same historical experience and tradition. The creation and integration of a group identity are directly connected with the institution of the church.

There are further assumptions involved in King's demand for the church to take responsibility for economic reforms. Through the institution of the church, King gives himself the opportunity to speak constantly with the voice of righteousness.

The actual speaking situation should be noted when I make this claim. There is naturally a difference between a sermon discussing the church and its place within the faith and a speech before The Southern Baptist Theological Seminary on the responsibilities of the church vis-à-vis the struggle of the civil rights movement. No matter how much a sermon is oriented toward the *Social* Gospel, it must in some way or other discuss religious faith and central Christian topics in themselves.

In the speech King speaks on another level; he speaks of the responsibilities of the church in the struggle against segregation. He does not have to explicitly define what the struggle itself is and what its religious meaning is. It is about what the institution of the church must do.

Hence, in the meeting between a shared religious faith and the demands for economic justice that King creates in the speech, a process of interpretation is necessary. King gives the Christian faith meaning from the social demands he makes, and "the church" holds this together within the discourse. King can therefore make specialized demands on the grounds of a shared understanding—the truth and faith of Christianity.

As a social agent, the church formulates social demands that ultimately have an ideological meaning because the church as an institution takes part in a particular social struggle in which different viewpoints are made possible through the different systems of truths they subscribe to. The use of the church as the central institution of this faith this context functions in the same way as religious meaning does for the civil rights movement discourse. It conceals and allows specialized demands through the almost unbreakable association with the inclusiveness of general truths. A "within," a discourse of shared meaning, is created.

King's rhetoric speaks of the abolition of segregation in the language of religious necessity by giving the concrete social situation meaning within the religious framework and by stripping it of meaning outside that framework. The responsibility of the church goes both ways. The church only has a meaning when related to the society it is a part of. But its capacity to harness a group identity, be it black Americans or even all followers of Jesus Christ, is dependent on refraining from activity as a "political" organ when it functions in a this-world context to structure the faith of its followers. This means that something must happen when the church mediates its faith in the language of the present society, when it relates directly to a distinct situation. It also means that the relationship can be explained the other way around: Society is given a special meaning when it is confronted by the church. When the church works for social reform it represents something different than when a "regular" political organization does so since the church can base its reform demands on a widely shared Christian faith deeply embedded in American structures of thinking and reasoning. The church must take advantage of this opportunity, King argues, because the church can work for reforms within the realms of a different discourse than that of other organizations.

This also implies limitations on the scope of the demands King can make. If his arguments are to gain strength he has to connect them with the strength of the initial demand of the movement: Racial discrimination is wrong and must be abolished. It is this King always ultimately speaks of. The problems he puts his finger on are problems that are solvable only if the values that the nation was founded on become actualized. Coming to terms with economic injustice is a method of solving racial tension. This discourse includes all who are familiar with and believe in the tenets of the founding democratic principles of the United States.

King speaks of the church as political agent and social institution because he needs to do so. The church was the only contemporary institution whose righteousness was widely accepted; the ideology of his statements had to be placed within the realm of faith statements. His arguments are based on the necessities of God, not on what any one particular group thinks. In order for King to communicate, the ladder of signification needed to be active. He needed to use his position as a preacher. When it acts as a social agent, the church inevitably takes part in a struggle that has ideological frontiers. Therefore it must find a way to see itself in relation to the ideological arena in which it is situated. King presents this as obvious in his speech; the responsibility of the church is to participate in courses of action that are much more specialized than the faith in its general form implies. This is a version of his discursive process: Interpretation and implementation are necessary, but it is of utmost importance that the actual interpretation—*ideologization*—is as invisible as possible. In this project, the church has an important role to play.

King's way of communicating through and within the construction of a discourse narrows his horizon of possibilities at the same time that it opens the opportunity to express ideological demands (economic justice!) that would have another meaning if presented in another discourse. That it is the church which must be active in this kind of reform work makes it a both specialized and a general demand at the same time.

This is also tied in with the critique of the persistence of segregation in American churches that King delivers in the speech.[59] Not only are segregation and Christianity fundamentally incompatible, but segregation within the churches is also what stands most blatantly in opposition to King's view of the church as a social agent. Segregation between and within churches poses a grave challenge to King's project of presenting specialized ideological arguments mediated through the church as an institution, using the sanctity of the faith it incorporates. A segregated church delivers a radically different message. It justifies the practice of segregation through its very structure and it legitimizes social claims through its own practices; in so doing, it links them to the Christian faith.

This is evidently a version of the continual struggle to determine the meaning of Christianity, a struggle that in this case has a history as long as the presence of Africans in the Americas. It is crucial for King to incorporate this discussion into his rhetoric since his rhetoric and the discourse need the institution of the church—in his and not the segregationist's sense—to formulate demands with ideological meaning under the flag of the truth of God, Jesus, and the Bible.

THE CONSCIENCE OF SOCIETY

There is also a third responsibility of the church: faith. How is faith connected with the previous responsibilities? To answer this question we once again turn to "The Church on the Frontier of Racial Tension."

The last area that King defines as the responsibility of the church in the context of racial tension is that it "urges all men to enter the new age with understanding, creative good will in their hearts."[60] Here he mainly speaks of the primary method of the civil rights struggle—nonviolence, its ethical foundations, and how these are intimately related to the new world that is about to be born. But we can also begin to see a further responsibility of the church. King says:

> Somebody must have the sense in this world, somebody must have religion in this world—sense to meet physical force with soul force, sense enough to meet hate with love. This is why I believe so firmly in non-violence as the way out. And I am convinced that if the

Negro succumbs to the temptation of using violence in his struggle for justice, unborn generations will be the recipients of a long and desolate night of bitterness, and our chief legacy for the future will be an endless reign of meaningless chaos.

There is still a voice crying through the vistas of time, saying to every potential Peter; "Put up your sword." History is replete with the bleached bones of nations. History is cluttered with the wreckage of communities that failed to follow this command. So I will say over and over again that our aim must never be to defeat or humiliate the white man, but to win his friendship and understanding. We must see that it is possible to stand up with courage and determination, organizing in mass action to break down the system of segregation, and yet not going to the point of hating and using violence in the process. There is this other way. So if we will but follow this way, I think we too will be able to aid in bringing this new order into being.[61]

To a degree King departs from the more distinct responsibilities of the church for a general description of the mission of the civil rights movement. But still, throughout the speech he does not define a dividing line between the two. Everything he says must be understood as a part of the civil rights struggle. But how does the responsibility outlined in this passage differ from the two previously presented? While the first responsibility was concerned with the church's ability to influence the individual and turn him into an active agent for the transformation of society's ideas and the second spoke of an institution that needed to take an active part in political processes using its position as a church to make room for ideological demands, this third role goes farther. It speaks of the production of ethics and the church's responsibility for the appearance of the future society.

Here the church is the source and upholder of divine ethics and morality. The church stands as the guarantee that the world is in tune with the moral structures of the universe of almighty God. We meet the church as the conscience of society, the religious institution. The passage not only speaks of what the church must do with its position of power in society, it also speaks of what it must do as directly related to God and as a modern intermediary for the divine ethics of Jesus Christ.

When King speaks of the duty to employ the methods of nonviolence in the struggle, he states that somebody has to "have religion." This squares with the last sentence of the passage, which says that something new will come into being. If this "new" thing is going to be born through the actualization of a particular ethic, through a relationship with the supreme morality of God as exemplified by Jesus Christ, somebody or something must give birth to it. This is the task of the church, the mediator of God's will, and, as such, responsible for its actualization in society. The church is what must "have religion" in a society, both in itself as an institution and as representing its members. If society is going to move in the right direction, the church must have a central place in both the actual transformation and in the end result that is produced.

In the speech, King expands this discussion through the set piece where he explains the difference between eros, philos, and agape and critiques the maladjusted contemporary society, another common King theme.[62] Finally, he reaches the goal of divine ethics when he says that the "creative minority that will stand firm on an issue will help bring into being the Kingdom of God, knowing that in the process, God struggles with us."[63] The "Kingdom of God" is what the struggle will finally lead to. And it is also, as we shall see, what determines the role of the church and its place in this aspect of King's manifested faith.

The sermon "Guidelines for a Constructive Church" further elaborates on the religious responsibilities of the church. The guidelines laid out in the sermon include three major responsibilities: to heal the broken-hearted, to free people, and to preach the acceptable year of the Lord. It is obvious that a different language is involved here than the language of "The Church on the Frontier of Racial Tension." This is a sermon and it is therefore more closely concerned with expressing faith in itself. King speaks to his congregation as the preacher, as the individual who has been vested with the authority of God.

The starting point is the elevated position of the preacher, which allows him to interpret faith adequately and apply it to a social situation. With the words of this faith, he can speak of the existing situation, the ideal situation, and the role of the church. While in the speech to the seminar, King needed faith as a general set of values shared with the listeners, here he needs the authority of the preacher to conceal the interpretation and ideologization of faith. The situation is different and therefore the function of "the church" is different.

This does not mean that there are no similarities. The church's responsibility to act ethically is one such point. Its job is to guarantee that every struggle it is involved in is compatible with the intentions of God's moral universe—in short, to "have religion." The church has the responsibility to guarantee that the civil rights struggle is not just based on religious values but that it also strives for an end result that can be defined in religious terms. Hence, in both this part of the speech and, as we shall see, in the sermon, the aim is to, in true Social Gospel fashion, establish God's kingdom on earth.

Naturally, both the church as an educator and the church as a social agent are manifestations of the Christian faith, but the church in the latter part of the speech and in the sermon goes beyond this. Previously we dealt with the church as an institution firmly placed within time and in a definite social context; here we deal with the church's typological function, its role within a sacred universe, its role not only as a manifestation of the ethics of Jesus but also as God's proxy on earth. This offers King rich possibilities for transforming the words of God into the existing reality of the congregation.

The first responsibility of the church is not of any great importance in this context. By healing the broken-hearted King simply means the church's responsibility to help people in pain. This is a general Christian view of the church as the extended arm of the loving God.

The church's responsibility to free people is more directly related to the practice analyzed here. In an intense passage after King has presented this responsibility and criticized in harsh words both white and black churches that are afraid to take a stand, he elaborates:

For the guidelines made it very clear that God anointed. No member of Ebenezer Baptist Church called me to the ministry. You called me to Ebenezer, and you may turn me out of here, but you cannot turn me out of the ministry, because I got my guidelines and my anointment from God Almighty. And *anything* I want to say, I'm going to say it from this pulpit. It may hurt somebody, I don't know about that; somebody may not agree with it. But when God speaks, who can but prophesy? The word of God is upon me like fire shut up in my bones, and when God's word gets upon me, I've got to say it, I've got to tell it over everywhere. And God has called me to deliver those that are in captivity.

Some people are suffering. Some people are still hungry this morning. Some people are still living with segregation and discrimination this morning. I'm going to preach about it. I'm going to fight for them. I'll die for them if necessary, because I got my guidelines clear. And the God that I serve and the God that has called me to preach told me that every now and then I'll have to go to jail for them. Every now and then I'll have to agonize and suffer for the freedom of his children. I may even have to die for it. But if that's necessary, I'd rather follow the guidelines of God than to follow the guidelines of men. The church is called to set free those that are captive, to set free those that are victims of the slavery of segregation and discrimination, those who are caught up in the slavery of fear and prejudice.[64]

Central in this passage are the guidelines of the church—the word of God and the preacher. To begin with, the phrase "to free people" can naturally have a double meaning in the Christian context, but King makes his this-worldly interpretation of Christianity clear. The church has a divine responsibility to take part in the freeing of individuals from any kind of oppression.

But how should this be done? In one way we can say that this demand incorporates both the educational responsibility and the social responsibility since the general demand is to free people from all aspects of oppression. But we are also on another level here since we are inside the context of a sermon. King speaks directly of how the church must free people because it is the tool of God. It must actualize the divine morality inherent in the universe.

We must remember that the preacher is vested with the truth

of God. This is what conceals the interpretation of the words of God into the language and facts of a contemporary reality. The preacher speaks the words of God and therefore it is not sufficient to speak of the church as an educational and reforming institution or even a social agent in this context. In this sense, setting captives free is a path to salvation that in the end must be collective. It is society that must be saved, and for this transformation to be possible society needs a conscience. The church has the obligation to preach the word of God so that it becomes relevant in the current situation and since it is through the preacher that God speaks, he has the central role.

By presenting the situation this way King does several things: He reinforces his authority as preacher, he gives the mission of the church a divine content by endowing it with typological meaning—a process that can be described as the social or civil rights struggle being sermonized, existing within the special logic and meaning of the sermon as a truth—and, finally, he opens up the possibilities for further specialized claims that become part of Christianity as words of God spoken by the preacher.

But to fully understand the process discussed here, the third guideline of the sermon must be approached, the one King defines as "to preach the acceptable year of the Lord."[65] The responsibility to preach the word of God sooner or later also confronts the reality that the church exists in. This confrontation can help us to see how the words of God become the words of the preacher and how these words also come to carry more specialized values and norms. It shows that the church is an institution that is a source of ideology as well as faith, not just when it clashes with the "false consciousness" of evil and untruth or when it interacts with other institutions in a political arena but also inside its own walls and in the very structure that makes it possible for it to deliver messages at all. It also shows that when the church assumes the position of the conscience of society, it rests upon the sanctification of reality that typology involves.

When defining "the acceptable year of the Lord" more directly, King blends the high and the low. He starts with the overarching and general definition:

> And then the church, if it is true to its guidelines, must preach the acceptable year of the Lord. You know that the acceptable year of the Lord is the year that is acceptable to God because it fulfills the demands of his kingdom. Some people reading this passage feel that it's talking about some period beyond history, but I say to you this morning that the acceptable year of the Lord can be this year. And the church is called to preach it.
>
> The acceptable year of the Lord is any year when men decide to do right.[66]

Thereafter nineteen further interacting definitions follow. The demands are of four kinds. First, there are concrete demands directly related to the civil rights struggle such as "the acceptable year of the Lord is when people in Alabama will stop killing civil rights workers who are simply engaged in the process of seeking their constitutional rights." Second, there are the congregational demands related to the everyday lives of the parishioners such as "the acceptable year of the Lord is the year when women will start using the telephone for constructive purposes and not to spread malicious gossip and false rumors on their neighbors." Third, there are the general ethical demands such as "the acceptable year of the Lord is that year when men will learn to live together as brothers." Finally, there are the typological demands such as "the acceptable year of the Lord is that year when men will allow justice to roll down like waters, and righteousness like a mighty stream" or "the acceptable year of the Lord is that year when every valley shall be exalted, and every mountain will be made low."[67]

Together these diverse claims form the utopia from which they are drawn. They are related to each other in several different ways. Naturally, they are related to each other through the speaking situation. But the claims are also interrelated in that they all both describe and prescribe something by contrasting "reality" and ideality and in that that they are parts of an interpretation that is needed to create the dichotomy between an existing reality and that what this reality must be changed into. If we further distinguish this interpretive act, it can help us to understand the function of the church and the preacher in this sermon. The church is that which transmits the will of God in the world. At the center of this process stands the preacher with the power of interpretation in his hand, an interpretation that goes both ways: He must receive *and* deliver the will of God. It is this tight connection between the assumption that the preacher speaks as vested with the authority of God, the actual content of the sermon, and the function of the church as part of this content as well as its disseminator that makes the varied content of the "acceptable year of the Lord" possible. It allows highly specialized demands such as "using the telephone for constructive purposes" and general demands such as "live together as brothers" to interact as parts of the divine message of God.

This illustrates the powerful position of the church in King's rhetoric. Its position as a religious institution—a place where faith is delivered, the word of God is spoken, and the ethics of Jesus can be encountered—means that all issues that can be spoken of within the boundaries of this meaning are bestowed with the same level of truth as other aspects of the faith for a believer. It also makes it possible for preachers (through the functioning of the church) to judge the world, society, or even an individual. The key is to make room for as much as possible within the walls of the church or, in other words, within the realms of the discourse. This strategy is what King expands in his rhetoric in its entirety, but it has its ideal form in this type of sermon context.

King's position as a civil rights leader in society is inextricably linked with his position as a preacher within a church and his relationship with his congregation. King establishes a position from which he can compare the facts of reality with the will and word of God, and when he uses this position optimally even the content of phone calls becomes the concern of God.

The importance of the typological technique for this process cannot be disregarded. Its sanctification of a contemporary reality acts both as a constant reminder of what the position of the preacher involves—the close relationship with God that makes it possible to see the structure of history—and as a creator of religious meaning—even if all statements are not directly related to a biblical truth, they all come to have a definite relationship with that truth.

finally, the comparison between the existing world and the will of God also needs a base from which this "will of God" emanates and where a grounding of the diverse demands can share a space. At the same time, it must guarantee the truth of the comparison between the actual world and the will of God. This is the function of "the Kingdom of God." King says:

> These are our guidelines, and if we only follow the guidelines, we will be ready for God's kingdom, we will be doing what God's church is called to do. We won't be a little social club. We won't be an entertainment center. But we'll be about the serious business of bringing God's kingdom to this earth.[68]

If the guidelines that King has presented are followed, God's kingdom will appear on earth. This is what the sermon as a whole leads up to. By criticizing the two extremes of the black church (snobbery and emotionalism) King positions the church on a level that goes far beyond these extremes. It is not a middle road he proposes, it is something beyond it. The conservative church and the emotional church are both defined not by a task or mission but by a particular character in a contemporary society. But when King defines his church as a definitively religious institution characterized by the guidelines previously outlined, he does so by defining its mission, a mission that determines its outlook. He totalizes the church, but the fine point is that when he does so he does not position it outside society. Instead, when the church is defined and referred to this way, King brings society into the church, or more correctly, inside the framework of the church and the structure of interpretation and truth that exists inside its walls. The interpretation of faith leads to a definition of the world and all that it contains, and this definition is vested with the authority that the preacher has when standing in his pulpit.

"The Kingdom of God" plays an important part in this, because it cannot be viewed solely as the sought-after end result. In fact it must be actualized long before the actual mission of the church is completed. When King interprets the word of God and compares the interpretation with the actuality of the world, he creates a dichotomy: "This must be changed" always consists of a polarization between "this is what is" and "this is what is not." The latter of these two poles answers to both the interpretation of God's will that has been made and that which will be the end result of the struggle.

King's characterization of the "Kingdom of God" falls into four categories. It is a this-worldly term that describes the ideal result of the collective struggle of humanity—a metaphor for the final success of the civil rights movement; a society that is not just transformed but saved in the religious meaning of the word. It is also an otherworldly term, a rhetorical altar call that describes where the church can lead the individual if he gives his life to its faith. It is also a term that is defined by the struggle. How the struggle is fought and how the movement interprets and legitimizes itself determines what the kingdom is, since that is what is striven for. Finally, it also defines the struggle. It is the silent place whence the urge to change emanates; it is what makes the interpretation and legitimization of the struggle possible.

"The Kingdom of God" can be defined here as a utopian superstructure: a term that can include, harmonize, and to give structure to a diverse ideological and religious body of thought that then comes to be defined by being a component of this term. "The Kingdom of God" is discursively created by King's demands, but as an idea that gives structure to the goal and as something tacitly defined and self-evidently true, it is already present in the translation of the words of God into the words of man.

Ideal and Utopia II: The Beloved Community

The term "the beloved community" does not appear very frequently in King's rhetoric, but it can be found sporadically in speeches, sermons, and writings throughout his career.[69] The speech "Facing the Challenge of a New Age," held before the First Annual Institute on Non-Violence and Social Change in Montgomery in December 1956, provides an early example:

> This love might well be the salvation of our civilization. This is why I am so impressed with our motto for the week, "Freedom and Justice through Love." Not through violence; not through hate; no, not even through boycotts; but through love. It is true that as we struggle for freedom in America we will have to boycott at times. But we must remember that as we boycott that the boycott is not an end within itself; it is merely a means to awaken a sense of shame within the oppressor and challenge his false sense of superiority. But the end is reconciliation; the end is redemption; the end is the creation of the beloved community. It is this type of spirit and this type of love that can transform opposers into friends. It is this type of understanding that will transform the deep gloom of the old age into the exuberant gladness of the new age. It is this love that will bring about miracles in the hearts of men.[70]

And there are late examples such as this from the article "Non-violence: The Only Road to Freedom" as published in *Ebony* in October 1966:[71]

> Only a refusal to hate or kill can put an end to the chain of violence in the world and lead us to a community where men can live together without fear. Our goal is to create a beloved community and this will require a qualitative change in our souls as well as a quantitative change in our lives.[72]

Both these examples are representative of how King discusses "the beloved community." The term is always vague to the point where it almost seems empty. It describes the happy situation when the present society has been rid of all its evils; it is the end result of the struggle waged. But "the beloved community" is more than this. It also represents a central key to the civil rights movement discourse as a discourse of faith.

Utopia and Ideal Society

In what way does "the beloved community" represent a concrete ideal society and in what way does it represent a utopian precondition for the ideology that King's rhetoric produces?

My starting point is that there is a difference between *ideal society* and *utopia*. The former represents that which is actively and consciously striven for in a social struggle. It involves specialized definitions of what a good society is. It also includes the perception that the ideal society is produced in a contemporary society which incorporates fundamental social antagonisms and it is therefore involved in a debate and struggle with other ideals that it must always take into consideration and, in the end, accept compromise with. Utopia, on the other hand, is a conceptual category that is ultimately responsible for how this ideal is manifested and what it comes to incorporate. Since it is not a "part of" society, it does not have to relate to anything but itself.[73] In other words, it cannot be signified since it is that which signifies. But, and this is crucial, it is through its signifying activity that we can detect it.

"The beloved community" should be understood as the mediation between the conceptual category "utopia" and the concrete category "ideal society." It transmits that which is not to that which is. Meaning is given and shared through a process of signification. What "the beloved community" is is therefore derived from two instances.

To make this point clear, let us discern the two levels that are intermediated. The utopia that is the place from which contemporary reality is given meaning is quite evidently the kingdom of God in King's rhetoric.[74] The kingdom of God is "that which is not" but what all of reality must strive to be. Just as God is the ultimate definer of the struggle, the kingdom of God is its ultimate goal.

It is not only, as one might think, in sermons that this kingdom of God stands as the final category from which King's rhetoric emanates. One of the clearest examples is the final sentences of "I Have a Dream." After saying (using the words of

Isaiah) "I have a dream that one day every valley shall be exalted, and every hill and mountain made low; the rough places shall be made plain, and the crooked places shall be made straight; and the glory of the Lord will be revealed, and all flesh shall see it together," King ends the speech with:[75]

> And when this happens, when we allow freedom ring, when we let it ring from every village and hamlet, from every state and every city, we will be able to speed up that day when all God's children, black men and white man, Jews and Gentiles, Catholics and Protestants, will be able to join hands and to sing in the words of the old Negro spiritual:
>
> > Free at last! Free at last!
> > Thank God Almighty, we are free at last![76]

The coming of the kingdom of God proposed here represents the utopian side, the view of the struggle from a temporal and conceptual position where it has ended. It reveals both what is the end result of the struggle waged and what therefore gives meaning to the struggle. This dichotomy is present in any ideology and in any political discourse.

But then there is also the other side, the actual struggle in itself. The demands are for just wage structures, just housing policies, even the right to eat a hamburger at the restaurant of one's choice. These are demands raised in a contemporary society, one that may be conceptually determined by an utopian superstructure but one which also will have to be changed at its own level. *This* struggle has as its goal a society or community that can be described as an ideal, the best possible solution in practical reality.

"The beloved community" represents the way the utopian notion of the kingdom of God becomes a definite feature of the daily struggles of King and the civil rights movement and it represents how the naming process of the movement discourse cannot be divorced from concrete movement activities. When we mix the kingdom of God with a reformed America, the name of the new entity is "the beloved community."

The term also shows King's practice of speaking of the two instances at the same time. The use of "the beloved community" as a name for what is striven for is political religion and religious politics at the same time, and this simultaneity produces characteristics that go beyond the individual characteristics of its two "parts." "The beloved community" represents a concrete reformed America at a level that makes it compatible with the religious level at the same time as it represents the kingdom of God at the concrete level of the struggle. It shows how meaning is transferred within the discourse.

NORMS AND VALUES

"The beloved community" is also related to King's faith as presented in his rhetoric. It represents a strong Christian idea of an ideal society with a long tradition and it must also as such be related to a praxis situation.[77]

The meaning of "the beloved community," if taken as a concrete term, is something that can be called a religious-moral society. The content of King's messages and the system of signification within the discourse both manifest that morality comes first and that the rights and values of the individual are more fundamental than those of the state. For society to be morally guided it must therefore guarantee the individual his freedom and constantly guard it, since it is in and through this freedom that his possibility to reach God lies.

These are norms related to "the beloved community" as a proposed ideal; ultimately, it is a name for what will emerge when the struggle is won. It will be a demonstration of what can happen when religious rhetoric is linked with a specific discourse of faith: the civil rights movement discourse. As King writes in *Chaos or Community*, in order not to be destroyed through "moral and spiritual bankruptcy," society needs to be based on what can be called Christian values.[78] It is important here to note both the breadth and vagueness of these terms. They gain their meaning precisely through their broad range of meaning. And the final guarantee that these values will be present in society and the institution that can guarantee the individual's personal relationship with God is the church.

If we want to speak of an ideal implicitly present in King's rhetoric, it would be the situation where political and economical power are balanced by, and maybe even subordinate to, the moral authority of the church. When this is coupled with what can be "taken for granted" when King's vague ideal society is first approached, some further consequences appear. No political, economic, or moral barriers can be allowed to exist between people, and society must be based on an all-embracing love and mutuality. These fundamentals can be expressed in several different ways, but when that is done another way of discussing it is required. When we speak of the ideal that is present in King's rhetoric, we can do so through restating the rather vague ideals about a society based on love and mutuality-the beloved community, but we must also speak of the ideal that is implicitly present in his rhetoric. We cannot stop at his "own" declarations. They must be analyzed in order to bring the implicit ideals to the surface.

To have a moral society, the state has to be moral or at least have moral qualities. But since the state does not have moral qualities in itself, its citizens must ensure that they are present in the corporate body. The church must therefore be the leading social institution in the same way that it was King's base throughout the movement years, in the same way that religion was an integral part of the struggle, and in the same way that religion is the ultimate definer within the discourse that both describes and is a part of this struggle.

This powerful position of the church also presents an interesting question. The fact that it produces a hierarchy cannot be ignored. To have direct contact with God in a Christian society or community, to be a preacher and a prophet, establishes an authoritarian position from which it is possible to define the natural order of God. To preach the word of God is also to claim that one is capable of rightly interpreting the word of God. Therein lies a potential for conflict in a religious-moral society.

The person that stands closest to God has truth and the right to decide in his hands, but who decides who is to occupy this position? How far the democracy King found so profoundly important should be extended into the domains of the church is an interesting question.

THE MISSION OF THE MOVEMENT

finally, there is also a direct relationship between the project of the civil rights movements in American society and "the beloved community." Since the motto of the SCLC was to "save the soul of America," is it therefore safe to assume that when this mission is completed, "the beloved community" will appear? The question is naturally hypothetical, but it shows how "the beloved community" itself is hypothetical at the same time that it is delineated as a proposed ideal. It is intimately tied to the actual civil rights struggle and the quest to force America to rid itself of that which stands opposed to the values that the nation was founded on. The "religionization" of the struggle means that the society in which the struggle takes place and which must be changed is also "religionized," a trope deeply embedded in the American self-understanding.

The definition of "the beloved community" takes place within the framework of this historically conceived self-understanding, and the term is as such involved in this double signification. The beloved community points to the different features that are involved in the discursive process, but it also shows its outer framework. Its vagueness means two things in this respect. First, the concrete struggle of the civil rights movement and the issues this struggle brings to the fore create frameworks around this emptiness and also to a large degree determine with what it can be filled. Therefore the ideal-society content of "the beloved community" varies slightly according to the different emphases of King and the movement. The meaning of, for example, "integration" is different in the segregated South of the 1950s and the northern ghetto of the late 1960s.

Second, because the term is connected with the struggle of

the civil rights movement it is also, like the rhetoric of this movement, connected with the distinct American tradition of political
religion. "The beloved community" as a term was a definite part
of the language that created a fertile soil for the initial arguments of the civil rights movement in the minds of many Americans.

As the rather vague ideal that anyone who ever heard and
read King could connect with, "the beloved community" was
congruent with a way of speaking and understanding that was
established within American political discourse. Therefore, almost by default, it also takes part in the process of creating con-
sent in mainstream America. Hence, the term was also encircled
by a meaning that was rather limited despite its vagueness. It
was tied to a way of speaking of America and American society
that rested on a specific foundation of what the nation was. Any
potential radicalness in the term was a radicalness that was already present and accepted as a part of the American tradition.

This discussion should not, however, shroud the other meanings and functions of "the beloved community." It was more
than a term that had an ability to connect the goals of the civil
rights movement with the divine mission of America and thereby
create acceptance for the movement's demands within the American culture; this was just one of its aspects and qualities.

King's use of the term "beloved community" in general reveals how his rhetoric functions and what it "consists" of: The
beloved community is as much the kingdom of God as it is the
integrated and equalitarian United States, and these characteristics are simultaneous. The positive vagueness of "the beloved
community" illustrates the strength of King's rhetorical strategy of using language that includes as many concepts and people
as possible. But since this strategy also rests on ideals that are
part of the general hegemonic structure, it is restricted to speaking of the necessity to fulfill a promise rather than speaking of
something new. Underneath its challenge lies an agreement that
was shaped through the centuries and ultimately signified by
its biblical origins.

2. Western Intellectualism
and American Ideals

King used other texts, other authors, and other historical situations to legitimize the civil rights struggle and to ascribe meaning to his rhetoric that went beyond the context of the speaking situation. King's dual background in the preaching tradition of the African-American church and the academic world positioned him to use a rhetorical technique in which the texts and thoughts of others were drawn into his project.

Who and what does King use as references in his rhetoric? How do the allusions and references function in concrete and complex historical situations? Furthermore, and to paraphrase Cornel West; what does it mean to subscribe to a discourse of significant signifiers in Western cultural history?[1] In other words, in what way is it possible to speak of a discursive formation tied to this often seemingly "innocent" rhetorical strategy, and in what ways does it represent an ideological act?

To find the answers I will begin with a brief look at King's account of his education and discuss it in relation to the various documents from that period. This does not mean evaluations of his academic work or long excursions into the content of the theology and philosophy he later used as references. Instead it is a necessary starting point for the argument that this education, represented in King's rhetoric from the simplest name-dropping to the signifying of knowledge and truth, serves specific functions in the civil rights movement discourse.

Education and Reproduction

The central text for this purpose is "Pilgrimage to Nonviolence," first published as part of *Stride toward Freedom* and later revised and updated in 1960 as an article for the journal *Christian Century* and once more for inclusion in *Strength to Love*.[2] The first version is of greater interest here since it is longer and presents in a more detailed way King's understanding of how he reached the theoretical position he was using at the time he wrote "Pilgrimage to Nonviolence."[3]

The essay is placed in the middle of *Stride toward Freedom*, between the story of the conception of the Montgomery bus boycott and the description of the methods the opposition used in that struggle. The chapter has a distinct place in the narrative structure of the book as both a breathing space and a momentum builder. But more important for our purpose is that it is centrally placed and is constructed to give form and prestige to the leading character of the narrative—King himself.

The three different Kings of the book meet in this chapter: King the author of the book, King the character in the book, and King the leader who stands at the forefront of the movement, both as an activist and, as "Pilgrimage to Nonviolence" establishes, a theorist. The intellectual journey presented in the chapter is a journey that tries to combine these three into one.

The chapter's autobiographical character raises some questions since this is how King wanted to present himself, his viewpoints, and the foundations for the struggle of the movement when he, at least theoretically, had the ear of the entire nation. This self-constructing is crucial when using "Pilgrimage to Nonviolence" as a way to understand King's rhetoric and discourse. Together with the overt purpose of the chapter—to establish a foundation for an already implied philosophy of nonviolence—comes the construction and presentation of the public figure Martin Luther King, Jr. The chapter is, therefore, in a way twofold: It is about the position and philosophy of nonviolence and its benefits as the method of the modern civil rights struggle, and it is also about who King wants to be, what he wants to be portrayed as, how he wants to be understood, what language and understanding he uses, and what kind of dialogue and argumentation he wants to establish. It is about initializing and stabilizing a discursive structure around his and the movement's project and establishing and incorporating a specific meaning into it.

This further distinguishes the relationship between the public figure King and the civil rights movement discourse. When the book was written and published King had not yet reached the absolute height of his national (and international) fame. His persona, his intellectual identity, and the meaning of the struggle were still in a quite early phase. "Pilgrimage to Nonviolence" can therefore be understood as a fundamental text for understanding both who Martin Luther King, Jr. is and what the new civil rights movement is. The intellectual journey of King becomes the theoretical framework of the movement and this theoretical framework gives meaning and content—identity—to the civil rights movement.

King starts the chapter by giving examples of his childhood encounters with racial discrimination (places where lynchings had occurred, actions of the Ku Klux Klan, police brutality, and injustice in the courts), which led him to become "perilously close to resenting all white people." Early in his life he understood that racial and economic injustice were "inseparable twins."[4] So when King entered the intellectual world, these problems and injustices were already a part of him and his understanding of the world. The pilgrimage is an intellectual journey embarked upon to find what the world of theories and philosophies had to offer the young man longing for freedom and justice.

King first stop on the journey is Henry David Thoreau's "Essay on Civil Disobedience," which he read while attending Morehouse College in Atlanta in 1944.[5] He calls it his "first intellectual contact with the theory of nonviolent resistance."[6] Thoreau's name would be frequently used in King's subsequent speeches and books. As is the case here, he seldom gives a lengthier interpretation of Thoreau's essay or argument. He quite plainly uses it as a legitimization for the right not to cooperate with an evil system. Thoreau's essay fixes a meaning and establishes a truth through its standing in an American canon.

The reading of Thoreau is also all King mentions of his years at Morehouse, and "Essay on Civil Disobedience" therefore becomes a symbol for his first contact with nonviolence and the combination of his academic and activist careers. It also establishes a known historical American figure as a starting point for his argument. However challenging that figure may have been to hegemonic American values, it has, in the contemporary situation, become a part of American tradition and history.

Instead of further elaborating on his early studies, King takes us to his tenure at Crozer Theological Seminary, beginning in 1948, and this period constitutes the major part of the chapter.[7] Here King tells of his encounter with Walter Rauschenbusch's *Christianity and the Social Crisis*.[8] He criticizes Rauschenbusch on two counts—his superficial optimism regarding the nature of man and the attempt to equate the kingdom of God with a particular political system—but on the whole, King clearly credits Rauschenbusch for his conviction that one has a religious duty to look beyond the soul of man and to address his material needs.

King writes that after Rauschenbusch he "turned to a serious study" of the traditional philosophers.[9] He mentions Plato, Aristotle, Rousseau, Hobbes, Bentham, Mill, and Locke.[10] But that is all he says about them. He does not utter a word about their more specific contributions to his current thinking. He states that they stimulated his thinking and that he both learned from them and criticized them on some matters. It seems it is not the content of these philosophies that is of interest to King here; he does not even try to connect them with his position or to nonviolence through anything other than their names. Instead, King focuses on the tradition they form—Western philosophy as such. King has not only studied these philosophers, they have become part of his public persona and the movement's project because they are part of a text that constructed the public persona's theoretical background. King understood them and mastered them. As the journey goes farther, it becomes clear that they did not provide the solutions King was looking for, but that is not the point. The point is that he is evoking a tradition. Through this, a dialogic space is created and a home for the public persona King and the meaning of the civil rights struggle is further developed.

Marx is awarded a lengthier discussion. King states that he studied *Das Kapital* and *The Communist Manifesto* during the Christmas holidays of 1949. He writes that he "carefully scrutinized" the books, but how well he studied them is a question that it is hard to answer.[11] The discussion of Marx in "Pilgrimage to Nonviolence" is roughly the same as all public discussions of Marx during King's career.[12] He cannot accept the ethical relativism of communism; he condemns it as "basically evil" because of its "deprecation of individual freedom." To King, history is spirit, not matter.[13] But the social goal of Marxism is something else. Herein lies the strength and challenge of the theory. King argues that this goal essentially consists of fundamental Christian values that are too often forgotten by churches and theologians and that Marxism is, in this respect, a legitimate criticism of the evils of capitalism.

The intellectual and political climate of 1950s America is of course important here. Marxism (or rather communism) was a constant presence during the Cold War. Fear of communism meant that Marxism was a theory that was in a way constantly present in American society. King discusses it more thoroughly and more directly than he does any other political theory. It had to be addressed and it had to be condemned, but in describing himself as a person who has carefully studied Marxism and is able to, in an analytical, academic and intellectual way, distinguish and address both its strengths and weaknesses, the public intellectual King takes further shape. A careful analysis of Marx is necessary in his project. But he defuses it politically as his public persona and the goals of the movement take precedence.

Three names are central in the rest of "Pilgrimage to Non-

violence": Gandhi, Niebuhr, and Hegel.[14] Gandhi holds a special place in King's project as the prime intellectual and political legitimization behind the early civil rights movement. The
story of how Gandhi became this central figure and how even
before the Montgomery bus boycott he was well integrated
into the African-American tradition can be read elsewhere, but
it is important to point out the prime example of legitimization that the use of Gandhi constitutes.[15] He became a part of
the Montgomery struggle primarily from the outside, largely
through Bayard Rustin, who viewed the ongoing boycott as
the perfect opportunity to inject Gandhian methods and theories into the struggle against segregation. Before Rustin came
to Montgomery in February 1956, the boycott had been a movement with a nonviolent method and ethic of love rather one
exclusively based on the teachings of Jesus.[16] With the introduction of Gandhian principles a further foundation was established. These principles quickly became an integral and often dominant part of the presentation and self-understanding
of the movement and its identity.

Even though King never formally read Gandhi during his
education, he had already encountered his thinking during his
Morehouse years. Mainly, however, he met it through the
strong Gandhian contingent at Crozer Theological Seminary
in the late 1940s. King states that he then studied Gandhi in-
tensively, but it is now clear that although he had a firm interest in and knowledge of Gandhi from his Crozer years, he did
not actually study Gandhi and Gandhian methods more systematically until February 1956, after the Montgomery boycott was instigated and had gained momentum.[17]

In "Pilgrimage to Nonviolence," Gandhi is the hero. Here
King found the final components of what he had been looking
for in all Western philosophy. His pilgrimage to nonviolence
becomes a pilgrimage to Gandhi. King writes:

> The intellectual and moral satisfaction that I failed to gain from
> the utilitarianism of Bentham and Mill, the revolutionary meth-
> ods of Marx and Lenin, the social contracts theory of Hobbes, the
> "back to nature" optimism of Rousseau, and the superhuman phi-

losophy of Nietzsche, I found in the nonviolent resistance philosophy of Gandhi. I came to feel that this was the only morally
and practically sound method open to oppressed people in their
struggle for freedom.[18]

This passage provides an opportunity to understand the function that the text and the long list of the names of important
figures in the history of Western philosophy have for the construction of King as a public intellectual and role of the rhetorical construction "Martin Luther King, Jr." as the leader of
the civil rights movement. It can be viewed from two angles.

In one sense, the passage is an accusation. What King says is
that the history of Western philosophy has not been able to
provide an answer to "oppressed people in their struggle for
freedom."[19] Instead, King found Jesus and Gandhi. Something
outside the Western tradition provided King with the methods
to attack the evils of segregation.

But even if this can be accepted as a first interpretation of
the passage and "Pilgrimage to Nonviolence" as a whole, there
is also another way of understanding it. The primary function
of the long line of philosophers is not to be repudiated as not
being enough. The names and references are crucial in themselves. Two areas of King's project meet here. Gandhian philosophy and Western philosophy do not fulfill the same function in King's attempt to create legitimacy for his struggle and
to establish himself as a public figure. Gandhi belongs to the
activity-centered moment of the discourse when the movement
is defined as a concrete social force, whereas the short references to a Western academic tradition represent a written moment of the discourse. They represent another form of justification. This duality is present in "Pilgrimage to Nonviolence,"
even though King tries to trace a single line of influence that
included everyone from Bentham to Gandhi. Gandhi is actualized in connection with concrete actions, the actual active moment of nonviolent resistance, while the line of philosophers
plays a different part in the struggle. This line of philosophers
is used and actualized before the active moment, as an appeal
to act and to legitimize the righteousness of the coming action

within the logic of the universe. They are also used *after* the active moment, again to legitimize the righteousness of the action.

But the philosophers still failed to provide King with an answer. That is true, but let us not forget the importance of the actual journey of the pilgrimage. The public intellectual who is constructed in the text does not in essence accuse Western philosophy when he states that it failed to provide him with a moral and practical answer. Instead he incorporates the tradition; he creates himself from the structure it forms. Two Kings meet: the intellectual who is well read in the history of philosophy and can initiate a debate about the movement at that level and the activist of the Montgomery bus boycott and future campaigns. How do you find a position from which to argue with this duality? Gandhi holds a central position in "Pilgrimage to Nonviolence," that much is incontrovertible, but it is not the only story of the chapter or, perhaps more correctly, the central function that the chapter comes to have. In addition to the story of how Gandhian nonviolence is the central theory that emerged from his quest, King reproduces and constructs his own education and establishes the special position that it has given him.

Reinhold Niebuhr is the next thinker King points to as important. He states that he became intrigued by *Moral Man and Immoral Society* about the same time that he studied Gandhi. Niebuhr offered a critique of the pacifist position that forced King to refine his own position. In general, he refutes Niebuhr's objections to the practice of nonviolence. What is important in Niebuhr's writing, though, King states, is his critique of the false optimism regarding the nature of man that prevailed in liberal theology. According to King, Niebuhr was able to critique this notion without falling into the trap of what he calls the "anti-rationalism" of Karl Barth or resorting to fundamentalist orthodoxy.[20]

King writes that Niebuhr made him aware of man's potential for evil.[21] He connects this realization with the next step in his intellectual journey. He moves on to his graduate studies at

Boston University and mentions the professors that inspired and influenced him and states that the idealistic Personalism he encountered there is still his "basic philosophical position."[22]

Then Hegel enters the narrative in a short passage.[23] King writes that he disagrees with certain points in Hegel's philosophy but only gives one example: "His absolute idealism was rationally unsound to me because it tended to swallow the many into one."[24] But he credits Hegel with two important contributions to his current position: "His contention that 'truth is in the whole' led me to a philosophical method of rational coherence. His analysis of the dialectical process, in spite of its shortcomings, helped me to see that growth comes through struggle."[25]

The obvious question is why King needed Niebuhr to see the potential for evil in man when he just could look out of the window in the South to see the evils of segregation. And was it because of Hegel that he understood that "growth comes through struggle"?[26] We must also go beyond this chicken-or-egg debate and understand the structure of King's texts and the structure of the discourse it both establishes and maintains.

When "Pilgrimage to Nonviolence" connects King's education with the struggle for civil rights, it makes them into one whole entity. It has three foundations: Western philosophy, modern theology, and Gandhian nonviolence. King describes his academic life as a search for answers he had yet to encounter. When he actually writes the chapter and presents it to the reading audience, the situation has changed. The writing about his education takes place inside the movement discourse, which the actual education did not. When we read of King's education as it is presented here, we also read of the intellectual climate of 1950s America. This is apparent if we study the later versions of "Pilgrimage to Nonviolence." In 1963, he has scrutinized existentialist philosophy, a philosophical school that he does not mention at all in the first version.[27]

What is important here is not King's actual education; it is his presentation of it. The education enabled King to create the connection between both traditional and (as in the case of existentialism) modern philosophy and theology and the struggle. King's presentation of his education is about establishing and solidifying meaning. The civil rights struggle takes place within the corpus of knowledge comprised of the history of philosophy and theology. It can and should be understood within the frames this creates.

"Pilgrimage to Nonviolence" is an example of King's technique of reference and allusion. His representation of his education constitutes and establishes a specific understanding of who he is, what the movement is, and what the struggle is about. And if he and the movement can be fixed in this position, they have won dominion over a crucial naming process. King's representation and reproduction of his education, under the guise of an almost deterministic journey to the theory and method of nonviolence, is an important element in the construction of the public figure of Martin Luther King, Jr. And it is an important element in our understanding of this figure.

His actual education is a quite another matter. Because King decided to archive all his material it is possible to follow his development. This material has been thoroughly analyzed in recent years and the picture of King the (graduate) student is now a familiar one. Always eager to impress his various professors, he often wrote what they expected; he was not a spectacular student and he had problems with the formal demands of scholarly writing, something that followed him through the years and came to a climax in the dissertation in systematic theology at Boston University: "A Comparison of the Concepts of God in the Thinking of Paul Tillich and Henry Nelson Wieman."[28]

But this is not a reason to dismiss his academic background and its importance for the public persona Martin Luther King, Jr. became. Although "Pilgrimage to Nonviolence" does not give a *true* account of his education, it must not be dismissed. This is, on the contrary, what gives it its special meaning and function. The philosophers and theologians, philosophies and theologies mentioned constitute a structure established to give meaning and identity to the civil rights struggle.

The next step is a broader look at King's web of allusions. Who and what does he draw into his project?

From Shakespeare to Behaviorism: Allusion as Technique

LITERATURE

King's rhetorical technique of referring to lines, phrases, and passages from literary history had deep roots. The practice stemmed from his profession as a preacher in which the sermon is the basic rhetorical form. Quotations are most often used as proofs of the thesis outlined in the sermons and speeches; they support an initial argument found in a preached text or a fundamental religious guarantee. The quotes from the literary history of the Western world in this way become evidential arguments.

One of the most frequently used examples of this literary argumentation comes in the form of a triad that King seems to love to use. It appears, with slight variations, throughout his career; the first time he used it was in his earliest known recorded sermon "Rediscovering Lost Values," delivered at Detroit's Second Baptist Church in February 1954 and the last time was in his last Sunday morning sermon "Remaining Awake Through a Great Revolution," preached at the National Cathedral in Washington, D.C., in March 1968.[29] The following example comes from this last occasion:

> We shall overcome because Carlyle is right—no lie can live forever. We shall overcome because William Cullen Bryant is right—truth crushed to earth shall rise again. We shall overcome because James Russell Lowell is right—as we were singing earlier today, "Truth forever on the scaffold, wrong forever on the throne, yet that scaffold sways the future, and behind a dim unknown, stands a God within the shadows, keeping watch above his own."[30]

The triad was often, although not here, combined with a line from the Bible ("You shall reap what you sow" or a similar passage) and together they formed a powerful rhetorical vehicle that King often placed at the climax of sermons and speeches. Although the authors of these three passages are not the most elite of the literary tradition, they have a clear place in American and literary history. When their words ring out in King's sermons and speeches, they are presented as the messengers of truth of the literary tradition. Their words have been carved into the structure of eternity.

The quotations form a proof that King's arguments are based on righteousness. He infuses them with the truth of God's moral universe and he gives the words almost biblical qualities. The sacred history of God incorporates the history of classical literature. The possibility to create and establish meaning is not exclusively limited to the actual words of the quotations themselves. Allusion also functions as a form. The struggle is being textualized at the same time that the text becomes a material reality. When King uses these quotes and passages, they are activated in a specific situation and thus have a specific function in the determination of what this situation is and means. This is also the case with other recurrent literary references and quotes. King frequently quotes Shakespeare, Donne, and Tolstoy, among others.[31]

It would be easy to argue that the use of literature simply fills the function of ornamentation; that, in contrast with his use of philosophy and theology, King does not use it to outline a specific idea, that it is not a part of any system of belief that proposes certain arguments. One might think that in King's rhetoric, literature gives form where philosophy and theology give content. It is "only rhetoric" as opposed to complex theories and ideas.

But this is a misunderstanding. The allusions help to build and uphold the specific moral universe that King continually refers to as a precondition for the struggle. They represent idealism in its most basic sense. The universe is moral, the world is spirit, the struggle is spiritual, and there is no fundamental difference between concrete material arguments and idealistic intellectual ones. Words, written or spoken, are always acts with a specific place in the moral universe upheld by almighty God.

Through this point of view we can detect two functions of King's literary quotes and references. One is to establish discursive boundaries within which a naming of the world takes place. The other is to manifest and consolidate religious belief in the moral universe of God. The quotes and allusions establish a particular form of understanding, a form into which the understanding of what the struggle is must also be fitted, and they also represent the content of the faith manifested in King's rhetoric: The universe is moral, reality is ultimately spiritual, evil will eventually be defeated by the forces of good, and so forth. And ultimately, these two functions are impossible to separate. They are what create and give meaning to each other.

PHILOSOPHY

In the field of philosophy, King's practice is roughly the same as with the literary allusions and quotes he uses. He often uses short lines, aphorisms, and thoughts as rhetorical tools. Prime examples are the Aristotelian syllogism, Hegel's dialectical method, and Martin Buber's distinction between "I-Thou and "I-It" relationships.

King uses the Aristotelian syllogism to demonstrate the absurdity of the logic of segregation. Aristotle becomes part of a tragic joke:

> Even philosophical logic was manipulated to give some intellectual credence to the system of slavery. Someone formulated the inferiority of the Negro according to the framework of an Aristotelian syllogism:
>
> > All men are made in the Image of God;
> > God, as everyone knows, is not a Negro;
> > Therefore, the Negro is not a man.[32]

Almost mockingly, King discusses here how the advocates of segregation have tried to do what he himself so often does: legitimize arguments and views with proofs from other fields. Of course, it is not Aristotle that is ridiculed here; it is the misunderstanding and misrepresentation of him. Aristotle is not important other than because of his name. King hardly ever refers to Aristotelian thought, but his use of the Aristotelian syllogism is one of many examples of this struggle over the interpretation of the Western tradition that takes place in the civil rights struggle, similar to the way that in the civil rights struggle in general there is a constant struggle over the meaning of the words of the Bible and the faith of Christianity. If segregationists use a simple syllogism this way, how can you trust any of their arguments rooted in or based on philosophy and the history and tradition it forms? Segregationists do not command the absolute knowledge that belongs to the history of the mind, a history that is also the history of the universe. To command this tradition is to command and understand this history and it is to situate it inside one's own meaning and definition of the struggle.

If the literary references can be seen as artistic proofs of King's arguments, the philosophical examples and references are often arguments in themselves. They become a method of legitimizing the struggle's claims to righteousness. The tradition becomes a part of the struggle and vice versa, and it gives a philosophical veneer to King's speeches and texts. King himself approaches the position of philosopher in this process, a position that creates the possibility of the definitional power of neutrality.[33] Through this position, King comes to represent an objective truth shaped through centuries of collective human intellectual achievement and knowledge.

King often uses Hegel in this way, often through the dialectical triad of thesis, antithesis, and synthesis. He uses Hegel to legitimize the principle of compromise, whether it be the compromise between communism and capitalism, the active and passive tactics of the concrete struggle, or the spiritual and material nature of man. This reconciliation, for which he often credits the Hegelian dialectic, is also the base from which King sees the history of philosophy as a whole. There are always two sides to every philosophy and philosopher, King argues, one you can criticize and one you can learn from. This is a central part of King's use of philosophy and philosophers; they come to represent the collective knowledge of the universe of idealism. When King uses philosophers as legitimization he not only uses them as rhetorical reference points to make the structure and argument of the particular sermon, speech, or text convincing; he also rhetorically ascribes them with a deterministic meaning in the history of the world. He connects them with the eternal wisdom of God and the truths of Christianity, and in his role as civil rights leader King defines himself as part of this wisdom and truth. This eternal wisdom is the perspective from which he views philosophy. He commands the history of philosophy in an earthly way—which is an important merit—but he can also view it from the position of having access to an absolute truth.

The third prime example of allusions and references to philosophy is King's use of Martin Buber's distinction between "I-Thou" and "I-It" relationships.[34] King often uses this as a pedagogical tool to explain the psychological terror of segregation. The use of the distinction often also forms an attempt to show the abstract aspects of the problem of segregation that concerns the deepest level of human existence. The following example, which King further bolsters by a reference to Immanuel Kant, is from the speech "America's Chief Moral Dilemma," which he made in Chicago in 1965:

> Segregation stands diametrically opposed to the principle of the sacredness of human personality. It debases personality. Immanuel Kant said in one formulation of the categorical imperative that "all men must be treated as ends and never as mere means." The tragedy of segregation is that it treats men as means rather than ends, and thereby reduces them to things rather than persons. To use the words of the late Martin Buber, segregation substitutes an "I-It" relationship for the "I-Thou" relationship. The colloquialism of the Southern landed gentry that referred to slaves and Negro labor as "hands" betrays the "things" quality assigned to the Negroes under the system. Herein lies the root of the paternalism that persists even today.[35]

Again, the question is why King needed Buber (and Kant) at all. The purpose is to explain and outline the wrongfulness of segregation, which to a King audience must be already obvious from the outset. So why discuss and develop it in this way? The answer reveals two specific, albeit interconnected, functions of this technique: King's desire to portray the actual dilemma as something deeper and part of a general human range of problems and his striving for a neutral position from which these problems can be judged and given meaning within an established structure.

The problems of segregation, racial discrimination, and injustice are never placed in just one specific context in King's rhetoric. It is the constant connection with higher issues that gives this rhetoric its specific character, quality, meaning, and consequences. So when he brings in Buber (as he did on this and many other occasions) to explain what segregation does to the value of the human being it is not because Buber makes the problem understandable in a basic sense. That is obvious to anyone in any way connected with the civil rights struggle. King thought that Buber had caught the essence of the problem in easily understandable and forceful phrases, but he referred to him because his thinking gave the struggle a further element of truth because it elevated the problem of segregation and its evils to the level of idealistic knowledge.

THEOLOGY

With Buber we encounter the border area between philosophy and theology, another major field of King's allusions and references. Here King sticks to the names and debates that stood at the center of his education—Rauschenbusch, Niebuhr, and Tillich; the debate between liberal theology and neo-orthodoxy and Personalism.

King also uses his formal theological background more as a entire entity rather than pointing to specific principles. It constitutes a central kernel of meaning and legitimization in many speeches and, above all, in sermons that are directly related to

the theological debates of the day.[36] Theology is closely connected with the public figure King, the civil rights preacher
who through his rhetoric presents a truth-claiming interpretation of Christianity that also is based on a deep knowledge of
theological problems and theories. While philosophy offers an
established canon for King to choose from, theology gives him
access to another range of ideas. He knows his classics—St.
Augustine and Aquinas are often mentioned—but he can also
relate to the contemporary discussion and thereby become a
part of it. When he incorporates references to this field of knowledge into his rhetoric, he elevates the civil rights struggle into
the realm of high ideals.

This is not to neglect the fact that King obviously wants to
discuss theological issues in his sermons—to argue otherwise
would be deeply unfair. But this practice also comes to have a
legitimizing function in his rhetoric. The references to and incorporation of theology and theological discussions enhance
the meaning-establishing features and character of his rhetoric. It not only sets the level for the discussion of someone who
wishes to oppose King's argument, it also lends to his viewpoints the force of the collected truth of hundreds of years of
discussions about God and Christianity.

THE AMERICAN POLITICAL TRADITION

The fourth area King draws on for his rhetorical references
is the American political tradition. He repeatedly refers to presi-
dents such as Abraham Lincoln and Thomas Jefferson, and
founding documents such as the Declaration of Independence
and the Constitution, not only to legitimize but to symbolize,
and in some cases even to serve as, the core of King's argument: The civil rights movement is an American movement.
Both the strategic and discursive meanings of this position in
the context of 1950s and 1960s America are central to understanding the effect of King's rhetoric and the civil rights movement in general. It defines a position within an American tradition and it creates the opportunity for a particular form of

righteousness; the movement and the political tradition are so closely linked that they become synonymous in King's rhetoric.

This aspect of his technique of using rhetorical references is somewhat different from his use of literature, philosophy, and theology. While these areas directly establish a connection with the moral and idealistic universe that stands above time as eternally valid truths, the use of the American political tradition is linked with King's and the civil rights movement's basic project of delivering an answer to the question of what America is, can, and should be. The demands of the movement are fused with the documents that ultimately constitute the nation and its creed.

His speech at the first mass meeting of the Montgomery bus boycott before the crowded auditorium of the Holt Street Baptist Church in December 1955 is the moment when King the movement leader can be said to be born. He establishes himself as this figure in a passage that in many ways is a typical example of the structure of King's rhetoric. The Bible and the Constitution become the two documents from which the movement is fed. The revolution against segregation is an utterly American act:

> There will be nobody amid, among us who will stand up and defy the Constitution of this nation. We only assemble here because of our desire to see right exist. My friends, I want it to be known that we're going to work with grim and bold determination to gain justice on the buses in this city.
>
> And we are not wrong, we are not wrong in what we are doing. If we are wrong the Supreme Court of this nation is wrong, the Constitution of the United States is wrong. If we are wrong, God Almighty is wrong. If we are wrong Jesus of Nazareth was merely a utopian dreamer that never came down to earth. If we are wrong justice is a lie. Love has no meaning.[37]

This example illustrates the different levels in King's rhetoric and how he places references to the central documents of American political history within this scheme. First King establishes that what the movement is trying to do is firmly placed within both the laws and meaning of the nation—no one will "defy the Constitution"—and then he legitimizes his claims through this same tradition and adds the truth of God and Jesus. He ends the argument with the incontestability of the divine values of justice and love. He establishes these values and the meaning they engender as the fundamental motives behind the movement's actions and claims. The idealistic and religious levels of King's rhetoric meet and form its characteristic network of signification.

These themes follow King through the years. The Constitution is a frequent point of reference. In the same way that the Bible makes the struggle ultimately righteous, the Constitution and the people and values it represents and evokes make the transformation of America righteous in a concrete sense. The relationship between these levels is thereby established.

At this first meeting of the Montgomery bus boycott King is anxious to place "America" at the center of the movement, with the promise of the nation on one side and the terror that the betrayal of its ideals has led to on the other. "America" must be incorporated into his and the movement's project. In this, names such as Jefferson and Lincoln are important. They become a way of staging an accusation while still remaining within the American political tradition, and the ideals of the movement come to symbolize the creed of America.

Science

The fifth area of references that can be discerned in King's rhetoric is more loosely categorized than literature, philosophy, theology, and the American political tradition, but it can be summed up in the term science (including human sciences). It can be divided into two different areas. First, King often points to the conflict between scientific progress and moral values. Second, he refers to academic disciplines, mainly anthropology, biology, psychology, and sociology.

King often uses the discussion of science versus morality in manifestly religious contexts, although it is a common set piece in his rhetoric in general.[38] King paints a picture of the grand technical and scientific achievements of our time and the benefits humanity has gained from them and contrasts this with the retardation of our moral standards and values. This is not so much a critique of modernity as a way of declaring that morality must always be in the forefront because it is that which is connected with God.

The discussion of science versus morality goes a bit beyond the practice analyzed in this chapter, but this legitimization (which it very much is—it promotes the values of the civil rights movement to the driver's seat in any social change and progress) relies on the Western tradition's deeply rooted trope of constant development and progress. The progress of science becomes an argument for the progress of morals. It also gives King's other references increased value. He describes the humanities, morals, values, ideas, art, philosophy, and so forth as being as important and "real" as natural and technical science. The discussion of science versus morality legitimizes the legitimization.

The second area belongs to the more concrete and sociological side of King's rhetoric. Here he wants to back his statements with the findings of modern research. He often brings anthropology and biology into his speeches, sermons, and texts to contradict any arguments that purport to establish racial inferiority with scientific evidence.[39] King uses the disciplines of psychology and sociology when he discusses the stigmas that slavery, segregation, and the ghettos have left in the black community.[40] In this practice we can read the scientific and intellectual climate of 1950s and 1960s America. The anthropologists he mentions are people such as Margaret Mead, Ruth Benedict, and Melville Herskovitz; as for psychology, he subscribes in the main to a behaviorist understanding of man.[41]

This is the final piece of King's legitimacy puzzle. Everything from classic literature to modern psychology is made part of his project. But how is the practice adapted to different situations and how does it vary over time?

Allusions in Context

King's practice of making allusions and using references does not have the same outlook in all speaking situations. It also changes somewhat during the course of his career. Three specific patterns can be discerned in his rhetoric: emotionalism, intellectualism, and a post-1965 pattern.

EMOTIONALISM

The first pattern can be found in the mass meeting speeches of the early (generally pre-1965) King. The first speech of the Montgomery bus boycott is an example of a quintessential movement speech: It is clearly and directly linked to a specific action (the boycotting of the buses), its audience is exclusively black (except for some police officers and journalists), and the fundamental rhetorical aim of the speech is exhortation (take action!) and legitimization (the action is righteous!). It is in a way a monologue within the black community surrounded by mute white American oppression. And even though the public figure King is yet to be established, King was already reaching toward the position that this figure later came to occupy.

The speech is exclusively based on Christianity and the American political tradition. Philosophers and literature are not mentioned, nor is Gandhi. The opening passage lays this framework bare:

> My friends, we are certainly happy to see each of you out this evening. We are here this evening for serious business. We are here in a general sense because first and foremost we are American citizens and we are determined to apply our citizenship to the fullness of its meaning. We are also here for our love of democracy, because of our deep-seated belief that democracy transformed from thin paper to thick action is the greatest form of government on earth.[42]

In this passage lies the nucleus of the speech. The boycott takes its righteousness from the glory, truth, and justice of the tradition of American democracy. Through this premise King establishes the fundamental dichotomy that throughout his career he would come back to in so many forms and shapes: The movement incorporates the beliefs of America in its demands and the enemies of the movement are thereby defined as outside the American common body. Movement participants would have to engage in struggle over these principles many times, as they did in Montgomery, since America and American tradition and values became such essentially contested concepts in the civil rights struggle, but King's use of the American political tradition in movement speeches is crucial in forming the identity of the movement, both inward—what we are doing is based on the equality given to us through our citizenship—and outward— what we are doing is not in any way a threat to what America is and stands for; it tries instead to uphold it. King's rhetoric represents a rearrangement of the relationship between the quest for civil rights, segregation, and the American tradition and values. The movement is connected with an idealistic level of truth that is then positioned within the framework of a religious truth. It is through this ladder of signification that King constructs the core identity of the movement.

At the same time, the direct context of the speech must be remembered. Since it is the first speech of the Montgomery bus boycott it is directly related to a concrete, specific, and practical situation. The interpretive and referential aims of the speech are therefore direct. King establishes and gives meaning to the righteousness of the upcoming protest through two illustrations: the tradition of American democracy and the love and justice of God. Intellectual reasoning must take the back seat.

An argument could be made that King speaks here to a relatively uneducated audience and therefore refrains from using references to philosophy and other academic traditions. But that is a problematic way of approaching the speech. King saw no problems in making such references in sermons before congregations of a similar demography.[43] Instead, the starting point of analysis must be the purpose and function of the rhetoric in the specific situation.

Here King's rhetoric is focused on an "emotional" interpretation of the struggle. The central elevating character of King's rhetoric has a specific form here. He does not have to emotionalize the injustice in itself—the church is already literally bursting with feeling; and he does not have to intellectualize it—that kind of legitimization would be superfluous here since its convincing effects are only needed with an audience that wants to see itself in a mirror that reflects that type of justification. Instead, the emotions are guided and structured into and in the speech. Its words and sentences reflect and develop the sense of anger and righteousness already there; hence the focus on Christianity and the American political tradition. God guarantees the ultimate truth, and this truth is in this worldly situation represented by the Constitution and democratic tradition of the United States.

The speech also represents a first step from isolated protest toward the formation of a movement. It gives the boycotting of buses a place in American history as well as in God's universe. He places the promise of America, the values of Christianity and Jesus, and the wrongs of segregation within the same field of meaning; he plays them against each other and understands them through their dialectical relationship. Here we find the beginnings of a discursive formation.

INTELLECTUALISM

The second pattern can be found in many speeches delivered outside the context of movement mass-meetings. It is apparent in fund-raising speeches, speeches held before other factions of the movement, and speeches before church audiences. It is the pervading pattern in the rhetoric of King's almost constant speaking tours across the nation. It can often be found in sermons to his own congregations, and it is often dominant in his written messages—articles, essays, and books. The rhetoric in these kinds of situations is characterized by the use of the full arsenal of references and allusions. The truth and legitimizing power of idealistic intellectual knowledge is a central feature of this kind of rhetoric.

Let us move on to July 1965, to the turning point of the civil rights movement, and the sermon/speech "America's Chief Moral Dilemma," given to the United Church of Christ's General Synod in Chicago. This message illustrates King's use of references to intellectual knowledge. King's position is different here; he is not speaking to foot soldiers at a campaign rally. The exhortation and legitimization are intellectual and rational rather than emotional and are not connected with a specific action. The purpose of the speech is to explain. It is roughly constructed as a Sunday morning sermon.

Furthermore, by this time King had risen to great national fame, and that also establishes a different starting point. Instead of the monologue he offered at the first Montgomery speech, he engages in dialogue here. White America and oppression play somewhat different roles in this speech. But why does using intellectual terminology to prove the righteousness of the civil rights movement seem so important to King?

King sets out to explain and justify his theory of necessary action not just in a manifestly religious context but also in a churchly and ecclesiastical context. If the obviousness of the wrongs of segregation and racism are not enough to make American churches act, he wants to structure his argument and fill it with meaning so that it becomes impossible to argue with it from both a Christian and an educated position.

The basic theme of the speech is that the acceptance of segregation is opposed to the fundamental values in the universe of God and that the church as the central moral institution has the responsibility to lead the struggle: "The task of conquering segregation is an inescapable must confronting organized religion" since churches are "called to be the thermostats that transform and regulate temperature in society, not thermometers that merely record or register the temperature of the majority opinion."[44] Segregation and racism is, ultimately, a moral problem.

To prove his argument and to justify that the problems of *this* world must be addressed by the church, King uses a long list of names and themes during the course of the speech: He refers to the problem of science versus morality, the Emancipation Proclamation, and Thoreau; he states that the problem "is not a political, but moral issue"; he quotes the Old Testament; he refers to Marx (he describes the otherworldly focused religion as the religion that "marxists like to see—an opiate of the people"); he refers to Kant and Buber; he quotes Tillich and Tolstoy; he refers loosely to contemporary theological debate; he paraphrases existentialists; he refers to Harry Emerson Fosdick; and he quotes Jesus, Amos, St. Augustine, and Whittaker Chambers.[45]

This is a typical example of how King creates and uses an idealistic level of meaning to position the struggle of the movement. All the names, references, and allusions lend a specific character to the speech as an intellectual disquisition carrying the weight of philosophical, theological, and academic knowledge. It reinforces the image of King as a leader who both embraces and represents this knowledge. King speaks from a position where he has access to this knowledge in the same way that the preacher has access to the world of God and is able to interpret and implement it in the concrete world of the congregation/audience. The references not only become argumentative proof that what King says is true and righteous, they also establish the position from which the speech is made. The history and knowledge of philosophy, theology, and other disciplines come to speak through King at the same time as he speaks through them.

Furthermore, his use of references and allusions in the speech draws its core exhortation—that the church must stand at the forefront of the civil rights struggle—into a particular web of meaning. The religious level of meaning is already established at the outset since the speech is held in a church. But within that setting further significations can be made and further meaning can be created.

The intellectual wisdom that King incorporates into his demands fixes the meaning of the struggle. It distinguishes and

defines the struggle's "home." This "home" is closely related
to an identity (in this case the church's) whose self-understanding can be mirrored in the references and allusions of the speech.
So the speech not only positions and presents King, it also positions the audience and it positions the struggle by endowing
it with meaning and identity from a long intellectual history
that is a part of God's moral universe. It reveals the idealistic
base and character of King's rhetoric.

The King we meet in "America's Chief Moral Dilemma" is,
depending on the angle we view him from, either King at the
high point of a triumphant nonviolent civil rights campaign
endowed with the ability to reach all of America, or King at the
crossroads—a leader who has taken his initial task as far as
possible and reiterates old rhetoric in the absence of new variations in a new situation.

The first angle is relevant if we consider the developments
leading up to this moment. The speech is a sort of formalizing
of what King had done throughout his years in the movement.
He had consistently tried to raise the issues of segregation and
discrimination, he had tried to reach the North, and he had
tried to involve white America and its establishment. This rhetoric formed a central challenge: "If you do not accept the problem when it is presented this way, then you cannot be who you
say you are."

My observation regarding the rhetoric of references and allusions is that King uses it in situations where he needs to create a kind of dialogue that differs from the emotionalism of the
mass-meeting situation, usually when he is addressing white
or mixed audiences, when a "rephrasing" of the quest is needed.
In "America's Chief Moral Dilemma," King has modified the
position he took in the bus boycott speech (as one of the oppressed accusing the oppressor). He is more clearly coming to
occupy his characteristic position *between* cultures.

He used this particular rhetorical strategy more and more
frequently during the period 1955 to 1965; it was a way for
him to open up a dialogue with white America. Using refer-

ences to the Western intellectual canon was naturally not exclusively a practice directed toward white America, but it was a
central way of relating the problem of racism to white, American, and Western identity. It constituted both a challenge and a
possible way for this identity and tradition to confirm its image of itself. To do so, it had to accept itself as a part of King's
project and accept the meaning that the discursive frames of
this project endowed it with.

THE POST-1965 PATTERN

There are some shifts after 1965, although it is problematic
to describe them as a break. The technique of allusion does not
disappear from King's messages. His sermons are in this respect quite similar throughout his career; he never abandoned
the strategy of proving by using references to other bodies of
knowledge.[46]

But still, the third tendency we encounter in King's messages belongs to these last years. After the legal victories of the
mid-1960s, King's position began to shift and he began to draw
upon different material in the references he made. He could no
longer sustain his position as the conscience of America in the
same way; he had to adjust to realpolitik, and in doing so he
began to rely on literature, philosophy, and theology less and
less. This shift in emphasis is clear in many messages from his
last three years. Gone are Hegel, Buber, and Tillich. They are
still to some extent present in the sermons from this period,
but the public dialogue has taken a new form. In the increasingly tough arena of political struggle, King returns to a focus
on America and he tries to justify himself and legitimize the
claims of the movement with hard facts from the human sciences.

In the posthumously published (1969) essay "A Testament of
Hope,"[47] King sums up the events of his last years and presents
his views on America's current state. In this text, the references
and allusions are of a different character than in the speech of
the first mass meeting of the Montgomery bus boycott and in

"America's Chief Moral Dilemma." They are accusations instead of promises, condemnations instead of guarantees. The
essay is also clearly directed toward white America and toward
an establishment from which King had become more and more
distanced since his criticism of the Vietnam War.

"A Testament of Hope" is characteristic of the later King's
referencing. Except for the use of American history, the only
pre-contemporary references are to Jesus and the Roman Empire, which is used as a warning of what may await America if
a change does not come. And in spite of the optimistic title, it is
a rather bitter King we meet. The problems have become more
serious and complex. Simple, sweeping solutions are no longer
a possibility. He uses this basic analysis in a number of areas:
the persistence of discrimination, poverty, education, health,
the pessimism and desperation of black America, the Vietnam
War, racial relations inside the remaining civil rights movement, the political system, and so on. He portrays America as a
prison that "must change."[48]

But the change of situation and the different argumentation
do not mean that the referential rhetoric has been abandoned.
It is still there, even if it is subtler. The Constitution again stands
at the center, but not as in 1955 when it was blended into one
with the struggle of the movement, guaranteeing its righteousness and eventual victory. Instead it has become the symbol of
the white backlash of the late 1960s, when King consistently
points to the contradiction between the values of the Constitution and the reality of black American life.

Otherwise King uses the political agenda of the day. He speaks
of Castro instead of Marx and Marxism. The politicians he discusses are not Lincoln or Jefferson; they are Kennedy and
Johnson, together with a number of contemporary senators, governors, and mayors. The only intellectual mentioned is Frantz
Fanon, whose work is recognized as the legitimization and theoretical foundation for black violence. But as was the case in the
first speech of the Montgomery bus boycott thirteen years before, the American tradition of protest is again the most basic
hope for the continued struggle for justice. King writes:

> This dissent is America's hope. It shines in the long tradition of
> American ideals that began with the courageous minutemen in
> New England, that continued in the abolitionist movement, that
> re-emerged in the populist revolt and, decades later, that burst forth
> to elect Franklin D. Roosevelt and John F. Kennedy. Today's dis-
> senters tell the complacent majority that the time has come when
> further evasion of social responsibility in a turbulent world will
> court disaster and death.[49]

This is a somewhat different tradition from the one that King
used in the boycott speech. There he wanted to position the
movement within the American political tradition; here he
wants to emphasize his and the movement's position outside
the system and outside the establishment. Dissent rather than
righteousness constitutes the argument. This is based on a different idea of America as a nation, as a system, and as an ideal.
Instead of the powerful ideals and ideas of the Constitution,
King refers to movements operating and acting on the fringes
of the system. It may seem obvious why King mentions the
abolitionists in the passage—their struggle was the "same" as
his—but having that said, the abolitionists as well as the popu-
lists and, to a degree, Roosevelt and Kennedy challenged the
ideals of America.[50] By the late 1960s, the American tradition
was no longer, as it had been in 1955, exclusively dependent on
the Constitution for the positive claim that the true and core
identity of the nation is just and righteous. The tradition that
King refers to here had been established during a long struggle
in a nation always divided by ideals and reality.

While King referred to the American tradition of protest as
the context in which the movement should be understood during the early movement days, there is a difference in character
here that must be understood as a part of King's general
radicalization. What King speaks of is *dissent*, not the right to
protest. He refers to "a long tradition of American ideals," but
he uses a different lens to give this tradition meaning. It is this
lens that changes a mere right to protest to a long history of
hard dissent. This lens also gives the reference points in the
rhetoric a different function. Instead of creating a common state
of mind, a whole identity representing inherent goodness in

the nation, King's references point to a duality. More clearly than before, they come to develop the central dichotomy in King's rhetoric; what America says and what America does are two different things. And in the development of this dichotomy the intermediary level of idealistic intellectual knowledge and truth comes to play a lesser part.

This is not to say that the dichotomy is something new after 1965. On the contrary, King had used it as a central rhetorical vehicle since the beginning of his leadership. The difference is how it functions in his rhetoric. What the references stress here is not solely, as often before, the schizophrenic personality of the nation that could be transformed into a whole and common identity. King's references begin to point out the refutation of this common identity that the white backlash since 1965 had revealed. King juxtaposed the two personalities of the nation in the form of a direct accusation rather than as an exhortative challenge: The core of this nation as revealed through its practices does not have the capacity to incorporate the truth and righteousness of an idealistic and religious universe. Therefore it must go through fundamental changes. It cannot simply find a way home; the old home does not harbor idealistic and religious ideals. America must find a new home that truly represents these ideals and values. King's late rhetoric increasingly comes to point an accusing finger rather than wave an easily recognizable hand of identification.

The Discursive Process:
Rewriting, Explanation, and Legitimization

The language and legitimization strategy of Martin Luther King, Jr. is an act of definition and a constituting of meaning which is locked in constant interaction with a world of social determinations and definitions. The rhetoric of reference comes to fill an important function in this process. The names, quotations, and allusions present in King's public messages in themselves form a particular understanding of how the world is structured. The ornamentation of the rhetoric and the attempts to strengthen its truth-claims through bits and pieces from intellectual history also mean that a particular world and particular truth are expressed. This is important with regard to who the public persona King is and what the social situation that he speaks of (and in) is.

Let us take a closer look at a prime example of this technique of allusion from the sermon collection *Strength to Love*, published in 1963 when King was at a high point as a national figure. The sermons in this collection are also interesting because they are adjusted to a white liberal Protestant audience.[51] In the sermon "Antidotes for Fear" King interprets the meaning of "courage" in the following way:

> We can master fear through one of the supreme virtues known to man: courage. Plato considered courage to be an element of the soul which bridges the cleavage between reason and desire. Aristotle thought of courage as the affirmation of man's essential nature. Thomas Aquinas said that courage is the strength of mind capable of conquering whatever threatens the attainment of the highest good.
>
> Courage, therefore, is the power of the mind to overcome fear. Unlike anxiety, fear has a definite object which may be faced, analyzed, attacked, and, if need be, endured. How often the object of our fear is fear itself! In his *Journal* Henry David Thoreau wrote, "Nothing is so much to be feared as fear." Centuries earlier, Epictetus wrote, "For it is not death of hardship that is a fearful thing, but the fear of hardship and death." Courage takes the fear produced by a definite object into itself and thereby conquers the fear involved. Paul Tillich has written, "Courage is self-affirmation 'in spite of' . . . that which tends to hinder the self from affirming itself." It is self-affirmation in spite of death and nonbeing, and he who is courageous takes the fear of death into his self-affirmation and acts upon it. . . . Erich Fromm has shown in convincing terms that the right kind of self-love and the right kind of love of others are interdependent.[52]

In what way is this passage a part of the civil rights struggle? In a written version of a sermon he has probably preached several times, King defines what courage is with the help of a number of historically and contemporarily significant intellectual names. In one sense there is nothing problematic about this. It gives the sermon a convincing effect, it intellectualizes the subject, and it gives the speaker in the text the position of an intellectual discussing the matter with other intellectuals. King defines courage by giving several examples before synthesizing them into a definition that includes general Christian ethics—a quite normal "academic" procedure, albeit a bit pompous.

But the context in which the text is offered is not neutral. King defines himself, he defines the reader/listener, and he defines the struggle of the civil rights movement in American history and society. The passage is a rewriting, an explanation and legitimization of the transformation of the system of segregation and oppression. The key is the tension between the universality of the names and quotations in the speech and the particularity of King's position and quest. The message gains specific meaning through this context. Plato and the others are positioned here within the context of a civil rights movement involved in a societal struggle in twentieth-century America.

The powerful intellectual wisdom of the philosophers and others mentioned in this text is encircled by the context of the civil rights movement project because it is the civil rights movement leader King who speaks. If it was ripped out of its context the passage could be perceived as a neutral discussion of what courage is. But because it is placed in the context of the civil rights movement, it is *not* a neutral discussion. It is a discussion from the perspective of the civil rights movement. And just as the philosophers and their wisdom are defined within the movement's project because of the situation in which the message came into being, this project also comes to be defined through these names and wisdom. If they lend their strength to a definition, they also leave their mark on that which is defined.

King uses rhetorical dramatization to change position—from minority to majority, from dominated to dominator, and from inferior to superior. It is an act of rewriting and rearranging as much as it is an act of definition. This rewriting act takes place between the centrality of "courage" as a fundamental feature of the concrete act of nonviolent resistance and the definition of courage given by the thinkers quoted. King rewrites the definitions of courage into the courage of the individual nonviolent protester. He gives the universal a particular identity through a typological use of the intellectual tradition. King draws all the names he cites, from Plato to Fromm, into his project. Through this act the sermon comes to have a double meaning.

Discursive transformation, however, takes place when this typological relationship is established. Although the white, Western intellectual tradition forms a part of the civil rights movement, it rewrites the conditions from which identity is determined, it rewrites the position of the segregationists as well as the northern liberal and the movement activist, and it rewrites the rules that surround the field of possible action. When King defines the same courage that has been discussed by the Greeks, Thoreau, and several contemporary giants as the act of protesting against oppression and discrimination, it is dramatized. It is given meaning as a part of the idealistic level of King's rhetorical structure and as part of this level's relationship to the ultimate religious truths—it is defined within the discourse of faith. At the same time, he undramatizes this definition of courage; it is made familiar, it affirms and reinforces a Western identity.

King defines the actions of both the individual protester and the movement as a whole by rewriting a linear intellectual history into ever-present values that the individual can find his own identity in. And when King underlines the necessity of action, the argument is turned the other way around. The courage that is needed in the struggle is a courage shared with everyone from Plato and Aristotle to Fromm. It is not only required from the individual human being, it is also a requisite for participating in a great intellectual tradition.

King positions himself at the center of this process. He is the one who through secular typology can give the situation its explanation and endow it with an understandable meaning. His journey through world history and his incorporation of the names he finds on his journey puts him in the position of a coordinator. King, not the southern segregationists or the northern establishment, defines and explains the basic meaning of the civil rights movement. This self-assigned role is crucial; with it, King attempts to create a *total* understanding in the sense of closing the discourse. Everything is to be understood within the meaning structures that King establishes through this explanation of what the movement and its struggle are.

The legitimizing act is related to the power to define. Ultimately, the legitimization is based on the existence of a personal and Almighty God. King uses allusion to give further meaning to the context of a legitimization that states that the struggle of the civil rights movements represents God's love and justice in this world. Clear thoughts and brilliant formulations are constitutive parts of the absolute and moral universe of God. The act of mastering the concrete fear experienced in the struggle through courage is possible; it is ultimately righteous and a necessity because everybody from Plato to Fromm has said so. And that is not such a simple line of argumentation as it may seem. In the idealistic and moral universe, ideas are never fixed, never permanent in a specific context. They determine the present. King rips them out of history and speaks through them. And when he does this he can define what the act of boycotting a bus, forming a picket line, or going to jail "is." He legitimizes the act of confrontation by holding the position of interpreter of the confrontation.

In this, the ladder of signification of King's rhetorical discourse can clearly be seen. Meaning is projected downward, and each step carries the truth and righteousness of the previous step. Idealistic intellectual knowledge is a part of God's universe and it is both given meaning through it and connected with it through its naming and elucidating powers. It is from this position that knowledge is related to the concrete civil rights struggle and comes to give this struggle a particular meaning, defining that which happens, explaining what it "is."

The key to King's success was his ability to reach many different areas of American society. He had the capacity (and the opportunity) to bring the white establishment, white liberal Protestants, and the black community into the same struggle. But what we also can begin to see at this point is something that has not been observed to the same extent: This communicative ability is also formative; it creates and expresses a particular understanding of the world and reality. The rewriting, explanation, and legitimization are normative at the same time that they create room to maneuver by strengthening the identity of the movement and infusing powerful idealistic meaning into its struggle. King strove to create clear boundaries around the discourse; he wanted to create an established *within* that could always be used to lend legitimacy and righteousness to the struggle. But closing the boundaries also confined the legitimacy and the righteousness to the established structure of meaning and truth in the discourse. For King to be able to use the strength of the established truth that the discourse constitutes, he also had to accept that the legitimacy is embodied in the very structure of meaning that has created and established this truth. Hence, the practice not only created legitimacy, it created a *specific* legitimacy.

King's practice of using references to other bodies of knowledge is, ultimately, tied to the fundamental dichotomy between sameness and difference that is central in King's project. If he was to be an effective leader, he needed to balance between two cultures in America. He uses figures from the history of Western intellectual achievements to evoke the common identity of humanity. He is creating a link being himself, the participants in the struggle, and the educated white North. When he makes the tacit assertion that "what we do is a part of you" he empowers himself by becoming part of a central American/Western naming practice. Established and unmistakable truths are put in a highly explosive situation and thereby King uses an existing discursive structure to give meaning to this situation. This naming of black America's struggle has the function of creating a basic common identity that also puts the tradition of Western and American values at the crossroads: If this sameness is impossible to accept, the way of naming must undergo a fundamental restructuring.

This leads to further complexity regarding the position of the persona King's rhetoric created. To put it bluntly: Does he speak the language of the oppressor and thereby become identified with it? Are the constant references to a white Western intellectual tradition and to historical American values forcing him into a system of meaning that he cannot break free from when he wants to change and, in some cases, even revolutionize his rhetoric? Does the use of common cultural knowledge mean that the civil rights movement rhetoric King constructed confirms rather than challenges? These are the problems that King faces when he takes up his position between cultures. How could he uphold a position of power in relation to both the White House and poor segregated black Americans?

King's struggle as a leader of the civil rights movement took place in a context that was larger than the fierce opposition of people such as Bull Connor and George Wallace or the angry and violent white mobs that confronted activists. His context included an America divided into a supposedly racist South and a supposedly anti-racist liberal North. His attempt to create a common Americanness from a clearly oppressed position in that society meant that to some extent he had to give up some of his independence as an outsider to become an insider. Positioning himself within the system and naming the world around him through the Western intellectual tradition could and does make him vulnerable to charges that he gave up some of his difference, some of his identity as black.

This is the *limiting* effect of the discourse and it is what becomes an acute problem for him later in the 1960s when the position between cultures gradually turns into a no-man's-land. When King tried during his last years to transform and expand his and the movement's aims, the public figure of Martin Luther King, Jr. was already established in a position dependent on the struggle against southern segregation. When trying to free himself from this position, he could not take the discursive power of that position with him.

The acts of defining and positioning are closely related to the different kinds of power in King's rhetoric. Even if King tries to adapt his rhetoric to different situations, this still means that the positioning in one situation affects others. It does not immunize King from the fact that through this very practice, through the effects it comes to have as being active in a field of public discussion and through the struggle over meaning and the right to define, his position is utterly ideological even when he refers and alludes to what is portrayed as general and absolute intellectual "truths."

The Ideological Effect: Power and Hierarchy

The ideological content of the references in King's rhetoric brings the close relationship between the ability to define and social and political power into focus. This relationship has two interconnected aspects.

The first aspect emanates from King's practice of using and expanding an already established way of naming. In one way or another, King ties his rhetoric and its way of naming to the assumed truths that are part of the already accepted signification system. The position between cultures that King occupies and tries to maintain cannot stand outside the two cultures. He must work within both cultures and create meanings that speak to members of both cultures. The position between cultures exists in a concrete historical situation and is integrally related to this situation, determining it as well as being determined by it. We must therefore look at the fundamental values of the power centers that King uses and see how he relates to them.

The second aspect is that this must be related back to where this chapter started; the public figure of Martin Luther King, Jr. In King's rhetoric, the ideological character of the referencing (and the very practice of referencing) represents a particular way of understanding the world, humanity, and society. This understanding is not least expressed by the public figure King that is constructed in the rhetoric. He represents an *ideal.* So when King uses this type of rhetoric to describe the world, he not only defines it, he not only names it, but he also states that this *way* of defining and naming is ultimately true.

THE POSITION BETWEEN CULTURES

A passage from a speech delivered during the Birmingham struggle in 1963 illustrates how incorporating an established way of naming is ideologically charged. Here a manifestly non-ideological position that arises in the context of a specific social situation becomes part of a web of understandings that has a distinctively ideological character. The specific demands and reassurances of the passage are not only related to themselves, they are also related to an ideological situation and an ideological understanding of history. King says:

> Years ago, Plutarch said, that if people in power will not speak out, then the common, ordinary people ought to rise up and speak, and who knows, but their voices represent the voice of God crying in the wilderness. So it becomes our responsibility to take a stand and save the fold of Birmingham. Make it clear that we are not going to stop until we gain freedom in this community. That's all we're asking for. . . . No, we aren't trying to dominate the nation's political scene, we just want to be free. We are not trying to do away with those things that are holy in our nation, we just want to remove those things that are unholy. We just want to be free.[53]

The idea of "America" has a central function in the emotionalism and intensity of this kind of movement speech. But King justifies something else here: The challenge to America is at the same time an act that preserves American values. The task is to keep the holiness "holy" and to force a removal of the "unholy" things. This is easily translated into freedom, democracy, and equality on the one side, and oppression, segregation, and racism on the other. King makes a clear distinction between the people involved in or actively supporting the civil rights movement and the segregationists and racists.

This distinction is part of the rhetorical strategy of allusion in the sense that the people who are part of the righteousness are also those that have access to and, in some cases, master the broad intellectualism that King employs. The opposition is de-intellectualized, de-culturized, and made into an inarticulate mob through the logic of the rhetoric.

But let us not forget that we have here a righteousness tightly knit to the "things that are holy in our nation." We have a social movement that does not want to "dominate the nation's political scene." The demands are minimized (we just want to be free); they are adjusted to an America that may feel threatened by large-scale social change. They are part of the self-evident truth that America is synonymous with freedom. This may seem to be suggesting that the speech is directed outward, and that its purpose is to create support from the general public and the establishment. But the fact is that this is a movement speech, delivered before the all-black nonviolent troops of the Birmingham campaign, and as such mainly directed inward.[54] The demand for "freedom" is carefully placed inside the framework of American values.

But what does King's persistent attempt to incorporate an American tradition into his position and his project really mean? A first conclusion is that it is based on the general key notions such as God, individual freedom, equality before the law, individual rights, and so on. It is obvious that especially King's pre-1965 rhetoric and the identity it gives the civil rights movement works inside these established American mainstay values. King defines himself and the movement and the struggle as something that constitutes an American locus. The opposition is kept at distance from a place *within*.

And let us not forget the meaning and importance of this generality of the mainstay values. The unspecified nature of the fundamental values that this locus gains strength and significance from means that their status is also unchallenged in the project that is launched from this place. The civil rights movement thus becomes, despite its concrete demands ("End segregation!" "Freedom from oppression!"), a social force defined and determined through this general American ideology. Placing "freedom" in the context of a larger structure of ideological belief (the Constitution) at once challenged that belief system (fulfill your promise!) and reaffirms it through the act of evoking it. King speaks as a *patriot;* the activities of the movement are expressions of its love of the nation. Through this self-understanding, the movement can more easily fit into the worldview of the American society in which it acts.

This leads to the second conclusion. The discursively limiting function of this practice is also limiting in an ideological sense. Evoking an existing social structure and understanding of history downplays the ultimate goals of the social movement, which actually involve a major restructuring of America. King also tries to reassure his listeners that the movement does not seek to become involved in the major national political struggles of the nation ("we aren't trying to dominate the nation's political scene"). In choosing these rhetorical strategies, King becomes part of the existing system. The change he proposes is a change aimed at upholding an established structure.

It is ironic that King limits the movement by declaring that its actions are both necessary and sanctioned by the American political tradition and system. This is both an act of empowerment—he speaks and acts from a position within and can use the strength of established understandings—and an act of fundamental powerlessness. To be able to sustain this position, King not only has to speak the language of the oppressor, he must also know and obey his rules. They must be his own.

The Ideological Ideal

If one effect of King's civil rights movement discourse is this acceptance of the basic ideological character of "America" and the American system, there is also another aspect where specific ideological effects regarding the understanding of the individual human being can be found.

From the earliest movement days, King was willing to address the class divisions within the black community and American society. The need to connect the problem of discrimination with the structural problems of the economic system was a constant in his quest, from 1955 to 1968, although he spoke of it more often during his last three years.

But even though King in this way argues that class position is irrelevant in terms of an individual's ability to take part in the movement, other features of his rhetoric point in a different direction. In a passage he often uses, he urges some segments of the black community to make the best of their abilities and through this to help themselves as much as possible. This passage is also constructed through the technique of allusion:

> Now I'm gonna holler a little tonight, because I want to get it over to you. I'm gonna be a Negro tonight. Now, we rush on, the hour is getting late. [*source tape damaged*] [. . .] must head out to do our jobs so well that nobody could do them better. No matter what this job is, you must decide to do it well. Do it so well that the living, the dead, and the unborn can't do it better. If it falls your lot to be a street sweeper, sweep streets like Raphael painted pictures; sweep streets like Michelangelo carved marble; sweep streets like Shakespeare wrote poetry; sweep streets so well that all the host of heaven and earth will have to pause and say: "Here lived a great street sweeper, who swept his job well."
>
> > If you can't be a pine on the top of the hill,
> > be a shrub in the valley—but be
> > The best shrub on the side of the hill.[55]

The emphasis on a protestant work ethic is obvious here. It is a religious, moral, and social duty to work. Work uplifts the black community and makes it into a powerful group in American society. The premise of this argument is an understanding of American society as a constant competition between different (ethnic) groups in which the ability to achieve political power is closely related to the economic resources within the group. So far the passage subscribes to traditional American ideology and protestant values.

But there is something else here. The ideals that are set up are Raphael, Michelangelo, and Shakespeare, and their connotations establish a special relationship with King's assertion that he is going to "be a Negro tonight," hollering to get through. Even if the examples may be chosen to give an enlightening and colorful picture of something artistic, of something beautiful, and even if the remarks about being "a Negro" and "hollering" have the character of internal jokes, they are still relevant. A hierarchy can begin to be found.

King's suggestion is that Raphael, Michelangelo, and Shakespeare are ideals of how the black community should carry out their work; he posits education, erudition, and knowledge as ideal human qualities. These are the qualities that legitimize King's leadership. King's rhetoric and writing demonstrates his command of the corpus of Western intellectual history and art again and again. In an idealistic and moral universe where progress is ultimately driven by spirit, the ability to achieve and the right to posses power is dependent on one's relationship with this body of knowledge. That is the macro-argument King is making when he alludes to figures in the Western canon of knowledge. By establishing his participation in and mastery of this shared knowledge, King places himself in a position of authority that white educated liberals share. And by placing himself *within* instead of outside this tradition, King can speak from a position of judgment.

This position becomes even clearer when it is related to the black community or, more specifically, the black congregation. King transfers the authority of the preacher from the pulpit and the church out into society and into the civil rights movement, where the questions "Who are we?" and "Who shall we be?" are central. King legitimizes his leadership in the same way that he legitimizes his position as preacher; the civil rights leader is sanctioned by intellectual knowledge in the same way as the preacher is sanctioned by God.

This sanction is ideological since it justifies a particular system of domination within the movement. The structure of the

movement and the leadership of King justify a distance between the speaker and his audience in the same way that the
church upholds a clear division between the preacher and the
congregation, the one mediating the gospel to the other. It is
no coincidence that King in another sermon calls God "a cosmic library" with an eternal catalogue in his mind.[56] The way
that God is able to command the "stacks of books" represents
the quality that man must strive to attain in his relation to the
intellectual tradition; a quality that is necessary if he is to earn
a position of leadership in his community.

The admonition to sweep streets like a Michelangelo is also
an admonition to become a specific person. This admonition is
central in the attempt to create a field of action through positioning oneself between two cultures. To be able to make the
transition from being segregated to occupying a position of
power, acculturation is necessary—on the individual level as
well as on the collective level. This does not necessarily involve
the suppression of one's own cultural identity, but it is based
on the need to gain power and identity inside the ideological
framework of the establishment.

There is therefore a crucial relationship here: King's position and his referencing draws ideological meaning from the
political and social situation in which the position is established
and the references are made. It is through the very effectuation that the ideological effect of the position between cultures
is created. King's rhetorical technique of allusion must be understood in its social context. The process of naming the world
and positioning oneself in that world does not take place in an
ideologically neutral situation free of systems of power. So although King challenges racist ideological systems by the way
he creates the identity and meaning of the movement with his
rhetoric, the meaning he creates is also determined by other
structures and systems of justification. Within the logic of the
discourse, King's position vis-à-vis segregation and racism represents "truth" in contrast to "ideology" that tries to cloud the
fundamental fact of human existence: The universe is ruled by

an almighty God and all human beings in his universe are created equal. But "truth" versus "ideology" is not the only relationship this position is involved in. Its non-ideological mask
also hinges on the fact that it is related to other constructions
and understandings of society. To be able to present itself as
neutral and non-ideological, to be able to present itself as representing the absolute truth of understanding racial oppression, the position must incorporate these understandings. But
the consequence of this incorporation is that the position becomes tied to the ideological structures and justifications that
are parts of these understandings. All that which is incorporated within the position is constitutive in forming the ideological identity of the position.

3. The Problem of Race

In the rhetoric of Martin Luther King, Jr., many meanings and functions are related to the presence and centrality of race. First and foremost, King's entire struggle, obviously, is in one sense about race. It is about black and white. The situation he tried to change was one where African Americans were discriminated against in one way or another by whites. But if this fact is more thoroughly analyzed, a further set of problems becomes relevant.

The first problem is the identity of "the Negro," "my people," "we," and "us," words and formulations that are as frequent as they are important in King's rhetoric. These identities often differ from situation to situation and from text to text. These shifting meanings constitute the second problem that this chapter is concerned with: the different functions the identities occupy in King's rhetoric and in the creation of a civil rights movement discourse.

These problems, then, include the issues of *sameness* and *difference* in King's rhetoric, the relationship between race and his directly religious rhetoric (especially with regard to its typological character), and the ways in which race, ethnicity, assimilation, and cultural pluralism are present in King's rhetoric, which demonstrates how this rhetoric works within a hegemonic understanding of race at the same time that it contains a theme that goes beyond and challenges this understanding.

Sameness and Difference: The Image of God versus the Moral Agent

A contradiction permeates all of King's works, from the first sermons delivered before the all-black congregations of Dexter Avenue Baptist Church and Ebenezer Baptist Church to the public speeches and the books aimed at a largely northern public: Although all men and women are made in the image of God and there ultimately exists no fundamental difference between peoples and individuals, at the same time some people have a special mission in history. The contradiction may seem to be easy to explain; as a Christian and as a preacher King has to declare the sameness of all God's children, and as an African American he cannot be blind to the facts of American society. Even though this explanation is in one sense true, it is quite superficial and raises more questions than it answers. How are this sameness and this difference situated within King's civil rights movement's discourse? Are they compatible?

King's articulation of the position of difference can be found in passages where "the Negro" is seen as a collective moral agent, destined to bring dignity to America and a new spirituality to the world. Passages of this kind are frequent throughout King's career. A typical example can be found in the closing paragraphs of *Stride toward Freedom,* where he writes that "this is a great hour for the Negro" since he faces the challenge to "give the new spiritual dynamic to Western civilization that it so badly needs to survive."[1] The "spiritual power" of the Negro can be used "so to challenge the nations of the world that they will seriously seek an alternative to war and destruction."[2] And despite all that happens during King's public career, a similar passage can also be found in his last book, *Where Do We Go from Here: Chaos or Community?:*

> So in dealing with our own particular dilemma, we will challenge the nation with its larger dilemma. This is the challenge. If we dare to meet it honestly, historians in future years will have to say there lived a great people—a black people—who bore their burdens of oppression in the heat of many days and who, through

tenacity and creative commitment, injected new meanings in the veins of American life.[3]

King equally frequently articulates the position of sameness. He states it quite simply throughout his career. The following comes from the written version of the sermon "How Should a Christian View Communism?" but it is by no means unique:

> Christians are also bound to recognize the ideal of a world unity in which all barriers of caste and colors are abolished. Christianity repudiates racism. The broad universality standing at the center of the gospel makes the theory and practice of racial injustice morally unjustifiable. Racial prejudice is the blatant denial of the unity which we have in Christ, for in Christ there is neither Jew nor Gentile, bond nor free, Negro nor white.[4]

How shall this simultaneous existence of sameness and difference in King's project be understood? In the first passage he speaks of a "black people" with the capacity to create "new meanings into American life," a particular people with both the capacity and ability to astonish future historians. In the second he speaks of the broad universality of the gospel, of the moral unjustifiability of racial injustice, and of humankind's unity in Christ. In a logical sense, the two positions seem to be mutually exclusive: How can there be a black people with a mission in history when there exists no Negro or white in Christ? How can there be a unity of humankind if a particular group within humankind can be distinguished as having special "spiritual power" and the ability to inject "new meaning" into American society? But this kind of reasoning leads nowhere. Instead it is the contradiction itself that is interesting. In this case, the contradiction between sameness and difference points to the ladder of signification within King's discourse and it points to the integrative and legitimizing areas of its ideology. Furthermore, the contradiction points to its own necessity to create a position between cultures. This position needs the space that sameness and difference create when they are situated beside and not necessarily against each other.

Both positions are connected with the construction of the

particular space King's rhetoric creates. The religious level of his rhetoric (here "the unity of man in Christ") determines its ultimate meaning and thereby determines other levels that nonetheless have power to define a social and political process. Difference—the moral agent—is related to these processes. This difference does not oppose the sameness proclaimed and defined by God; this difference is present *because of* that sameness. It is racial injustice that stands in opposition to the ultimate religious meaning that this difference strives toward—its ultimate goal is to reinstate the balance of the sameness created by God. The duality of sameness and difference therefore functions to both integrate and legitimize African Americans in struggle. Difference integrates (Who are we?) and legitimizes (Why are our actions righteous?) the struggle by creating an identity directly related to the sameness of all humanity. Sameness, in turn, also legitimizes. It is the fundamental belief of the core demand of the movement: freedom and equality for *all* humanity. But it also integrates; it evokes a set of religious symbols central to the self-understanding of Americans. Sameness also answers the question "Who are we?" without negating the answer difference provides. Instead, it incorporates that answer.

In these senses, both positions address the same issue: What is the relationship between race and the struggle of the civil rights movement? The answer is that the relationship between race and the struggle is characterized both (and simultaneously) by the sameness of all men and the difference of the African Americans.

But the passages also discuss different issues. In the examples from both *Stride toward Freedom* and *Chaos or Community*, King speaks about the future struggle—the responsibilities of and possibility for the movement born in Montgomery. Its meaning in history legitimizes its importance. And when speaking of the importance and meaning of the movement, King of necessity starts with the difference that is its precondition: the division of people in America into different races. Without this division there would be no civil rights movement to speak of. Here King is not placing the concept of "the Negro" in the position where the notion can be criticized and, ultimately, abolished. Instead, he is concerned with filling the category with a new and special meaning.

In the example from "How Should a Christian View Communism?" King speaks of a future ideal—he compares the stateless society of communism with the promises of the gospel— and while the connection with God embodied in the position of difference is strictly related to the Negro (it is his "spiritual power" that has the power to create "new meaning"), the connection with God embodied in the position of sameness expresses a different idea. In this respect, human beings were created without any racial differentiation. Man created racial discrimination *against* the will of God.

For King there exists something *absolute*. There is something more fundamental than the sociological difference created through history and experience: an ontological sameness. This is the understanding he establishes with the network of meaning he creates. Therefore, it is problematic to categorize and understand King solely according to the theme of moral agency without regarding the relationship that difference has with another cornerstone in his messages, the unity of man in Christ—the sameness. The relationship between these two poles creates the possibilities of meaning in King's messages about race. Together, the concepts of difference and sameness constitute the discursive realms of possible understandings.

King is active in a historical process in which race is the very question and object of struggle. The struggle is in one sense about how society should be constituted in relation to race. And King uses the term "race" in several distinctly different ways. It has a southern segregationist meaning, a northern liberal meaning, a black meaning, and so on. King is bound by these definitions; the field of meaning is already circumscribed. His task is to rearrange the meanings, to both use them against each other and bind them together in various ways. Even though it was not created by God, race is a reality. Otherwise King would not be needed at all. An interesting passage in "I Have a Dream" illustrates this point:

> There will be neither rest nor tranquility in America until the Negro is granted his citizenship rights. The whirlwinds of revolt will continue to shake the foundations of our nation until the bright day of justice emerges.
>
> But there is something that I must say to my people, who stand on the warm threshold which leads into the palace of justice: In the process of gaining our rightful place, we must not be guilty of wrongful deeds. . . . The marvelous new militancy which has engulfed the Negro community must not lead us to a distrust of white people, for many of our white brothers, as evidenced by their presence here today, have come to realize that their destiny is tied up with our destiny. And they have come to realize that their freedom is inextricably bound to our freedom. We cannot walk alone.[5]

Here King excels in invoking the simultaneity of sameness and difference. The field of understanding about race is already established, but rearrangements can still be made within it. The sentence "there is something I must say to my people" is crucial in this respect.[6] King states that difference is something so fundamental that you must choose whom you are speaking to. The activity of the oppressed Negro can never be entirely the same as the activities of the liberal white. But this manifestation of *difference* is delivered in a speech that evolves into a celebration of the *sameness* of all men (and women), most specifically in a passage that calls directly for the necessity of unity and states that men (and women) are "inextricably bound" to each other.

King simultaneously assumes that humanity is an image of God and that "the Negro" is America's savior. He does it through speaking to "my people" about whites, who here are the "white brothers" who are supportive of the movement. King speaks of the connection between the two races—the white can never be free without the Negro being free—but still, there are "we" and there are "them." Race relations in American society constitute and define the speaking situation itself and a duality comes to structure this situation: We are the same, yet we are different—we are different, yet we are the same.

But King still works and exists within a racial hegemony that has established that there are different racial groups in the United States, and he does so from a position where one group is oppressed by another. The basic conflict in America is positioned around race and the only way to eradicate, or at least to come to grips with, this conflict is to change or rearrange the understanding of the conflict.

King's aim is to change, even to create something new. The sameness of the races is related to God and the moral universe against which racial prejudice stands in opposition. *But the difference is the source of action.* If there had not been any racial oppression, there would have been no reason for action. But from this concrete situation a particular project is formed and a particular meaning is created: The difference of "the Negro" is the admonition from God to take action.

Through this King creates space where the divine origin of all human beings, the source of their sameness, can be combined with the designation of a particular group as God's moral agent. The difference is the reason to act while the sameness is the guarantee that anyone who opposes these actions opposes Christianity. Through this, a rather strange circle is created. Races exist in social reality and in the relationship between man and God, but they have no basis in God's creation as such. This situation warrants further discussion.

"The Negro" and Typological Rhetoric

A further meaning of the difference of "the Negro" is inevitably connected with the theme of moral agency. While the difference is in one sense related to a concrete situation and is fundamentally a sociological difference, created in time and not in eternity, in another sense it also has a more directly religious meaning.

I have already suggested the sameness of all human beings as the ultimate religious signifier within the discourse because it represents the absolute truth of God and it is, and remains, the anchor of meaning in the sense that it is what all difference is always linked with. But the position of moral agency cannot be explained and understood solely as a this-worldly construction and manifestation of difference. It also has religious dimensions. This is where the rather strange circle of meaning is again actualized: Race "exists" in the social reality and in the relationship between man and God even though it has no basis in God's creation as such.

It is the relationship between man and God that is central in this context. Its position in the circle shows that the relationship, in addition to being related to the sociological world of difference created in history, is also related to the absolute religious ontology of God. A particular religious quality in the racial identity of African Americans is manifested in King's messages and it is a definite part of the theme of moral agency. But this does not mean that the structure of the discourse falls apart; it still hinges on the interplay between sameness and difference. King does not challenge the unity that we all have in Christ as an absolute truth; instead he vests black people with a religious meaning through the special access to this truth the struggle endows them with. In this respect, the position of moral agency represents both the interplay between time and eternity and the fundamental dual citizenship of man. Nowhere is this clearer than in King's use of typology. It is here that we can find the religious meaning of the position of moral agency.

The use of typology and its creation of a sacred time where characters and narratives from the Bible move through time as eternal patterns of understanding allows King to create a special understanding of "the Negro" and the "we" and it gives us an opportunity to find the meaning that is the primary one when he addresses predominantly black audiences.

A typical example can be found in the sermon "Paul's Letter to American Christians," as delivered at his Dexter Avenue Baptist Church in November 1956. The title tells us two things. First, King removes himself from his own historical position

by evoking the name of Paul; the title serves notice that King
has entered the realm of typology. He thereby occupies a speaking position where he is both Martin Luther King, Jr. the
preacher and the civil rights leader, and Paul, a biblical character and a founder of the Christian church. This creates rhetorical and moral authority and gives King the opportunity to be
both inside and outside the specific historical situation. Second, he addresses all Americans of Christian faith, but he does
so before an all-black congregation. This also creates a position
where King is inside and outside at the same time.

King opens the sermon with the set piece of science versus
morality. Paul stands astonished before all the scientific achievements that have been accomplished since his age but he contrasts this with the moral degeneration of America: "Your moral
progress lags behind your scientific progress."[7] To the congregation this is, of course, related to the real issue: the wrongness
of segregation, the prime example of the moral retardation of
the nation. King/Paul follows this course through a number of
examples before he openly turns his attention to segregation.
Here we find the sameness of all humanity that I discussed
earlier: "Segregation is a blatant denial of the unity which we
all have in Christ."[8] In the absolute moral universe no racial
categories exist. Even if King/Paul is defining segregation as
the blasphemy and not directly the racial categories in themselves, the argument is derived from the fact that all men are
sons of God and therefore inherently the same. King/Paul states
that American Christians, like the Philippian Christians, are "a
colony of heaven" and have dual citizenship in heaven and on
earth, but with ultimate allegiance to God.[9] This basis is given
its full meaning when he turns exclusively to the victims of
racial oppression:

> May I say just a word to those of you who are struggling against
> this evil [segregation]. Always be sure that you struggle with Chris-
> tian methods and Christian weapons. Never succumb to the temp-
> tation of becoming bitter. As you press on for justice, be sure to
> move with dignity and discipline, using only the weapon of love.

Let no man pull you so low as to hate him. If you succumb to the temptation of using violence in your struggle, unborn generations will be the recipients of a long and desolate night of bitterness, and your chief legacy to the future will be an endless reign of meaningless chaos.

In your struggle for justice, let your oppressor know that you are not attempting to defeat or humiliate him, or even to pay him back for injustices that he has heaped upon you. Let him know that you are merely seeking justice for him as well as yourself. Let him know that the festering sore of segregation debilitates the white man as well as the Negro. With this attitude you will be able to keep your struggle on high Christian standards.[10]

This is of course an admonition to use nonviolence as the weapon against segregation, but this admonition is placed within a typological situation. By letting Paul not only enter but become a part of the civil rights struggle, King makes space for himself. This creates an opportunity to speak in a dual language. At the same time that he addresses a large part of the nation with the formulation "American Christians" and speaks of the unity of all mankind, King can open a specific dialogue with the black congregation. Through the civil rights struggle "the Negro" becomes the agent who works between God's universe and American society. Religious and racial identity become one. Religion becomes race and "the Negro" becomes "the Christian" through the combination of statements such as "American Christians" and "the unity we all have in Christ" with the fact that the speaker is both Paul and King, that he speaks outside logical time, and that he is able to speak several languages at the same time. The American racial situation becomes a religious situation and to be a Christian is to be active in the movement.[11]

Through being oppressed, "the Negro," even if those words represent a category created in time and not in eternity, is vested with a particular religious essentiality. When this is manifested in the struggle, "the Negro" will be able to implement the fundamental denial of the division between people that "debilitates the white man as well as the Negro." Sameness and difference presuppose and need each other in the meaning structure of King's thetoric.

But there are further elements of making "the Negro" into a religious entity in this speech. Typology in itself creates meaning.

The genre of the sermon makes the language here religious. It is a clear example of the axiomatic structure of King's rhetoric: The political is given meaning through the religious. But the concrete situation is also fundamentally political. King positions himself so that he can demand social action from his congregation and at the same time legitimize the struggle in the eyes of northern America. Two factors that enable him to inhabit this position are already there before the sermon is preached: It is offered by a preacher in a black community in the South, and the struggle against legal segregation was seldom a problem in the North.

The southern segregationists are another issue. But even if segregation can be viewed as evil in "Paul's Letter to American Christians," segregationists do not play a primary role in the part of the sermon that explicitly discusses race. King/Paul points to a struggle about the meaning of the Bible—and therefore about the meaning of race—but the rhetorical function of the segregationists' wrongful interpretation of the Bible is not primarily to reveal its evil morality. The primary function of their beliefs in the rhetoric is to *provide legitimacy* for King's struggle and his conflation of religious and racial identities and categories. The general meaning of the sermon evolves out of its dichotomies—Negro (Christian)/segregationist, morality/amorality, good (God)/evil—but the specific meaning evolves from its typological themes.

When King creates the situation where race becomes a religious quality he justifies his own position, he justifies the struggle for civil rights, and he gives meaning to the historical suffering of the black Americans. To advise an oppressed community to engage in struggle may not seem to be that difficult an assignment, but the duality of the sermon leads to a situation where the struggle has meaning for all American Christians and not just for King. In the name of Paul, King can criticize the white Christians who do not take part in the struggle for civil rights from a biblical and sacred standpoint. He is not confined to the position of one of the oppressed trying to end segregation. Typology makes the preacher righteous by transcribing him and the situation into a system of archetypal biblical meanings and situations.

In the sermon, the definition of "Christians" becomes "those who are active in the civil rights struggle." This means that African-Americans have, through their historical and social situation, the ultimate Christian qualities. But this does not mean that whites are defined as non-Christians. That is not the issue. Instead King invites them to *become* Christians, like the Negroes, through being the agents that work between the actual American society and the moral universe of God. The struggle comes to represent salvation.

The legitimizing strength of typology as a rhetorical vehicle must not be underestimated here. The most obvious function of the religious quality of the positioning of civil rights workers as moral agents and defining the struggle as an opportunity for salvation is to draw a mantle of righteousness around the project of the civil rights movement—legitimization at its fullest. The meaning of racial identity is an important aspect of this legitimization, and it is organized by a ladder of signification. You cannot disagree with even one rung on this ladder of meaning—if you refute the struggle, you will ultimately refute the absolute truth of God. The struggle to become those who represent this truth is therefore fundamental in the social and political project of the movement.

This can be seen most clearly in the segregationists' and the movement's different interpretations of the Bible, but perhaps more interestingly in the relationship of these two groups to the federal government. Here the struggle is about the power to posit the interpretation of the Bible in relation to the movement. If the identity of the movement's struggle can be established as mediation between the kingdom of God and American society,

King's rhetoric argues that it becomes mandatory for the federal government to act in accordance with the intention of God's moral universe. King's rhetorical dramatization goes hand in hand with the concrete dramatization of the evils of segregation which are manifested, for example, in vicious police attacks on nonviolent protesters.

But King's strategy of forcing the "power structures" to listen and act should not be overstated. The creation of a discourse of inclusion involves more than opening up the discourse to include whites or the federal government. The definition of "the Negro" serves a crucial function in a discourse that is fundamentally grounded in religious truths and meanings. Typology is the key. It transforms the Bible from a holy text to sacred events forever recurring in history. Common King metaphors for the struggle such as "light versus darkness" (instead of "Negro versus white") and the contrasting of "content of character" with "color of skin" are also typical of this attempt to raise race from its previous as well as contemporary positioning in hegemonic mainstream thought by evoking other features of an established hegemony. The reality of racial oppression enables King to transform "race" from a social category (and in the extreme case a biological category) to a religious category. Through this he can at the same time integrate blacks and America as a whole and he can legitimize the struggle by demanding action that is not only acceptable but necessary.

But the religious definition of racial identity does not stand alone in King's rhetoric. We cannot avoid a discussion of how King handles sociological difference. Here we meet the discussions of race and ethnicity, of assimilation and cultural pluralism, and the possibilities and impossibilities of the relationship between "the Negro" and mainstream American society of the 1950s and 1960s.

Different Paradigms

In their book *Racial Formation in the United States from the 1960s to the 1990s,* Michael Omi and Howard Winant provide a map for what "race" has been and has meant in the United

States in different historic periods, including what the concept meant at the time of the activities of King and the civil rights movement activities in relation to the dominant meaning of the term.[12] Omi and Winant argue that two paradigms dominated "race" in America until the second half of the 1960s. The first paradigm was constituted by the biological notion of race that began to be challenged in the 1920s and that had definitely been undermined by the 1940s (the South, of course, was the exception). What instead emerged was the paradigm of ethnicity that reigned until the civil rights legislation of the mid-1960s. What developed after 1965, Omi and Winant argue, was a struggle for hegemony, a struggle to establish a new dominating paradigm. Three concepts contended for dominance: the remnants of the ethnicity-based conception of race, a class-based conception of race, and a nation-based conception of race. Their description of the ethnicity paradigm and its struggle with both the biological conception of race and the problems it encountered in the late 1960s that can provide an illuminating background to my discussion.

The ethnicity paradigm arose as a challenge to the biological paradigm during the 1920s but did not reach hegemonic status until the 1940s. Omi and Winant point to Myrdal's *An American Dilemma* and the confrontation between integrationists and segregationists within the Democratic Party in 1948 as starting points for the paradigm's attainment of hegemony. It assumes that all minority groups can in one way or another be assimilated into American society like white European immigrants and it assumes the fundamental goodness of America. Omi and Winant define the paradigm as "an insurgent theory which suggested that race was a social category. Race was one of a number of determinants of ethnic group identity or ethnicity. Ethnicity itself was understood as the result of a group-formation process based on culture and descent."[13] In this paradigm, American society is available to anyone who wants to get in and African-American identity and history are ethnic in the same way as white European immigrants are ethnic.

What this eventually would lead to was a matter of debate among proponents of the ethnicity paradigm. The dominant position was that of the assimilationists, who argued that the differences between ethnic groups would be gradually erased in the process. From time to time the assimilationists were challenged by the cultural pluralists, who argued that different ethnic identities could live side by side in American society. Instead of merging into one, they would form a mosaic.[14] An attempt to reconcile the two positions was made in 1963 in Nathan Glazer and Daniel Moynihan's famous study *Beyond the Melting Pot.*[15]

Where did this leave King and the civil rights movement? It must be remembered that their starting point was the segregated South, which was still largely dominated by the biological paradigm. The challenge to this paradigm posed by the demand for integration therefore almost by default came from a position from within the ethnicity paradigm, which, in the context of the South, was a very radical idea. As in other areas, King incorporated and used the power of established hegemonic notions and understandings to establish a position between cultures. King and the civil rights movement were clearly positioned within the ethnicity paradigm—but there was still a great deal of room to maneuver within that paradigm. But how did King view the ethnicity paradigm and his position within it when it was severely criticized, not only by others but also by himself, and began to disintegrate after 1965?

Like Others: Ethnicity and Assimilation

The ethnicity paradigm offers a way of challenging segregation through a challenge to its fundamental racial division. It offers a way of challenging "color of skin" with "content of character."

Because King's project exists in and through the dichotomy of black and white, he does not use the actual terms "ethnic" and "ethnicity". But that does not mean that he does not define "the Negro" in accordance with the ethnicity paradigm's

model of explanation. But to understand the relationship between ethnicity and race in King's rhetoric, we cannot take the
meaning of ethnicity for granted. King's understanding of
ethnicity is tied to a notion of social, political, and economic
power and it is formulated in a context—the segregated South—
where it is both offensive and explosive. And because the newly
hegemonic ethnicity paradigm's understanding of race challenged the premise of the segregated South, King and the movement, almost by default, came to embrace (at least parts of) the
paradigm.[16]

Even if assimilation and cultural pluralism were the two
antitheses within the ethnicity paradigm, it is not an especially
constructive approach to simply ask whether King's rhetoric
supported assimilation or ethnic pluralism. Both views can be
found in his language, but what primarily must be understood,
and what primarily gives meaning to "the Negro" as an ethnic
identity, is the context in which King's and the movement's
mission took place—the structure in which blacks were oppressed and whites were the oppressors. To define and understand "race" from the viewpoint of ethnicity therefore has a
particular function in the context of oppression. It defies the
hierarchical nature of race-based categorization since it relates
the characteristics of "the Negro" to the characteristics of other
ethnicities. In King's rhetoric, an understanding of identity
based on *both* ethnicity and race exists in a dialectical relationship with an understanding of identity based *only* on race that
supersedes any questions of assimilationism and cultural pluralism.

Having that said, the central demand for integration in King's
rhetoric is related to assimilation,[17] not least through two contextual preconditions. The way that segregationists understood
integration was based on their assumption that it equaled assimilation—at least this thought was the central motif in their
objections to it. To be integrated was to be assimilated into
mainstream America as smoothly as possible. The assimilation
standpoint was therefore discursively powerful for King. The

shared American identity he so often evokes represents the main anchor in his demand for integration.

But in his positing of "the Negro" as an ethnic identity, King does not entirely incorporate a straight assimilationist strategy that is based on the history and experience of white European immigrants. Many times he carefully points out that integration to him is a fundamental sharing of power and that special measures are needed in order to give "the Negro" the chance to acquire this power. This represents another type of demand than assimilation.[18]

A further theme in his rhetoric is the recognition of the situation of black Americans as unique—how is it relevant to speak of assimilation when "the Negro" has been in America since long before even the birth of the nation?—and that special efforts therefore must be made if they are to become integral parts of American society.

But what is important, even if a straight dichotomy of assimilation and cultural pluralism is problematic, is that King often uses methods of explanation that place "the Negro" side by side with other ethnic groups, not so much based on what they are as an ethnic group (or even what an ethnic group really is) but rather on the fact that they *constitute* such a group. This positioning is focused on the form of identity that ethnicity constitutes and it is directly connected with the contemporary political strength of the ethnicity paradigm. The category "ethnicity" offers King a way to legitimize the struggle ("the Negro" shares with other groups the status of an ethnic identity and all the concerns that accompany that identity) and to politicize the goals of the movement within an established structure (democratic freedoms). By embracing "ethnicity" as an identity for African Americans, King can position them inside the American mainstream; he can remind audiences that they have other identities than "segregated Negro." The ethnicity paradigm appeals to northern liberals as well as southern moderates and it is almost by default a constitutive part of the political demand for integration.

But what then happens to the meaning of race and racial identity in a method of legitimization that ties them to ethnicity as a form of identification? Does King have to downplay race to promote ethnicity?

The positing of race and racial identity within and as determined by ethnicity is closely tied to the idea of assimilation. This is true in King's rhetoric. But for this positioning to be relevant for King's project, he has to make the connection through a comparison with others. The fundamental fact is that the "the Negro" is part of an ethnic group—it is the categorization in itself that is significant. The other half of the comparison is either society as a whole, as in rhetoric discussing assimilation, or other ethnic groups, as in rhetoric discussing the meaning and consequences of ethnicity as identity in itself.

The first type of comparison can be illustrated by the article "The Time for Freedom Has Come" (1961), where King discusses and explains the sit-in movement:

> Inevitably there will emerge from this cauldron a mature man, experienced in life's lessons, socially aware, unafraid of experimentation and, most of all, imbued with the spirit of service and dedication to a great ideal. The movement therefore gives to its participants a double education—academic learning from books and classes, and life's lessons from responsible participation in social action. Indeed, the answer to the quest for a more mature, educated American, to compete successfully with the young people of other lands, may be present in this movement.[19]

For this "mature man," assimilation will be no problem since his race is no more than a subordinate fact of his ethnic identity, which in turn is subordinate to his identity as an "educated American"—he will be assimilated into and will represent a whole. King speaks of "a young man" without even mentioning race; there is no essential conflict in assimilating a young man into adulthood. The young individual's opportunities for assimilation and his future contributions to American society are what is central. So it may seem a bit awkward if we

view and understand ethnicity solely through its distinguish-
ing aspects and qualities. The components of King's rhetoric
that discuss ethnicity, in which he subordinates racial identity
to ethnic belonging, illustrate the sameness category in his discourse. When he uses these types of patterns of explanation in
his rhetoric, African Americans constitute an ethnic group just
like other groups do. What is important in this explanation is
not what this ethnicity consists of; what is crucial is that it
states it is the same *form* and *type* of identity as that of other
ethnic groups. Here race is not a quality in itself, it is one of
several ethnic denominators. This form and type of identity is
much easier to assimilate than an identity in which race is the
primary basis.

The civil rights movement strategy of the sit-in is a striking
metaphor for assimilation. The participants were largely, like
King himself, black, middle-class, and college-educated young
people who wanted to get inside American society. In "The Time
for Freedom Has Come," King writes that the Negro of today
is "college-bred, Ivy-League clad, youthful, articulate and reso-
lute."[20] He is, in short, the future of America.

The article was published in *The New York Times Magazine*
and was primarily directed at the North; its purpose was to
present and legitimize the sit-ins. The identity of "the Negro"
whose time has come is clearly related to this audience. King
paints a picture of an evil system not fit for a modern and free
nation and of an upwardly mobile ethnic group. In the article,
segregation is personified by a "stubborn, rude bus driver"—
an illuminating contrast to the Ivy-League student.[21]

In this article, the demand for the abolition of segregation
becomes intertwined with the assimilative aspirations of the
young "new" Negro. And this kind of assimilation, its function as an argument, is related to the goal of the civil rights
movement. The initial position was that of being oppressed
because of an established racial difference. The sameness dimensions of the ethnicity paradigm's assimiliationist aspects
therefore represent a discursively powerful way to disarm this

oppression. The demand to end segregation becomes a demand for the entire South to assimilate into mainstream America. This rhetorical strategy has one pitfall that becomes extremely apparent after 1965. In using language that subordinates racial identity to ethnic identity, the concept of an integrated society becomes confused with the concept of an assimilated society. After the laws were passed that "let African Americans in" to mainstream society, it became clear that just stepping over that "warm threshold" that King spoke of was not enough. It quickly became apparent that where one was positioned within the mainstream was almost as important as being allowed to be a part of it.

There is also internal debate within the movement about this strategy, highlighted in the late 1960s by the militance of SNCC and the debate over the use of the phrase "Black Power" in particular. It is in this context that more direct comparisons between blacks and other ethnic groups most often come to the fore. The militant wing of the civil rights movement did not agree that the assimilation of "the Negro" is possible and inevitable, and it rejected that argument that giving ethnicity primacy over race would help African Americans reach their goal of equality. Instead it spoke of the ethnic reality of American society and how the problems of "the Negro" mirrored the problems of other ethnic groups. This wing of the movement is closer to the cultural pluralism version of the ethnicity paradigm but it also sees the limits of the paradigm itself.

In *Chaos or Community*, King discusses the issue of Black Power at length. Here the problem of combining ethnicity and race becomes clear. King jumps back and forth between different understandings of what "the Negro" of American society is:

> No one has ever heard the Jews publicly chant a slogan of Jewish power, but they have power. Through group unity, determination and creative endeavor, they have gained it. The same thing is true of the Irish and Italians. Neither has used a slogan of Irish or Italian power, but they have worked hard to achieve it. This is exactly what we must do. . . . We must use every constructive means to

amass economic and political power. This is the kind of legitimate power we need. We must work to build racial pride and refute the notion that black is evil and ugly. But this must come through a program, not merely through a slogan.[22]

The centrality of the subject "we" and its interposition with "they" in this passage reveals that the ethnicity paradigm is a contested issue among African Americans and that King's awareness of the segmented reality of American society had grown stronger and stronger. In the book this passage is a part of a dialogue with Black Power advocates Stokely Carmichael and Floyd McKissick, and even if we remember that this is King's version of the discussion, it definitely shows that his position within the civil rights movement has changed and that the movement has changed its position within American society.

There is a strong discrepancy between King's comparison of African Americans with Jews, the Irish, and Italians—and the recommendation that African Americans emulate those groups —and the outspoken focus on *racial* pride. It shows the crisis that King's discourse confronts in the context of the political and social environment of the late 1960s. He can no longer maintain the position where he can integrate several questions into one. This is evident in his attempt to both oppose and support the Black Power slogan at the same time.

As different meanings and positions of "the Negro" meet in the discussion of Black Power, King tries to give the figure an ethnic *and* a racial identity. This can be viewed as a concrete post-1965 application of the fundamental dialectical relationship of sameness and difference: From one viewpoint we are an ethnic group like other ethnic groups, and from another viewpoint we are a racial group (*black* Americans) and that makes us different from the various white ethnicities. This also speaks of how King's position changes after the legislative victories of the mid-1960s. As legal segregation is abolished and radicalism in the movement grows stronger and stronger, King becomes more the defendant than the accuser within the movement. The double identity formulated as above shows the movement and King himself at a turning point. He tries to maintain his inclusive discursive project by speaking simultaneously of ethnic-group power and racial pride while at the same time arguing against the combination of the words "black" and "power," understanding them as impossible within the structure of the discourse. As he said, "You just can't communicate with the ghetto dweller and at the same time not frighten many whites to death."[23] His problem was that it was becoming more and more difficult to find rhetoric that created a common identity for both the militants and the assimilationists in the movement that at the same time welcomed white allies into the movement with open arms.

The relationship between the phrase "black power" and the ethnicity paradigm therefore contains an interesting duality, particularly given the slippery meaning of the phrase.[24] "Black Power" came to mean everything from actual physical separation from whites to black-owned business and black-controlled institutions. When it is used across the full political spectrum it can in one sense be seen as the "race as part of an ethnic belonging" position taken to its extreme and in another as a rejection of the ethnicity paradigm itself. In the first sense, Black Power is about guaranteeing its own group as much political and economic power as possible. In the second sense, Black Power is not just a revolt against oppression; it is a revolt against the civil rights movement, its forms of protest, and its perception of "the Negro's" place in American racial society.

King's rejection of the phrase is to a large degree pragmatic. He foresees that the offensiveness of Black Power will make the dialogue with the white America of political power impossible and therefore considers that the nature of the appeal in the phrase is overshadowed by the fact that it will be counterproductive in the attempt to achieve power.[25] Although pragmatic, this also shows that King still has a foot firmly planted in the ethnicity paradigm. His criticism is in one sense a fear that Black Power will be understood by white America as precisely the rejection of the hegemonic perception of race that was one of its meanings.

But the King who speaks of racial pride is not just a new persona who has been created by the demands and accusations of the young radicals and nationalists. Throughout King's career, although with shifting focus and emphasis, he stressed the uniqueness of black Americans in relation to other ethnic groups. Even if he closely related that uniqueness to the position of moral agency, he focused on what concrete existence as a "Negro" in American history and society means. This focusing is about establishing a common black identity and self-understanding and it represents yet another aspect of "the Negro's" difference.

Not Like Others: History, Suffering, and the "Stigma of Color"

At the core of the ethnicity paradigm stands an internal contradiction. The understanding of the paradigm was that race was one ethnic denominator among others and thus a subordinate identifier. Race belonged to an ethnic identity, not the other way around. However, the ethnicity paradigm's name for this *ethnic* group was that of "Negroes"—a *racial* name, definition, and category.

Even if this was the conventional contemporary name for Americans of African descent, and therefore perhaps not consciously spoken of as a racial rather than ethnic category within the ethnicity paradigm, it is nevertheless a term that describes a racial group—the ethnic group is still finally formed and delineated by racial characteristics. This demonstrates two things. First, the ethnicity paradigm is modeled upon the history, experience, and situation of white immigrants. Blacks are identified within this scheme without having their primarily racial identity redefined. They are still determined by the color of their skin. Second, race, in its American sense, cannot be contained within the term "ethnicity." Race is one way of categorizing people, and in the history and structure of the United States it is crucial. Ethnicity is another way of categorizing people (by descent, culture, traditions), and even if the two often are seen as overlapping in different constellations, they are categorizations with different meanings and with different relationships to the society in which they are used. In the United States, race has a meaning and quality in itself that is something more and different than ethnicity.[26]

King may not seem to be the primary spokesperson for the black experience. That role is generally given to individuals with personal experience of the American nightmare's deepest darkness, such as Malcolm X. But still, King's relatively privileged background does not hide the fact that he was a victim of segregation. He often recapitulates childhood memories of being unable to play with white friends and seeing his father being humiliated in stores and harassed by the police.[27] The identity given to the black people of America through slavery, segregation, and more subtle forms of oppression is central for King from the start of his public career. As a "Negro" he is part of this experience even in his most triumphant moments.[28] Furthermore, King's leadership position demands that he always refer to this experience. It is crucial for creating the necessary bond between himself and the grassroots participants within the movement. To be a leader he had to speak of the uniqueness of the blacks. He had to once again emphasize their *difference.*

To be defined as a "race," as a deviation from the norm of whiteness, and throughout history to be subjects of an oppression based on this definition, is what in the American context and in King's rhetoric makes the black experience different from the history, experiences, and identities of other ethnic groups.

There are many examples of this racial experience in King's rhetoric. It is frequently a theme when he explains the motivation and force behind the movement (often symbolized by the birth of a "new Negro"), and he used it in the central formulation of the first mass meeting of the Montgomery bus boycott: "There comes a time when a people gets tired of being trampled on by the iron feet of oppression." It is also a defining element of King's description of the experience of the segregated South and how it is related to the history of blacks in America. A famous passage in "Letter from Birmingham Jail" warrants a long quotation:

> Perhaps it is easy for those who have never felt the stinging darts of segregation to say, "Wait." But when you have seen vicious mobs lynch your mothers and fathers at will and drown your sister and brothers at whim; when you have seen hate-filled policemen curse, kick and even kill your black brothers and sisters; when you see the vast majority of twenty million Negro brothers smothering in an airtight cage of poverty in the midst of an affluent society; when you suddenly find your tongue twisted and your speech stammering as you seek to explain to your six-year-old daughter why she can't go to the public amusement park that has just been advertised on television, and see tears welling up in her eyes when she is told that Funtown is closed to colored children, and see ominous clouds of inferiority beginning to form in her little mental sky, and see her beginning to distort her personality by developing an unconscious bitterness toward white people; when you have to concoct an answer for a five-year-old son who is asking: "Daddy, why do white people treat colored people so mean?"; when you take a cross-country drive and find it necessary to sleep night after night in the uncomfortable corners of your automobile because no motel will accept you; when you are humiliated day in and day out by nagging signs reading "white" and "colored"; when your first name becomes "nigger," your middle name becomes "boy" (however old you are) and your last name becomes "John," and your wife and mother are never given the respected title "Mrs."; when you are harried by day and haunted by night by the fact that you are a Negro, living constantly at tiptoe stance, never quite knowing what to expect next, and are plagued with inner fears and outer resentments; when you are forever fighting a degenerating sense of "nobodiness"—then you will understand why we find it difficult to wait.[29]

King relates this reality to the history and future of black people in the United States and, by extension, to the history and future of the nation:

> Abused and scorned though we may be, our destiny is tied up with America's destiny. Before the pilgrims landed at Plymouth, we

were here. Before the pen of Jefferson etched the majestic words of the Declaration of Independence across the pages of history, we were here. For more than two centuries our forebears labored in this country without wages; they made the cotton king; they built the homes of their masters while suffering gross injustice and shameful humiliation—and yet out of bottomless vitality they continued to thrive and develop. If the inexpressible cruelties of slavery could not stop us, the opposition we now face will surely fail. We will win our freedom because the sacred history of our nation and the eternal will of God are embodied in our echoing demands.[30]

To be fully understood these themes should be related to the more metaphysical theme of suffering that runs through King's works. The theme of suffering is not just a legitimization for proposed changes, it is also an important part of King's religious belief system, for which redemption through suffering is central.[31] It is no coincidence that King mentions the word "suffering" in the second passage from "Letter from Birmingham Jail." He develops this theme in a slightly different direction in other texts. Here, the real and mystical sides of the black experience meet. As King writes in *Chaos or Community:*

> The central quality in the Negro's life is pain—pain so old and so deep that it shows in almost every moment of his existence. It emerges in the cheerlessness of his sorrow songs, in the melancholy of his blues and the pathos of his sermons. The Negro while laughing sheds invisible tears that no hand can wipe away. In a highly competitive world, the Negro knows that a cloud of persistent denial stands between him and the sun, between him and life and power, between him and whatever he needs.[32]

The passages are obviously from different contexts; the letter was written to justify the movement's activities in Birmingham 1963 and the passage from *Chaos or Community* forms the introduction to the discussion of the desperate situation in the northern ghettos, but together they are significant for the position of "the Negro" I want to emphasize here.[33]

In the long first passage, it is not an ethnic group or identity King speaks of. He does not speak of the need for assimilation or cultural pluralism in a society where this is possible and in the long run inevitable. Instead King directly speaks of *racial* oppression. He speaks of the systemized terror called racism and segregation that equates skin color and identity. This constitutes the area where the civil rights movement creates its identity; it is in this context that the righteousness of their demands is legitimized. It is this black experience that so clearly states that to wait is not an option or possibility.

King is pointing out that throughout history and in the contemporary social situation, identity and self-understanding—with all that these concepts include in terms of culture, traditions, experiences, history, and so on—have been and are defined along racial lines. In King's rhetoric, "the Negro" comes to mean another thing in relation to the history and reality of *white* oppression than what it does in relation to Irish Americans, Italian Americans, and even Jewish Americans. This difference forms the constitutive part of what distinguishes "the Negro" from other ethnic groups in American society. "Black," "nigger," "Negro," and "colored," all used by King in the long passage from "Letter from Birmingham Jail," are names for this difference and they are all constructed in a racist society. They have one common counterpart: white.

The historical positioning of "the Negro" in the second passage from the letter has a quite obvious meaning: Both as a Christian and as an American, "the Negro" is righteous. The physical and mental brutality of slavery not only justifies the actions of the movement, it also lends a particular quality to the heirs of the former slaves; they will endure in their struggle just as their enslaved ancestors did. "The Negro's" ineradicable part in the building of the nation and the inner qualities he has inherited are, in combination, a central way of legitimizing the civil rights struggle. The experience of slavery is different from the experience of immigration. "The Negro" is not someone who has come from the outside to be assimilated into the nation; he has been a part of this nation since even before its very conception. In this aspect, too, "the Negro" is not like other ethnic groups.

The context of "Letter from Birmingham Jail," its intended audience and its purpose, is such that the final tone must be one of optimism. It must guarantee not only that the actions of the movement are righteous but also that the movement is unstoppable and undefeatable. And when the difference of "the Negro" is approached from this angle, that of a special quality created through the experiences of slavery and the claim that he stands at the core of the American nation, we approach the position of moral agency. But how should this be understood in relation to the passage from *Chaos or Community,* which can seem to be one of total disillusion? What is the quality of pain in the black experience that King emphasizes?

first, the pain has a political meaning. The meaning of slavery is essentially the same in the passage from *Chaos or Community* as in the second passage from "Letter From Birmingham Jail," but it has a different function. It represents another justification for the movement. The same history of suffering that gave "the Negro" a special quality that legitimized the struggle in Birmingham emerges here in the new historical situation of the late 1960s. Here it represents a legitimization for special treatment for blacks. It is a way to distinguish them from other ethnic groups. A few sentences later, King writes that while other immigrant groups had language and economic handicaps when they came to America, no other group had to face "the stigma of color" and no other group had been a "slave on American soil."[34]

King challenges the ethnicity paradigm from within the paradigm. He still speaks of the similarity between black Americans and other immigrant groups in the context of the possibility of an integrated society—which suggests that he believes that the groups at least in part share a common set of problems. But "the Negro" has a special position because of the historical pain of the black experience in the history of America. The contemporary frustration of "the Negro" is embedded in this history. And as part of that which constitutes America, it is also a pain within the nation. This calls for and justifies a change in the social structure that is much deeper than the abolition of segregation in the South, and it challenges the hegemonic understanding of race.[35]

Second, the quality of pain has a religious meaning in accordance with the theme of redemption through suffering. In King's rhetoric this is often connected with the birth of the movement and to what happens when "the Negro" becomes involved in the struggle. This internal function of the black experience can be further illustrated in the early article "Our Struggle," which describes the background of the Montgomery bus boycott:

> We discovered that we had never really smothered our self-respect and that we could not be at one with ourselves without asserting it. From this point on, the South's terrible peace was undermined by the Negro's new and courageous thinking and his ever-increasing readiness to organize and to act. Conflict and violence were coming to the surface as the white South desperately clung to its old patterns. The extreme tension in race relations in the South today is explained in part by the revolutionary change in the Negro's evaluation of himself and of his destiny and thereby his determination to struggle for justice. We Negroes have replaced self-pity with self-respect and self-depreciation with dignity.[36]

The description of the birth of a "new" Negro as the reason for the civil rights movement becomes more and more rare in King's post-1965 rhetoric. But the theme does not disappear entirely. King still tries to point to a qualitative change in "the Negro" as the central act of the struggle. But instead of speaking of "the new Negro" he increasingly comes to speak of "manhood." In "Where Do We Go From Here?" his last presidential address before the Southern Christian Leadership Conference in 1967, he says:

> To offset this cultural homicide, the Negro must raise up with an affirmation of his own Olympian manhood. Any movement for the Negro's freedom that overlooks this necessity is only waiting to be buried. As long as the mind is enslaved, the body can never be free. Psychological freedom, a firm sense of self-esteem, is the

most powerful weapon against the long night of physical slavery. No Lincolnian Emancipation Proclamation, no Johnsonian civil rights bill can totally bring this kind of freedom. The Negro will only be free when he reaches down to the inner depths of his own being and signs with the pen and ink of assertive manhood his own emancipation proclamation.[37]

Both of these examples contain a transforming act and both depict an identity-creating act. "The new Negro" is not a personification of a people finding a missing identity, it is about a people growing into an identity, of becoming what their history has made them. When King writes "we could not be one with ourselves without asserting it," he describes this process.

That there is a spiritual, almost mystical, side to the birth of the movement is a consistent theme in King's rhetoric: When "the Negro" fully understands the history and consequences of his suffering and starts to act, a redemptive moment occurs. This is both a strong challenge to act, directed inward, and an expression of the power inherent in the movement that is mainly directed at white society. The experience of being black from 1619 to (in this case) 1956 has created an individual with the ability to make contact with God through this self-transformation.

The manhood metaphor has the same function. It too speaks of this self-transformation. The difference is the position from which King speaks. In 1967 it has become evident that the accomplishments of "the new Negro's" civil rights movement were not enough. There is still an oppressive gap between "the Negro" and the true qualities of his identity. To King, the urban riots and the new militancy represent a misguided search for this identity. They reveal an emptiness within "the Negro" just as they reveal the impossibility of the whole political, economic, and social structure.[38]

But the necessary self-transformation, the search for assertive manhood, is still possible. The change from "the new Negro" to "manhood" represents a shift in King's focus. He does not concentrate as much as he did before on the first step out of oppression—the active moment—as he does on the need for new definitions of the problem. King's new definitions of the central problem of African Americans are attempts to address the crisis he faced in the creation of the discourse.

4. THIRD WORLD, COLD WAR, AND VIETNAM

Throughout his career King spoke and wrote of international situations and circumstances. King's basic understandings determine the way he sees foreign countries and international politics; the language he uses to discuss such issues can in turn help us to get a clearer view of the structure of King's rhetoric and civil rights movement discourse. This also raises the issue of how King's rhetoric is inextricably bound to what he can and cannot say to his different audiences.

The analysis in this chapter closely examines four central King texts. The starting point is the essay "My Trip to the Land of Gandhi," which illustrates how the structural opposites of known and unknown function in King's rhetoric. This discussion forms a basis for the continuation of the chapter, which takes us through King's views on anti-colonial struggles in Africa, the international landscape of the Cold War, and, finally, the Vietnam War.[1]

Holding Up a Mirror: India's Problems as a Reflection of America's Problems

Between February 2 and March 10, 1959, King and his wife Coretta and his good friend Lawrence D. Reddick, a history professor at Alabama State University, visited India on an invitation from Prime Minister Jawaharlal Nehru.[2] The connection with India was, of course, no coincidence. Even if the explicit reference to Gandhian nonviolence was something that was brought into the struggle as it developed, it had by the time of 1959 become one of the most frequently used sources of legitimization for the civil rights movement. The ethic of Christ's love that dominated King's earliest speeches of the Montgomery boycott had gradually been enhanced by Gandhian theories of nonviolence. King and his advisors used the connection between King and Gandhi to its fullest, and the identification was a central way to mold and fine-tune the public figure of King during and after the Montgomery bus boycott.

The trip to India can be seen in the light of this fine-tuning. King welcomed the heroic aura of Gandhi and Gandhiism, a philosophy that was hard for King's antagonists to condemn. It was in a way immune to the usual arguments of Cold War ideology and as rhetorically forceful as it was strategically fruitful. Gandhiism also carried a definite if undefined religious quality. It provided proof of the struggle's divine righteousness that King always reminded his audiences of. In this respect Gandhi is a typological trope, just as Moses, Jesus, and Paul are typological tropes in King's rhetoric.[3]

Gandhi and Gandhiism also have a more concrete function: the practicality of Gandhian nonviolence in the struggle of the civil rights movement. Gandhiism became synonymous with nonviolence in such a way that they could not be defined without each other. So while it was an almost unfailing source of outward legitimization for King, a way of creating himself and defining the civil rights movement, it was also important inwardly as a way of making the tactics of nonviolence function in concrete situations. Gandhiism was an example that nonviolence could and would indeed work.

The trip to India can also be seen as evidence of King's success in establishing the intimate connection between Gandhi, Gandhiism, himself, and the burgeoning civil rights movement. That the prime minister of India invited him speaks of this. As Gandhiism became an integral part of King's rhetoric and the civil rights struggle, the idea of King as the American Gandhi began to spread throughout the world.

When King came back from the trip he wrote a short essay

on the visit (with the assistance of Reddick) entitled "My Trip to the Land of Gandhi," published in the black weekly magazine *Ebony* in July 1959.[4] This essay allows us to examine how King used Gandhi's thought and how he perceived his connection with Gandhi. It also allows us to analyze how King pictures himself, America, and the American civil rights struggle in relation to foreign nations and international affairs and how he presents this aspect of the struggle to the U.S. audience.

"My Trip to the Land of Gandhi" can be divided into five parts: the background to the trip and King's expectations of it, the actual journey in itself, a romanticized picture of the visit to India, a more sober discussion of the concrete social problems India is faced with, and an account of India's attempts to solve these problems.

The opening paragraphs of the essay announce the fundamental dichotomy of known versus unknown that structures the text:

> For a long time I had wanted to take a trip to India. Even as a child the entire Orient held a strange fascination for me—the elephants, the tigers, the temples, the snake charmers and all the other storybook characters.
>
> While the Montgomery boycott was going on, India's Gandhi was the guiding light of our technique of nonviolent social change. We spoke of him often. So as soon as our victory over bus segregation was won, some of my friends said: "Why don't you go to India and see for yourself what the Mahatma, whom you so admire, has wrought."[5]

The two paragraphs stand in direct opposition to each other. The first two sentences contains the classical Western view of "the Orient" as something mysterious, as the Other, as a counterpart to Western civilization and ways of life. In these two sentences King, knowingly or unknowingly, paraphrases hundreds of stories and renderings of "the Orient."[6]

But in this unknown milieu there is also something utterly known. The second paragraph connects this wide-eyed child-like anticipation with the concrete memories of the Montgomery bus boycott and the tactic of nonviolence used during that campaign. King's visit to India and his use of Gandhi combine the known and the unknown.

This gives a specific stature to King as the leader of the movement. He becomes the interpreter who understands the unfamiliarity of foreign countries yet has the ability to familiarize it and to place it within the civil rights movement discourse.

King then describes the background to the trip, how he had wanted to undertake it since 1956, when the first invitation came. Different circumstances had stopped him from going at the time, though. At first he was unable to make the trip because of a previous commitment in Ghana, then he was stabbed during a book signing in Harlem. It was through that incident, however, that the possibility of visiting India came about. After he was released from hospital it occurred to him "that it might be better to get in the trip to India before plunging too deeply once again into the sea of the southern segregation battle."[7]

In one sense it is easy to understand what King means; if he wanted to go to India he had better do it before something came up that would make the trip impossible, but in another sense his meaning is more problematic. The sentence clearly states that the trip to India was not a part of the southern segregation battle. So what is it then? Surely King cannot have viewed it as a purely recreational visit. Instead this becomes a typical example of how King signifies the struggle in his civil rights movement discourse.

The struggle can be divided into two different parts. First, there is the concrete struggle of the different campaigns, the day-to-day work of the Southern Christian Leadership Conference (SCLC), the court battles, the strategies at the national political level, and so on. This is what he signifies by the "southern segregation battle." But in King's rhetoric and in the civil rights movement discourse, this is never what "the struggle" is. "The struggle" is always a representation of something more fundamental. As determined by the ladder of signification, the

struggle has idealistic qualities and ultimately religious meaning and legitimization.

One should therefore understand the notion of the trip to
India as not part of the "southern segregationist battle" in the
context of this ladder of signification.

In this signifying process—this actualization and stabiliza-
tion of the ladder of signification—an interpreter is needed,
and this is the position that King occupies. He stands in a symbolic pulpit, speaking to a congregation, intermediating the
truths of God that are attainable to him in his role as a preacher.

The second part of "My Trip to the Land of Gandhi" consists
of the actual journey. King presents his traveling companions,
gives an account of who financially supported the trip, points
out that the Gandhian Memorial Trust of India extended an
official invitation "through diplomatic channels," and generally builds up the tension with assertions such as "my true test
would come when the people who knew Gandhi looked me over
and passed judgment upon me and the Montgomery movement."[8] The result of this test plays a central, albeit less explicit, role later in the essay.

Then the reader meets India through the eyes of King and
the third part of the essay begins. We are presented with an
idealized picture of the country. After "a grand reception" that
included the "most generous hospitality imaginable," King's
party met with the president, the prime minister, and the deputy
prime minister. King describes the welcome his group received:
"Virtually every door was open to us. We had hundreds of in-
vitations that the limited time did not allow us to accept."[9]

The picture of the reception that King presents to readers
reinforces the portrait of India as a whole. The reader immediately gets the impression of a humble and loving nation that
stands in sharp contrast to the "southern segregation battle"
that King left behind when the plane took off from Kennedy
Airport. It is a picture of a romanticized unknown and King is
the messenger of this "something else."

But immediately after his encounter with this almost unattainable idyll, King makes a connection between the known and unknown. They can never be entirely separated; they execute their structural function in the essay through their connection. The humble hospitality and the importance of the visit of King and his friends are placed within the framework of the idealistic struggle represented by both a worldwide uprising against colonialism and the movement to end segregation in the United States: "We were looked upon as brothers with the color of our skins as something of an asset. But the strongest bond of fraternity was the common cause of minority and colonial peoples in America, Africa and Asia struggling to throw off racialism and imperialism."[10] The two aspects of sameness King points out are ranked by importance and strength. He mentions the concrete aspect of skin color, but he rates it as inferior to "the strongest bond of fraternity," which represents the common goal the people of these three continents share—to be free from oppression.

Then Gandhi and nonviolence enter. This forms the bridge between the third and fourth part of the text, the bridge between King's personal experiences and the discussion of India's history and social and economic problems.[11] The main character from now on is a combination of King and Gandhi and this persona's relationship with history and historical change. In King's writing, the theory and practice of nonviolence unites the struggles in India with the struggles in the American South. Through this the contradiction between known and unknown comes together to form a new entity that gains meaning in its relevance to the battles on the streets of Montgomery, for example. King writes:

> I left India more convinced than ever before that nonviolent resistance is the most potent weapon available to oppressed people in their struggle for freedom. It was a marvelous thing to see the amazing results of a nonviolent campaign. The aftermath of hatred and bitterness that usually follows a violent campaign was found nowhere in India. Today a mutual friendship based on complete equality exists between the Indian and British people within the commonwealth. The way of acquiescence leads to moral and spiritual

suicide. The way of violence leads to bitterness in the survivors and brutality in the destroyers. But, the way of nonviolence leads to redemption and the creation of the beloved community.[12]

The description of how successful nonviolence was as a method in India is an argumentative guarantee here that the same thing applies to American circumstances. It is through this connection that further meaning is created within the essay. Since two fronts are established in one argument—the factual success of nonviolence in India and the impending success of nonviolence in America—the identity/meaning of the struggle is ultimately determined by something more than these two situations in themselves. The struggle for justice, represented here in both the Indian and American versions, is connected in the text with the ultimate forces of the universe and the moral power inherent in history's way forward.

This text gives the argument that nonviolence is the ultimate method available to achieve lasting and positive social change even greater meaning. The text establishes the ideals that connect the Indian and American struggles, which King uses to signify "the struggle" in its most idealistic sense.

King's attempt to portray and define the struggle as beyond ideology by naming as its source a universal and righteous higher authority is thus laden with ideology. King defines nonviolence as a universal method of goodness with a string of ideological keywords: morality, spirituality, redemption, and the beloved community. These ideals are manifested in the text and they represent what a social struggle leads to if it is allied with a religious power.

King relates these ideals to the role that certain individuals must take upon themselves. After positing this meaning of nonviolence, King immediately connects it with the person and role of Gandhi. King freely uses superlatives to describe the figure of Gandhi in India: "The spirit of Gandhi is very much alive in India today," King writes. He states that "nobody today . . . comes near the stature of the Mahatma" and that "India can never forget" him. He concludes: "Posterity could not escape him even if it tried. By all standards of measurement, he is one of the half-dozen greatest men in world history."[13]

The text states that history is moved forward through the activities and responsibilities of great individuals who by being these special individuals, associated with the ultimate truths of human existence, come to represent something more than themselves. Their spirits can float over time, history, and situations and they function as typologies in King's rhetoric. In a seemingly humble way, King tries to identify himself with the figure and spirit of Gandhi. When he writes that "the Gandhians accepted us with open arms" and "praised our experiment with the nonviolent resistance technique at Montgomery" which they saw as "an outstanding example of the possibilities of its use in Western civilization," King translates Gandhi-nonviolence-India into King-nonviolence-America.[14]

This translation continues in the fourth part of the text, where King discusses India's social problems. Even though he is mostly factual, discussing topics such as infrastructures, annual incomes, unemployment, overpopulation, housing problems, and so forth, these discussions are also structured by comparing what his readers know with the unknown situations in India. King ties the known to the unknown in the following passage: "And then there is, even here, the problem of segregation. We call it race in America; they call it caste in India. In both places it means that some are considered inferior, treated as though they deserve less."[15] Here the two different struggles become one to the point where they can be described and explained in the same terms. King does more than compare the struggles; he makes them one and the same. This signification of sameness through caste and race forms the bridge to the fifth part of the essay: a discussion of India's attempts to come to grips with its ills.

A further theme can be found in this next part of the essay. King discusses whether India should be westernized as quickly as possible so that she can raise the standard of living for her citizens or if this would be harmful because of the vices of westernization: "materialism, cutthroat competition and rugged individualism."[16]

In the end, King proposes some kind of compromise without really offering a clear solution for India's complex problems. What may be a bit eye-catching is King's cautiously positive view of the socialization projects that the Indian government had initiated.[17] He also seems to sympathize with the so-called Bhoodanists, whose program included large landowners giving up holdings to landless peasants, smaller landowners giving up individual property to cooperatives, and an economy based on domestic production.[18]

These ideas may seem to be far removed from an upwardly mobile black middle class trying to make it in American society. But King structures his text in such a way that the new ideas seem less threatening to American readers. He positions the new ways of social organization he saw in India in the context of Indian history and traditions—"such ideas sound strange and archaic to Western ears"—and tiptoes around them carefully enough to be able to avoid mentioning the word "socialism."[19] Second, the meaning of "My Trip to the Land of Gandhi" is already firmly established when this discussion takes place and he does not attempt to make a one-to-one correlation of known and unknown here as he did in earlier parts of the text. At the concrete political level India and America are different and separate here; they represent two different entities. The contradiction between Indian ideology and American values can therefore be maintained without tearing the text apart. We are back in the India of snake charmers and tigers.

But the text does not end there. To end with a separation of known and unknown and without the possibility of creating meaning by letting the opposites determine each other would be contradictory to the gist of the text. Instead King ends by tying together all the threads that have been outlined: "Today India is a tremendous force for peace and nonviolence, at home and abroad. It is a land where the idealist and the intellectual are yet respected. We should want to help India preserve her soul and thus help to save our own."[20]

The Legitimizing Power of Decolonization

The decolonization movements of the 1950s and 1960s, which occurred mainly in Africa, had a tremendous effect on the civil rights movement in America and the rhetoric of Martin Luther King, Jr. They were important for the movement in several different respects.

On the one hand, they played a widespread political role as part of the general international situation after World War II and during the Cold War. On the other hand, decolonization was also important inside the movement, both for its self-image and as a source of inspiration. The effects of decolonization abroad, however, meant different things to different segments of the movement.

It had the least effect on traditional organizations such as the National Association for the Advancement of the Colored People (NAACP) and the Urban League, which often ignored the connection between Africa and America. But it was extremely important for the growth and development of the younger and more radical organizations, primarily the Student Nonviolent Coordinating Committee (SNCC). During the first half of the 1960s, decolonization came to mean new things to SNCC; at first SNCC viewed it as a lens through which to view their own situation and as a source of inspiration; it was the brotherly struggle. But gradually SNCC came to see decolonization in the same way as black nationalists and pan-Africanists did.[21] In that view, the struggles in America and the struggles abroad constituted a worldwide black revolution that was essentially one and the same. Adherents of this view felt that every individual and every group that was part of this struggle should use the same methods and the same theories. This was the position of Malcolm X, who became highly influential in SNCC's development mainly after his defection from the Nation of Islam.[22]

King's SCLC generally stood somewhere between these two positions, but King never hesitated to use decolonization in Africa and Asia in his rhetoric. The theme was present from

Montgomery and onward. It would later be one of his main points of reference with SNCC. On many occasions he pointed out the close affinity between the student movement and decolonization movements.[23] But he did not limit his use of decolonization as a legitimizing argument to that context. He also used the rhetoric of decolonization in two other areas: when he spoke to the (white) liberal North and when he preached from the pulpit to his own congregations.

It is not difficult to understand why he would use the rhetoric of worldwide decolonization in the first context. Here King spoke before people who were often engaged and interested in these international affairs, and it was strategically important to help them see the interrelatedness of decolonization and the American struggle. References to Africa in these speaking situations are not overly ideologically charged or rhetorically unique. King speaks of a world and a history that is about to change and a new world that is starting to emerge.[24]

In the other context, in which King speaks about decolonization to his own congregations, we can find certain elements that are harder to discern in the other situations, especially if we focus on the early movement years. The sermon "The Birth of a New Nation" preached at Dexter Avenue Baptist Church in April 1957 offers an example of King's use of the rhetoric of decolonization in a sermon.[25] It is structured similarly to "My Trip to the Land of Gandhi"—it connects the known and the unknown—and King's role as the interpreter, the mediating link between the forces of history and the individual listeners, can clearly be seen.

Because it is a sermon for King's own congregation, it has a different starting point than his more public speeches and sermons. Such sermons took place in a context that had fewer restrictions about what King could or could not say, and he was able to gauge very accurately the capacity of his congregation to hear and understand what he was saying. The sermon is also interesting because King uses typology. How does decolonization in Africa relate to the Bible and the civil rights movement?

In the sermon King describes his visit to Ghana in 1957 when, as an official visitor, he participated in the new nation's independence celebrations. The sermon can be divided into two major parts. In the first part, King introduces the theme of the sermon and describes the geography and history of Africa and the Gold Coast/Ghana. He also tells the story of Kwame Nkrumah and the eve of independence celebrations in Ghana. The second part consists of King's explanation of what the story of the Gold Coast/Ghana means and a disquisition in which he discusses the history and situation of the British Empire and colonialism in general. Even though the sermon does not explicitly revolve around a biblical text, scripture is still the central structuring function of the text. As with most of King's sermons, he first outlines a scripture text, then he interprets the text and explains what knowledge his congregation can draw from it. In this sermon, the "scripture" part of the text consists of the story of the colony of Gold Coast and its liberation by Kwame Nkrumah into the nation of Ghana. But the subtext of the story is clearly an actual scriptural text: the story of the exodus of the Jews from slavery in Egypt.

King opens the sermon by presenting its topic:

> I want to preach this morning from the subject "The Birth of a New Nation." And I would like to use as a basis for our thinking together, a story that has long since been stenciled on the mental sheets of succeeding generations. It is the story of Exodus, the story of the flight of the Hebrew people from the bondage of Egypt, through the wilderness and finally, to the Promised Land. It's a beautiful story.[26]

Here the entire framework of the sermon is outlined. Everything that King says in what follows is determined by this "basis for our thinking together." The story of Exodus gives meaning to a contemporary situation. The exodus is the basis from which every struggle that involves breaking free from oppression and reaching the land of freedom can be understood and explained.

By opening the sermon with these words and this story, King signals to his listeners that is should be understood in terms of their own struggle. He also immediately establishes the connection between known and unknown. The sermon will take the listener to a foreign country and a seemingly different context, but by making it a version of the known story from Exodus, it will mean something more than itself.

After this introduction King turns into an educator. He explains that the former Gold Coast is situated in "the very vast continent known as Africa" which, he says, is also the continent of Egypt, Ethiopia, Tunisia, Algeria, Morocco, Libya, and a host of other countries.[27] It is difficult to determine the necessity for this geography lesson, but at least it implies that King had a certain notion of the knowledge level of his congregation regarding these matters. It also makes the unknown and unfamiliar pole of the structural opposition clear. Even though the obvious identification with Africa is present in the situation, an identification that exists not least through the fact that every individual in the congregation has African ancestors, when King talks about Africa, he is talking about something strange, something very far away. Africa is a largely unknown entity to this congregation.

When King finally reaches the Gold Coast in the sermon, the subject turns from geography to history. He describes how the European settlers came in 1444 and how the former colony was established.[28] Here his congregation hears of something they know about; the connection to slavery in Africa forges a connection to their own family histories. King uses this point of sameness—a shared knowledge—to merge the story of breaking free from colonialism in Africa with the struggle against slavery in the United States in the past and the struggle against segregation in the present.

King repeatedly links the actions of the characters in the story he tells with details from the story of the exodus, sometimes more explicitly than others. King ends the first section of the sermon with the following words:

There seems to be a throbbing desire, there seems to be an internal desire for freedom within the soul of every man. And it's there; it might not break forth in the beginning, but eventually it breaks out. Men realize that, that freedom is something basic. To rob a man of his freedom is to take from him the essential basis of his manhood. To take from him his freedom is to rob something of God's image.[29]

This passage has several layers of meaning. It may appear that King draws this conclusion solely in relation to the revolt against colonialism he has just discussed. But it also points to the opening of the sermon, where the structure was determined by making the story in Exodus "the basis of our thinking." We are, in this way, still in the scripture part of the sermon. Ghana is a part of biblical sacred reality.

This opens up the potential for King to make more specific claims in the second section of the sermon. He begins to offer definitions of man, society, and history.

King begins the story of Kwame Nkrumah: "About 1909, a young man was born on the twelfth of September. History didn't know at that time what that young man had in his mind."[30] This story illustrates how some individuals play an important role in shaping history. King uses the rhetorical strategy of discussing the characters of his story without naming them. He does not reveal Nkrumah's name until he has told the story of his upbringing, education, and general development. Even though King speaks of a concrete individual, he speaks of all the individuals involved in the struggle. The quest for freedom needs individual acts to become actualized. Just as the decolonization movement would have been impossible without the personality and activity of Nkrumah, every struggle for freedom is impossible without a version of him. Special leadership and unique individuals are needed. King reminds his congregation that the story of the exodus is the basic text of the sermon. He knows that everyone in the pews will understand this reference.[31] Every exodus must have a Moses.

After explaining that history did not know that this individual was about to change its course, King describes how even though Nkrumah was brought up by illiterate parents ("humble people"), he finished school and "decided to work his way to America." When he finally arrived "with about fifty dollars in his pocket," he began his education at Lincoln University in Pennsylvania, where he read "the great insights of the philosophers" and the "great insights of the ages." Finally, he got his theological degree and preached in the Philadelphia area and in other places in America at the same time that he obtained master's degrees in philosophy and sociology. Throughout all this time of intense study, "he was poor," King says, "he worked as a bellhop in hotels, as a dishwasher, and during the summer . . . he worked as a waiter trying to struggle through school."[32]

This story of Nkrumah's life and education acquires special meanings in the speaking situation. First, it stresses the importance of education and the possibility that one can move from an upbringing in poverty to an elevated position in society—a version of the American dream. Nkrumah—this still nameless and therefore generally applicable individual—was born of illiterate parents in the wilderness of Africa, but he made a social journey through sheer will and individual strength. King presents his experience as a model for the possibility of individual growth and the individual strength that is necessary. For Nkrumah the social journey was the precondition for his influence on the forces of history, but it also becomes a metaphor for how success can be achieved within American society: through hard work, endurance, and morality. In other words, King preaches traditional Protestant values to the congregation at Dexter Avenue Baptist Church.

Second, King describes a particular kind of knowledge and education. He mentions theology, philosophy, and sociology and equates these disciplines to "the great insights of the ages," thus stressing the importance and relevance of intellectual and idealistic knowledge. One needs this kind of education if one is to play the role of the heroic individual leader who can influence history; this kind of knowledge represents the eternal truths of God's universe. Insight into these truths enables one to become an interpreter, to become an individual who can mediate between eternal universality and concrete situations.

King describes *an ideal* to his audience, a normative story of personal and professional development. He, as well as Nkrumah, fulfils these norms. King confirms his position as interpreter and leader of the movement.

Third, the structural opposites of known and unknown are determinative in this part of the sermon. When King mentions Nkrumah's parents, who not only were illiterate but also were "not part of the powerful tribal life of Africa, not chiefs at all," we are in the unknown Africa.[33] This is where the journey starts, a journey that is not just Nkrumah's physical journey or the intellectual journey from illiteracy to a university degree, but also a rhetorical journey from the unknown to the known. Nkrumah comes to America, he receives his education there, and he also works as something as secular as a dishwasher in Philadelphia, Pennsylvania. The story of the exodus is given concreteness in a modern-day context, and the bond between the struggle for freedom in the two contexts of Ghana and the United States becomes very concrete. In the process of acquiring an education, Nkrumah learned how hard work and discipline were necessary for success. The known and unknown meet through the fact that the methods and the necessary steps one must take to achieve the goals in the respective contexts are the same.

After this passage the recording is interrupted and some sentences (how few or many is impossible to say) are missing, but the structure of the text indicates that Nkrumah's name is mentioned for the first time during this interruption. The pronoun has changed from "he" to "I" as King says, speaking as Nkrumah: "I want to go back to West Africa, the land of my people, my native land."[34] Back to the unknown with the knowledge of the known as ammunition.

When Nkrumah comes home the central phases of the struggle begin. King summarizes the events. Nkrumah worked as secretary for the United Party of the Gold Coast but soon found himself in conflict with other leading persons within the party who "thought he was pushing a little too fast and . . . got a little jealous of his influence."[35] Instead he organized the Convention People's Party; from that point on the struggle took clearer form and began to move more rapidly. Nkrumah united his people and tried to convince the British Empire to give them their freedom. He also began to write. He was confined to jail for several years but continued to influence the people outside prison walls; he was elected prime minister while in jail. Finally, the British realized that they "had better let him out."[36] Thereafter the struggle for independence took further form and on March 6, 1957, Britain had to let the new nation go; it would "no longer be a colony of the British Empire."[37] The festivities, the actual reason for King's visit, could begin.

It may appear a bit odd that King devotes more time to describing the independence celebrations than to discussing the history of the struggle, but there are several possible reasons for this choice. The reason for King's visit was the celebration, and the celebration in itself is the actual birth of the new nation that is the theme of the sermon. The speaking situation also was neither the time nor the place to give a more detailed account of the history of Africa and the Gold Coast. King uses the celebration to further strengthen the ties between known and unknown, to give the struggle an idealistic meaning, and to give a special meaning to the word "freedom"—a concept that connects both the congregation in the United States and those who struggled against colonization in the Gold Coast. That King himself becomes a character in his own sermon—one who is openly taking part in the story—is not to be neglected either. His physical presence forms a bridge between the known and unknown.

Kings mentions the names of prominent guests and tries to convey the magic of the situation: "We sat there that night, just about five hundred able to get in there. People, thousands and thousands of people waiting outside, just about five hundred in there, and we were fortunate enough to be sitting there at that moment as guests of the prime minister."[38] King says that when Nkrumah began to speak, "there was something old now passing away" and continues:

> The thing that impressed me more than anything else that night was the fact that when Nkrumah walked in, and his other ministers who had been in prison with him, they didn't come with the crowns and all of the garments of kings, but they walked in with prison caps and the coats they had lived with for all of the months that they had been in prison.[39]

That King points out that Nkrumah and his ministers still wore their prison clothes further establishes the connection between the struggle in Ghana and the struggle against segregation in the South, where going to prison for a just cause had become both a central strategy and a noble mark of involvement. It was something thoroughly familiar to the congregation and also to King himself; he too had been imprisoned during the Montgomery bus boycott. This detail serves to connect the characters in the sermon with the congregation in the pews.

This detail further reminds the congregation that at the concrete level of the struggle all men and women are the same and all are equally subjugated by a system of oppression—they all wear symbolic prison clothes. To remember this in the moment of triumph is crucial. By retaining this common identity even in a situation where it is Nkrumah's individuality that is central demonstrates that he is an individual with a special place in history. Even in triumph he represents the unbreakable bond that exists between his newly freed Ghana and the still-unfree segregated South. The story of the exodus is still being told.

This is further emphasized in the crescendo of the sermon's first part. The Union Jack has come down and the new flag of Ghana has just risen. Nkrumah has finished his speech to his people with the words "We are no longer a British colony, we are a free, sovereign people." King says that he himself cried for joy.[40] He continues:

After Nkrumah had made that final speech, it was about twelve-thirty now. And we walked away. And we could hear little children six years old and old people eighty and ninety years old walking the streets of Accra crying "Freedom! Freedom!" They couldn't say it in the sense we'd say it, many of them don't speak English too well, but they had their accents and it could ring out "free-doom!" They were crying it in a sense that they never heard it before. And I could hear that old Negro spiritual once more crying out "Free at last, free at last, great God almighty, I'm free at last." They were experiencing that in their very souls. And everywhere we turned, we could here it ringing out from the housetops. We could here it from every corner, every nook and crook of the community. "Freedom! Freedom!" This was the birth of a new nation. This was the breaking aloose from Egypt.[41]

In this passage, as well as in the sermon as a whole, the word "freedom" has a central position. Freedom is the general objective that unites the exodus, Ghana, and the American South; they are examples of the sure movement toward liberation in God's universe. In this passage, King makes clear that there is a special relationship between the individual and this force within the universe. The moment of freedom, the actual moment of liberation, represents individual salvation.

The force of freedom in the universe speaks through individuals, even young children who do not know the language. Freedom takes human shape, first in the struggle and then in the moment of liberation; human divinity is actualized in the almost hypnotic chanting of "freedom." Earthly redemption and otherworldly salvation go hand in hand. When King describes the scenes of the night that followed Nkrumah's speech it reflects this moment of joy.

The passage is also loaded with the significance of the meeting between the known and the unknown that makes the story tell as much about the American South as it does about Ghana. The necessity for and success of liberation in Ghana legitimizes the quest for freedom in America. King is explicit when he actually moves from Ghana straight into the words of the famous Negro spiritual. Freedom is the same necessary redemptive feature of both situations. Like the exodus, Ghana is a model of the struggle being waged in the segregated American South.

Overall we are still inside a biblical time and context. The congregation is still being presented with the religious situation that knowledge will later be drawn from. The story of the exodus is still being told. King concludes the climax with the words "this was the breaking a-loose from Egypt." The story in Exodus has been told in the story of decolonization in Ghana and vice versa. Now the time has come for the American South to manifest this recurring historical theme.

King then comes to the turning point of the sermon. He says, "Ghana has something to say to us."[42] King concentrates his interpretation of the text on what it says about freedom. He has thoroughly laid the groundwork for this interpretation in the first part of the sermon, and the ideas and their ideological interpretations are the same in both parts of the text. What is added is King's role. He moves from being a participator in the festivities surrounding the independence of Ghana and the voice of the Bible to become the preacher of Dexter Avenue Baptist Church situated in the American South. The fusion between known and unknown has been made and King can concentrate on implementing the norms of the scripture in the context of the speaking situation.

What does Ghana's story of decolonization tell King, his congregation, and the civil rights movement? He says:

> We've got to keep on keeping on in order to gain freedom. It never comes like that. It would be fortunate if the people in power had sense enough to go on and give up, but they don't do it like that. It is not done voluntarily! It is done through the pressure that comes about from people who are oppressed.[43]

And

> Ghana reminds us that freedom never comes on a silver platter. It's never easy. Ghana reminds us that whenever you break out of Egypt, you better get ready for stiff backs. You better get ready for some homes to be bombed, you better get ready for a lot of nasty things to be said about you, because you getting out of Egypt. And

whenever you break aloose from Egypt, the initial response from
the Egyptian is bitterness.[44]

King underlines this point by speaking of how Nkrumah's
prison cap was a reminder that freedom never comes easily,
that there is no crown without a cross and that one must confront the Red Sea before one can reach Canaan.[45] King's interpretation of the scripture has the purpose of projecting the
meaning of that story into the congregation and the movement. The success of liberation in Africa demands freedom in
America. That is the first statement of the interpretation. But
it does not stand alone.

The interpretation also includes the biblical milieu of the
book of Exodus. The guarantee of Exodus extends the promise
of Ghana to the struggle in the south. Pharaoh, the colonizer,
and the segregationist are ultimately one and the same. So just
as the lesson of Ghana legitimizes demands for freedom in
America, it also guarantees the religious quality of the struggle
and, ultimately, victory. The cause is just. The struggle is endowed with a biblical, God-given quality.

When King discusses the hardships of the struggle, religion
is central. King focuses on this. The "bitterness of the Egyptian" will be part of any exodus, just as setbacks will be a part
of the experience. The civil rights movement must go through
all this, and King carefully names examples of setbacks that he
places directly within the context of the movement: the house-
bombings, the smear campaigns, and so forth. But there is also
a guarantee that liberation will come:

> The road to freedom is difficult, but finally, Ghana tells us that the
> forces of the universe are on the side of justice. That is what it tells
> us, now. You can interpret Ghana any kind of way you want to,
> but Ghana tells me that the forces of the universe are on the side
> of justice.[46]

King goes on to place events in Ghana in a larger international
context: the downfall of colonialism itself. This is another version of secular legitimization of the sermon. The death of colo-

nialism symbolizes a new world coming into being, and the impending death of segregation is a part of this new world.

Cold War:
Rhetoric, Strategy, and Ideology

The importance of the Cold War for the emergence and development of the civil rights movement is in itself unquestionable. But there are conflicting views regarding exactly *what* it meant. The most common argument is that the Cold War had a positive effect on the movement. The realities of World War II, the struggles against colonialism, and the constant propaganda war between the United States and the Soviet Union opened up possibilities for change in America and pushed these forces of change forward once they had been set in motion.

But there is also the negative view that the consequences of the Cold War delayed the civil rights struggle by a decade. The changes that had been on their way before and during the war were seriously hampered by the Red Scare. Furthermore, the internal American political climate forced the civil rights movement to choose a path that could be accepted in that environment. To be heard and accepted, the movement had to subscribe to certain ideological values.[47]

Both of these positions are important when discussing King's relationship with the Cold War and its impact on his rhetoric. To do so I will use the speech "The Montgomery Story," delivered at the forty-seventh annual convention of the NAACP at the San Francisco Civic Auditorium in June 1956.

The speaking situation here is different from when he was addressing the congregation at Dexter Avenue Baptist Church. This is an "official" speech; here King speaks in the way he usually did when addressing northern audiences in such circumstances. He speaks of the Montgomery bus boycott to people who are not actually taking part in that activity. Therefore King's way of representing is different than it was in "The Birth of a New Nation."

It could be argued that a speech before an NAACP convention is not the ideal situation in which to study this kind of interpretive act. The NAACP was not only a civil rights organization—it was the biggest and the most influential civil rights organization. In that sense, King still speaks to his own; he addresses an audience that is involved in the struggle. But even though the NAACP was a part of the civil rights movement, there was a gap in ideology, tactics, and strategy between that organization and King and "his" organizations. Furthermore, King went to San Francisco as an "outsider" to the NAACP. The position from which he speaks to the convention is in many ways the same as the position from which he spoke to northern liberal (often all-white) organizations. He justifies his actions by naming his struggle using their language. He wants to stress the similarity between what may seem to be different struggles and thereby overcome the gap between him and his audience. On this specific occasion King plays a double role: He speaks from both the inside and the outside, both as a "part" of the NAACP (the civil rights movement writ large) and as a part of a struggle that had been waged from other starting points and with other strategies than those the NAACP was using.

To this, two further circumstances must be added. First, the NAACP was a participant in the Red Scare purges of the Cold War. Under the hegemonic rule of the national political powers, the NAACP was the guardian against socialist influence in the civil rights arena.[48] Through guaranteeing that their mission was anti-communist and anti-socialist, the NAACP guaranteed its own survival and importance; it defined its struggle within the framework of the hegemonic order of Cold War America. In the interpretation of the NAACP, the struggle against racial prejudice was also a struggle against communism.

Second, an NAACP convention was a national event. When King spoke, he addressed many more people than the audience in the San Francisco Civic Auditorium. He of course knew that any controversial utterance would quickly would find its way to the national newspapers, that the NAACP was the sole civil rights organization that at this time had the ear of the government, and that it was not only closely connected with the liberal North but in fact a part of it.

THE GUARANTEE

King opens the speech by presenting the background to the Montgomery bus boycott, a narrative that features many of his standard rhetorical elements: He puts Montgomery in the perspective of Negro history, he speaks of how a new Negro has been born in the South, he uses both the Bible and Aristotle, and he excels in phrases such as "every man, from a bass black to a treble white, is significant on God's keyboard."[49] He concludes this first part of the speech with the words "you can never understand the Montgomery Story without understanding that there is a brand new Negro in the South, with a new sense of dignity and destiny."[50]

In this way King establishes the interpretive framework before the story itself is told. The different levels of the civil rights movement discourse are also present here. The history of the Negro evokes the idealistic and religious levels and solidifies the meaning of the concrete examples that are about to follow.

One can also sense some caution in this introduction. The contexts King places the Montgomery story within are historical, religious, and intellectual. He does not speak of a political context. He speaks of the Negro's place within America, the wrongdoings of the past, the false intellectual proofs of the Negro's inferiority; he says that God stands on the side of the Negro's demands and that blacks and whites can and should stand and work together. Thus, he clearly connects his introduction, and thereby the framework for the way he wants the Montgomery struggle to be understood, with the structure, strategy, and ideology of the NAACP as a racially mixed organization that worked within the judicial system rather than through political action, an organization that was always eager to place itself within the general American political consensus. The only thing that goes beyond this framework is the focus on the birth of the "new Negro." This focus constitutes a legitimization for King's and the Montgomery Improvement

Association's activities (the SCLC was yet to be founded) before an NAACP that was often suspicious of any form of direct
action. But this focus on the birth of the new Negro is more
than a legitimization in the sense that it explains and makes
the actions in Montgomery necessary and righteous; it also
serves as a kind of guarantee that the forces behind the struggle
and the concrete action of its participants does not have any
other background, history, or motive than those of the audience at the NAACP convention. As well as offering a guarantee, this also makes the frames of interpretation clear.

King then tells the story of the boycott in a quite detailed
way; it is a summary of what would later form *Stride toward
Freedom*. But some aspects of the story reveal that it is specifically directed toward the NAACP audience: the emphasis
that nonviolence is the "basic philosophy undergirding our
movement" and the clear assurance that the struggle does not
in any way aim to win a victory over or to humiliate white
people.[51]

King speaks here from a position outside the NAACP; he
legitimizes his actions within the ideological constrains of the
NAACP. The focus on nonviolence guarantees that there is no
hidden agenda behind the boycott. The "built-in" radicalism of
the concrete action of the Montgomery Improvement Association draws upon what King depicts as the ideologically neutral
philosophy of nonviolence. He defines the boycott in Montgomery in a way that the NAACP can accept.

But what does this tell us about how trustworthy the ideology in King's rhetoric is? Is his rhetoric a vacuum that fills
itself up with the ideological notions of his audiences, there
only to be understood, accepted, and supported? Of course not.
King's audiences were not that diverse. He did not speak to
Leninist revolutionaries one day and conservatives the next.
He spoke to U.S. audiences that were in one way or another
involved in the civil rights struggle. There was a common denominator. Furthermore, King's speeches were, generally, never
that contradictory. He did not advocate separation one day and
integration the next. The key is the space between these ex-

treme opposites. King adjusted his rhetoric to the situation he spoke in by emphasizing different parts of the struggle.

This means that there are fundamental ideological assumptions involved in King's rhetoric. But there is also space within this relatively loose structure to adjust it in special ways in different situations. But when he adjusts it, when he emphasizes different things, there *are* ideological effects. The structure that language creates or upholds is real in the sense that it defines the speaker himself in the same way that it defines the world or the specific situation.

This is relevant in reference to what happens in the speech when King openly confronts some of the features of Cold War America. Toward the end of the speech, when the story of Montgomery has been told, King discusses the future of the civil rights movement and he defines the role of the NAACP he is speaking before. Here he relies heavily on Cold War–era language:

> The underlying philosophy of democracy is diametrically opposed to the underlying philosophy of segregation, and all of the dialectics of logicians cannot make them lie down together. Segregation is an evil, segregation is a cancer in the body politic which must be removed before our democratic health can be realized.[52]

A bit farther on he adds

> We cannot afford to slow up. We have the moral obligation to press on. We have our self-respect to maintain. But even more we can't afford to slow up because of our love for America and our love for the democratic way of life.
>
> Out of two billion, four hundred million people in this the world, one billion, six hundred million are colored. Most of these colored people have lived under the yoke of colonialism and imperialism. Gradually most and all of those people are gaining their freedom, and they are determined not to follow any nation that will subject [*word inaudible*] citizens to second-class citizenship. And if America doesn't wake up, she will discover that the uncommitted peoples of the world are in the hands of a communistic ideology. So, because of our love for America, we cannot afford to slow up. But even more, but [*sic*] we can't stop there. The motive for America giving freedom and justice to the Negro cannot be merely to com-

pete with godless communism. We must do it because it's part of
the ethical demands of the universe.[53]

We can here recognize several different aspects of the Cold War
context. King points to the blatant incompatibility of democracy and segregation—if America wants to remain (become)
democratic and thus be able to claim to represent the "free
world," segregation must be abolished. He further emphasizes
this point in the second passage. He relates the urgency of the
situation to both morality and self-respect in order to map out
the general framework of meaning. The map is finalized when
the meaning of the passage is determined in the last sentence:
The freedom of the Negro is a "part of the ethical demands of
the universe." These demands are what ultimately determine
the nature of America's situation and its role in the scope of
international politics, the Cold War, and decolonization.

In this process both "America" and "communism" are highly
charged words. They form a continuation of the guarantee that
King offered at the beginning of the speech: the "radicalism"
of Montgomery did not have any ties to left-wing activism.[54]
But it also goes beyond this.

The constant surveillance of the FBI, their attempts to red-
bait King and the movement, and the segregationists' persistent claims that any demands for changes came from communist outsiders are also factors here. From the beginning, King
had to be exceedingly careful not to be associated with communism or socialists of any kind. In this speech he exploits the
threat of this accusation by reversing its meaning. Instead of
the movement being a socialist risk, it becomes the only available way to save America from the threats of the Cold War. He
manages this reversal by expanding the scope of the Cold War
from the internal Red Scare in America into a worldwide
struggle.

Through this way of defining desegregation's role in history and its role relative to concrete Cold War strategy, King
defines the movement as a social agent. He legitimizes the
movement's actions by positioning them in a context where

their meaning comes to be inherently acceptable to the national political demands of the day, a meaning that also eases the eventual fears of the moderate NAACP.

But this is more than a process in which King establishes a particular way of discussing and understanding the issues. His rhetoric also has ideological effects.

THE TRADEOFF

The civil rights struggle was aided by the Cold War because it became harder to justify the acceptance of segregation within American democracy, especially as related to the propaganda war between the United States and the Soviet Union. In this respect, the Cold War was highly useful for King's rhetoric. It enabled him to place "love for America" and the struggle against "godless communism" at the heart of the civil rights quest. But the movement was also stifled by the Cold War because it had to form its identity and mission in the language of Cold War discourse and was thereby deemed to share its central ideological values. This means that there is an inherent demand— a tradeoff—in the decision to use the Cold War as an incentive for change in the civil rights arena. The rhetoric King chose upheld and emphasized the stability of America.

King stresses that the abolition of segregation is an instrument that can shore up America's world dominance and a weapon America can use to win the battle over the decolonized areas in Asia and Africa. King thereby pledges to support the stability and righteousness of America. The civil rights struggle is waged *because* of American values, not in spite of them. In order to be heard and understood, King speaks within the limits of the hegemonic orders. His view of humanity, of history, and of society does not challenge established notions; it is identical with them. King supports individualistic capitalism in a society based on personal success and a general, if vague, notion of liberal democracy. This enables him to occupy the position between cultures.

COLONIALISM AGAIN

Another aspect of the ideological meanings created by King's rhetoric can be seen if we return to the sermon "The Birth of a New Nation."

As a conclusion to the sermon King discusses the worldwide collapse of colonialism. He takes the congregation with him on his journey from Ghana back to America. During this trip, he stopped in London and this event provides King the opportunity to develop the theme. King's imagery is almost too explicit here, as when he sees how the splendor of Westminster Abbey is a symbol of a dying system.[55]

In the sermon King does not structure the world in terms of the Cold War vocabulary that he uses in the NAACP speech. But still, the revolts of the oppressed peoples in both texts are placed within the ladder of signification and thereby ultimately religiously determined. The situations never stand alone. Colonization and oppression stand in opposition to the ethical demands of the universe; they are against the will of God. King says:

> God has injected a principle in this universe. God has said that all men must reflect the dignity and worth of all human personality, "And if you don't do that, I will take charge." It seems this morning that I can hear God speaking. I can hear him speaking throughout the universe, saying, "'Be still, and know that I am God.' If you don't stop, if you don't straighten up, if you don't stop exploiting people, I'm gonna rise up and break the backbone of your power. And your power will be no more!" And the power of Great Britain is no more.[56]

The prophetic warning to America emphasizes the necessity for concrete action both from the movement and from the government. King uses the example of Britain to say to America that if it does not change, God will destroy its powers. But even if this may seem to be a long way from "the love of America and democratic way of life" that he stresses in the NAACP speech, the argument in fact has the same core: The abolition of segregation is the only way to save America. The central aim of the movement in both speeches is to uphold the America displayed in the values of the Constitution.

In the sermon it is an open threat and in the speech it is an implicit warning, but they both insist that the central American ideological beliefs are not the problem, but the solution. And if the struggle against segregation is lost, then so are the core values of America. In the sermon this leads to God's vengeance and in the speech it leads to communist world dominance. In both cases the movement participants stand as the defenders of America, as the true patriots.

But something changes when King and the movement confront the post-1965 situation and the Vietnam War.

Vietnam and the Evil Triplets

When King finally officially and nationally spoke out against the Vietnam War in April 1967, it was no sudden decision. Several contexts informed a decision he had been considering for some time.

World War II had brought with it a consensus around the two fundamental assumptions of U.S. foreign policy: internal security and the moral obligation of the United States.[57] The assumptions were tightly knit together. The internal security argument was based on the belief that the United States always had to be prepared to defend itself against the ever-present threat of communist world domination. This called for permanent international activity. Associated with this was the fear of what in the debate about whether or not to enter Vietnam would be called the "domino effect": If one country fell into the hands of communist powers, another, probably its neighbor, would soon do the same. To protect itself, America had to protect the world.

Herein lies the second assumption: America believed it had a moral duty to defend freedom and liberty all over the world. America's position as the world's greatest superpower implied that it had to take responsibility to defend the values that the nation was founded on wherever it felt they were threatened.

This was the logic behind the proclamation of Vietnam War as a "just war."

During the initial stages of the conflict, the security and moral aspects of the war indeed went hand in hand, as they had done during the whole postwar period. The fight to secure U.S. interests was a fight for democracy and freedom. The war was morally just since its aim was to stop all the evils that communism represented.

The first major escalation of the war began in the last months of 1964 and lasted into 1965. During this escalation a new debate over the war began. In this debate, the two U.S. foreign policy assumptions gradually became as separated as they had been interconnected before. The opposition to the war sprang from a questioning of its moral purpose. How could killing women and children, burning villages, and using weapons and methods such as napalm ever be morally justifiable? The proponents of the war based their stand on the security argument: The war was necessary for holding communism at bay. The opening of a gulf between the two foreign policy assumptions had begun.

VIETNAM AND BLACK AMERICA

Black America and the civil rights movement were both divided on the war issue. In many camps, a sense of loyalty to Lyndon B. Johnson prevailed because of his role in the passing of the civil rights and voting rights laws of 1964 and 1965. He was also the president who had launched the Great Society, and in the 1964 election he received over 80 percent of the black vote. To many blacks, Johnson was a president who continued to lead the nation toward racial equality.

The ties between the movement and the president meant that the traditional division between domestic civil rights issues and U.S. foreign policy was maintained. Several movement participants as well as the political establishment argued that what took place within one context should not affect another, and a mutually agreed upon, yet unspoken, tradeoff stated that as long as the movement did not overstep its bounds, it would have the ear of the president. This made the movement a part of the establishment and it was also the background to the condemnation King received from many black leaders after he openly criticized the war.

Another fact that became important during the debate about Vietnam among black leaders was the disproportionate numbers of black soldiers fighting in Vietnam. In 1966, 22 percent of the soldiers killed were black, yet on the whole blacks constituted only 11 percent of the population.[58] This reality brought two arguments to the fore. For the prowar blacks it was an incentive to step up the war efforts; they felt that the United States was not doing all it could to win the war. If only the right funds and efforts could be made available, a victorious ending would come sooner rather than later. But mainly, the fact that blacks made up a disproportionately large percentage of the U.S. troops became the basis of the opposition of antiwar blacks, and as a whole the black population was more critical of the war than were other demographic groups. Nobody gave this a public voice better that Muhammad Ali, who when refusing the draft said, "I ain't got no quarrel with those Vietcong anyway; they never called me a nigger."[59]

That statement's emotional sentiment became the central nerve of the opposition to the Vietnam War that grew rapidly in the more radical circles of the civil rights movement, especially among the students in SNCC. The fight for freedom should be waged at home, not in some foreign land where soldiers were forced to kill other oppressed people of color. Others pointed out that the war diverted resources from Johnson's Great Society programs, which in the long run meant that a black American soldier killing, as Stokely Carmichael put it, a "colored brother" also bit by bit killed the chances of social and economic improvements in his home town.[60]

King had become increasingly troubled by the war around the time of its first major escalation in 1964–1965 but was caught from the beginning between these two positions. On the one hand, the moderates of the movement urged him to respect the deal with the Johnson administration. The president's importance for the passage of the Civil Rights and Voting Rights Acts called for loyalty and a "hands-off" guarantee when it came to issues that were not related to civil rights, such as Vietnam. To speak out against the war would not only step outside the designated area of civil rights, it would betray the political establishment as a whole and the president personally and it would seriously hamper the movement's cause. Possibly, King was also held back by the FBI, which, as some reports claim, threatened to publicize damaging information on King's private life should he go public with his opposition to the war.[61] On the other hand, the young radicals urged King to take a stand against the war. How could a nonviolent crusader such as King silently watch children being burned to death by Americans in Southeast Asia?[62]

On a combined vacation and writing trip in Jamaica in January 1967, King came to the conclusion that he could not remain silent on the war issue. He had in fact expressed mild criticism of the war in speeches as early as in 1965, but his 1967 position was something else.[63] He wanted to place himself as a central figure in opposition to the war. He initially intended to make a speech outlining this position at a large protest meeting outside the United Nations building, but this was vetoed by some of his advisors, who argued that the venue would be too risky; King could not take the chance that his views, which he would have only ten minutes to expound, would be confused with those of other much more radical speakers. If King wanted to speak out against the war, he should do so in the forum he knew best and where he would be able to state his arguments in his own way: the church.

THE SPEECH

"Beyond Vietnam" was delivered at The Riverside Church in New York City on April 4, 1967. The speech is naturally central for any understanding of King's position on the war issue, but it can also be read in another sense: Here too King uses a foreign situation to give meaning to the civil rights movement.[64] The speech also reveals some central themes of King's later rhetoric. Something has happened to the discourse that was previously so clearly defined. The way King speaks of Vietnam mirrors the way he views the civil rights movement—as a transformer of American society—while the way he describes the aims of the struggle defines how he speaks of Vietnam.

King's introductory words are carefully chosen and establish the structure of the speech. After declaring that it is not an easy task to oppose the policies of one's government, especially in time of war, he says:

> Some of us who have already begun to break the silence of the night have found that the calling to speak often is a vocation of agony, but we must speak. We must speak with all the humility that is appropriate to our limited vision, but we must speak. And we must rejoice as well, for surely this is the first time in our nation's history that a significant number of its religious leaders have chosen to move beyond the prophesying of smooth patriotism to the high grounds of a firm dissent based upon the mandates of conscience and the readings of history. Perhaps a new spirit is rising among us. If it is, let us trace its movement and pray that our inner being may be sensitive to its guidance. For we are deeply in need of a new way beyond the darkness that seems so close around us.[65]

This is a guarded opening. After explaining the great agony of coming to the conclusion that he must oppose his own government, a government that had been instrumental in helping the civil rights movement to succeed, King seeks a position of moral authority that is so high that its judgments supersede those of any government. He wants to take up a position that parallels the righteousness of the civil rights leader. As a way of reassuring that he speaks with moral authority, King uses strategies of legitimization from the struggle against segregation: The ultimate forces of the universe demand that he take the position he takes in this speech. Therefore civil rights and Vietnam share the same meaning and cannot be divorced from each other.

King is explicit about this issue a little farther on. When criticizing the view that civil rights and foreign policy do not mix, he states that "I believe that the path from Dexter Avenue Baptist Church—the church in Montgomery, Alabama, where I began my pastorate—leads clearly to this sanctuary tonight."[66] This relationship between the two movements is a rhetorical tool, and the explicit aim of the speech is to reveal that connection. Accordingly, the stand against Vietnam must be incorporated into a larger framework.

As in many speeches from this time, it is not an America of promise and hope in which King situates himself. When he speaks of "a darkness that seems so close around us" he does more than aim at the Vietnam conflict that casts its shadow over America. The nearness of the darkness suggests that it exists *within* American society. Vietnam is not the cause of the darkness; Vietnam is an outgrowth of a darkness that resides in the nation.

Here King uses an international situation to speak of a domestic situation. The focus may not be on America as obviously as in the other texts analyzed in this chapter—Vietnam is the "real" issue, the motive behind the speech—but his rhetoric still uses the connection. The rhetorical strategy of drawing a straight line between Dexter Avenue Baptist Church in 1955 and The Riverside Church in 1967 states this explicitly. But what makes this speech different, what gives it another meaning, is the different position from which King speaks.

The values of "my beloved nation" no longer represent the ethical demands of the universe.[67] The values of King's criticism and the central values of America are not only separate; they have become opposites. This means that he steps outside the hegemony of the landscape of Cold War America.

The terms and values King had used in previous speeches were based in shared identity. They were comprehensible, and were given meaning, within mutual points of reference. But with regard to the Vietnam War the incontestability of the terms and values was more difficult to achieve. They are not as easily comprehensible as when they were given meaning through the Constitution and Christianity. King's ability to appeal to a shared identity is seriously hampered when he is attacking instead of celebrating patriotism.

Before King gets to the concrete aspects of the war, he sets the frames for the interpretive possibilities of the speech and endows his position with a context of his own choice. He uses the same technique he used in the NAACP speech. When he opens with the words "since I am a preacher by calling, I suppose it is not surprising that I have seven major reasons for bringing Vietnam into the field of my moral vision" he states two things.[68] King speaks as a preacher and his standpoints thereby incorporate the truths of Christianity. Since his standpoints represent these truths, the horrors of the war must ultimately be understood and morally judged in relationship with the "moral vision" of King the preacher.

King puts forward seven reasons for his opposition to the war. The hopes of civil rights reformers and the social programs of the Great Society have been shattered by the economic demands of the war. Black and white boys can burn villages in Vietnam together but they cannot live in the same neighborhood in an American city. It is impossible to speak against the use of violence in American ghettos without condemning the government's use of violence in Southeast Asia. The SCLC has a responsibility "to save the soul of America." King has a personal responsibility as a Nobel Peace Prize recipient to oppose the war. He has a responsibility as a minister who was committed to the teachings of Jesus to oppose the war. And finally, he says: "I must be true to my conviction that I share with all men the calling to be a son of a Living God."[69]

Here he begins at the most basic level—the effects of the war on the domestic economy—and through steps that incorporate all the essentials of the civil rights struggle moves upward through a hierarchy of morality: integration, nonviolence, the attempt to cure America, the legitimacy bestowed upon King's leadership symbolized by the Nobel prize, and the Christian roots of the movement and its fundamental notion that every individual is sacred as a child of God.

King directs these arguments toward those within the movement who argued that it was in their best interest to remain silent on the war issue because that strategy would enable them to draw upon the power of the struggling hegemonic powers of the nation as they had done before 1965. King's arguments represent a break with this strategy. He has moved his criticisms and demands from the inside to the outside.

After King has established his position and set a framework for interpretation, he discusses the actual war. His aim is clearly to refute the claim that Vietnam is a "just war." This aim takes him directly into the restructuring of U.S. foreign policy assumptions. In two central passages he says:

> They watch as we poison their water, as we kill a million acres of their crops. They must weep as the bulldozers roar through their areas preparing to destroy their precious trees. They wander into the hospitals with at least twenty casualties from American firepower for one Vietcong-inflicted injury. So far we may have killed a million of them, mostly children.[70]

And:

> If we continue, there will be no doubt in my mind and in the mind of the world that we have no honorable intentions in Vietnam. If we do not stop our war against the people of Vietnam immediately, the world will be left with no alternative than to see this as some horrible, clumsy, and deadly game we have decided to play. The world now demands a maturity of America that we may not be able to achieve.[71]

In the first passage King discusses the morality of the activities of the United States and in the second he turns the assumption of the need for security against itself. He upholds the notions of moral obligation and the guarantee of security, but he places them within another network of meanings.

King argues that if American foreign policy is to be based on morality, the Vietnam War is diametrically opposed to that principle. If morality is the issue, the war must be stopped immediately. The divine ethics involved in his role as a preacher and "the son of a living God" stand opposed to U.S. actions. King attacks his "beloved nation" with all the moral force that he once used against the most hardened and vicious of segregationists. The actual words may be the same, but the meaning is different.

Then he responds to the argument that the war is necessary to protect American security: America has nothing to fear from Vietnam, he says; only a minor proportion of the "Vietcong" were communists. He turns the security-based justification for war on its head by noting that the war creates the risk that other nuclear powers will become involved in the deadly game.

But King does not stop there; he reserves his most severe criticism of the war for the final part of the speech. It is here that the straight path between Dexter Avenue Baptist Church and The Riverside Church is drawn out in full and it is also here that we can most clearly see how Vietnam is a symptom of an American social sickness that cannot be cured with anything less than a radical medicine. The goal is no longer about individuals changing places within a society and thereby making that society better and more moral. The goal is now about changing the fundamentals of that society to give individuals another context, another moral space, to live and act in. King's moral vision cannot be achieved in a society whose own inner darkness is manifested not just by starving children in Mississippi or the abysmal conditions in the Chicago slums but also by the butchering of innocent people on the other side of the world.

As in many speeches from his last years, King speaks of the giant triplets of racism, materialism, and militarism as the interconnected causes of the injustices of the world. They depend upon each other to stand between humanity and the moral vision. To be on the right side of what King calls "the world revolution"—the uprisings in the Third World—the United States must change. It must undergo a radical "revolution of values." This expression demonstrates that King's vision is still idealistic, but the scope of his demands is different. He says:

A true revolution of values will soon cause us to question the fairness and justice of many of our past and present policies. On the one hand we are called to play the Good Samaritan on life's roadside, but that will be only an initial act. One day we must come to see that the whole Jericho Road must be transformed so that men and women will not be constantly beaten and robbed as they make their journey on life's highway. True compassion is more than flinging a coin to a beggar. It comes to see that an edifice which produces beggars needs restructuring.

A true revolution of values will soon look uneasily on the glaring contrast of poverty and wealth.[72]

The Vietnam War is an expression of America's moral wrongdoings in the international arena and the fundamental problems that must be faced domestically. The use of the parable of Good Samaritan in this passage is not coincidental. King uses typology to make his point. Even the America of the late 1960s has biblical meaning. All the connections King makes—between the quest for civil rights and Vietnam, between the moral and structural problems of the United States and the immoral cruelties of its war machine, or, for that matter, between racism, materialism, and militarism—are given the comprehensible name of the biblical story, the same story that King had used over and over again when speaking on the more confined issue of segregation.

But something is different here. When King uses civil rights signifiers to formulate and legitimize his opposition to the Vietnam War, they come to have a different meaning. Instead of laying the foundations for an American dream, they create, in the words of Malcolm X, an American nightmare.

Vietnam and Radicalization

King's opposition to the war is connected with the general development of his rhetoric after the legal victories of the mid-1960s. King moves from the use of international ideas and developments such as Gandhiism to the struggles against colonialism in Africa to the boundaries created by the hegemonic rules of Cold War America to the use of another international situation, the Vietnam War, as a way to formulate and legitimize an accusation against America.

The new situation offers King the "opportunity" to use the war as a further creator of meaning in his project. This is a project that during 1967 and 1968 comes to include demands ranging from calls for massive civil disobedience actions to the nationalization of large industrial corporations. And the fundamental issue of the early civil rights movement, that every black individual should be guaranteed the possibility to reap the fruits of American social opportunities, is replaced by the task of ridding American society of all the obstacles that stand in the way of economic, social, and racial equality.

The effects of this can be seen in and through "Beyond Vietnam." The horrors and consequences of the war legitimize the revolution of values that America must undergo. But the speech cannot be viewed alone. The next chapter discusses the roots, components, and effects of King's process of radicalization.

5. Radicalization

Over the course of his career as a civil rights leader, King went through a process of radicalization. The points of view he put forward during the Montgomery bus boycott and in *Stride toward Freedom* are not exactly the same as those he put forward during the struggle for fair housing in Chicago and in *Chaos or Community.* As the civil rights struggle changed, King changed too.

But what parts of King's rhetoric changed and what stayed the same? In which ways did its system of signification change? Which new and more radical ideas are expressed in his later rhetoric?

A New Mission: From Desegregation to Radical Restructuring

Toward the end of *Stride toward Freedom,* King used a passage that recurred in many of his speeches and sermons. Almost triumphantly, he wrote:

> This is a great hour for the Negro. The challenge is here. To become the instruments of a great idea is a privilege that history gives only occasionally. Arnold Toynbee says in *A Study of History* that it may be the Negro who will give the new spiritual dynamic to Western civilization that it so desperately needs to survive. I hope this is possible. The spiritual power that the Negro can radiate to the world comes from love, understanding, good will, and nonviolence. It may even be possible for the Negro, through adherence to nonviolence, so to challenge the nations of the world that they will seriously seek an alternative to war and destruction.[1]

There is a similar passage in his last book, the posthumously published collection of speeches called *The Trumpet of Conscience* that, despite its slender size, gives a quite comprehensive picture of the attitudes of the later King.[2] At the end of "Impasse in Race Relations," King states:

> We may now be in only the initial period of an era of change as far-reaching in its consequences as the American Revolution. The developed industrial nations of the world cannot remain secure islands of prosperity in a seething sea of poverty. The storm is rising against the privileged minority of the earth, from which there is no shelter in isolation and armament. The storm will not abate until a just distribution of the fruits of the earth enables man everywhere to live in dignity and human decency. The American Negro of 1967, like Crispus Attucks, may be the vanguard in a prolonged struggle that may change the shape of the world, as billions of deprived shake and transform the earth in their quest for life, freedom, and justice.[3]

These two passages, although they discuss the same theme, illustrate the changes in the way King presented his ideas over time. The later King was more willing to use radical allusions and metaphors; his rhetoric is not the same as it was in his early career.

Although both quotes discuss what actions "the American Negro" can and must offer the world at large, the demand of one speech is for the end of segregation; the demand of the other is to change the entire social structure of the United States. One speech sees the United States and the Constitution as a symbol of promise and hope; one defines the nation through the desperation of its poverty-stricken ghettoes. In one speech the American Negro is the spiritual hope of the Western world; in the other black people have become revolutionary agents that, together with the oppressed and poor all over the world, accuse and threaten the very structures of Western power. The triumphant optimism of the earlier quotation does not have a counterpart in the second passage, although an obstinate belief in the possibilities for change remains. But there is a clear contrast between the great hour of challenge and the threat of the rising storm against the privileged minority. The optimism of the passage in *Stride toward Freedom* stems from the experiences of the South and a successful struggle there (the bus boycott), while the scope and firmness of the demands of the passage in "Impasse in Race Relations" is the result of the loss of false illusions and naïve hope that accompanied the expansion of the struggle to the North.

In the early passage there is no concrete enemy. It merely states that the Negro has the possibility to end war and destruction and that Western society is in need of something new. What must be challenged is evil, the almost metaphorical force of darkness that *Stride toward Freedom* has earlier made synonymous with segregation; the evil is not individual segregationists but a system that opposes God's will. Because the Negro has successfully challenged segregation, he can also challenge its spiritual cousins, war and destruction. The enemy is an evil *idea*, just as the agents of change are the instruments of a great idea.

In the second passage, the adversary is much more concrete—the privileged minority. This passage speaks of we and they, you and us, rich and poor, just and unjust. It connects the problem to social, political, and economical structures. His use of the word "minority" is a radical act in itself. In using the word "minority," King was reminding white people in power that if you expand the lens to the entire globe, *they* are the ones who are in the minority, not people of color.

These two passages illustrate the change in King's rhetoric from a belief in the transforming possibilities of nonviolence to the necessity for large-scale civil disobedience. They point to another shift in his thinking toward a greater understanding of the importance of a distinctly black heritage and a different understanding of the position of African Americans in U.S. society. King has also changed how he understands white people in power. Finally, the way he defines "freedom" and "equality" has changed; he is now much more focused on the world of material reality.

America?

To describe this development more fully I will let the perception of the United States in King's rhetoric stand as a center from which I will point to several other aspects of his radicalization. The shifting meaning and position of the concept "United States" are fundamental in King's radicalization, since its many aspects are in one way or another related to it. As we will see, the Constitution and values of America come to form an accusation in his rhetoric instead of a yet-to-be-fulfilled promise and that he defines the nation through its ghettos, poverty and violence instead of its noble idealistic values touches upon most areas of King's radicalization.

The Meaning and Reality of the Nation

To fully understand the King we meet in the speeches of the Chicago campaign for fair housing, the opposition to Vietnam, or *The Trumpet of Conscience*, it is necessary to remember that the seeds of the ideas he expressed in these venues were present in the King of the Montgomery bus boycott and the March on Washington. During the boycott, for example, he stated: "If peace means a willingness to be exploited economically, dominated politically, humiliated and segregated, I don't want peace" and "I never intend to adjust myself to the tragic inequalities of an economic system which takes the necessities from the classes to give luxuries to the masses. I never intend to become adjusted to the madness of militarism and the self-defeating method of physical violence."[4] The March on Washington was a march for jobs and freedom, and while the "I Have a Dream" speech was linked with the promise of the United States and the Constitution, it also included a passage that said that "the life of the Negro is still sadly crippled by the manacles of segregation and the chains of discrimination. . . . The Negro lives on a lonely island of poverty in the midst of a vast ocean of material prosperity. . . . The Negro is still languished [*sic*] in the corners of American society and finds himself in exile in his own land."[5]

These are issues that in the latter stages of King's career come to define his quest: Poverty is the evil twin of discrimination and inequality, unemployment, materialism, and militarism reinforce the structure of inequality, and these factors keep the Negro outside the mainstream of American society. But in King's early rhetoric, the problems he defines surround a specific nucleus: *racial* discrimination. They are civil rights issues, defined through their relationship with that struggle. And when that struggle was won, which it would be since it answered to the intentions of God's moral universe, America would live up to the great promises of its Constitution. The civil rights struggle was a struggle *for* America, not against it. This hope is something that gradually disappears from King's rhetoric.

Up until the mid-1960s, the hope and the promise formed one pole in the central dichotomy between the real and the ideal America: The segregation of the South not only stood against the moral laws of God, it also stood against the ideals of the United States. In the final analysis, what held the United States together and made it into a nation was not politics, the economy, or even its boundaries. It was its status as an unfinished project, a promise waiting to be fulfilled. "America" was a moral entity.

In this formulation, segregation could be defined as a practice that was not part of the ideals of the United States. The oppression of segregation worked against the intentions behind the Constitution and stood between the promise of freedom and equality and its realization as reality. And since blacks were the victims of this oppression, they, as agents of change, became the embodiment of the nation's ideals. During this phase of King's career, he asked of his country that it fulfill the ideals of its founding documents.

During King's last years, the goal of demanding that the nation live up to its inherent ideals could not be maintained. Saving the soul of America came to mean something else. The dichotomy between the promise of the Constitution and the reality of the nation was no longer relevant. After 1965, all King sees is the reality, one that had not changed even when its promises, as ideals, were fulfilled through the signing of the Civil Rights Act and the Voting Rights Act.

This does not mean that the dichotomy between "that which is" and "that which should be" disappears from King's rhetoric. On the contrary, he still, and more than ever, wants America to change. The difference is that in his earlier rhetoric, the hope and promise of America was a part of American reality; it was only necessary to awaken it fully.

But "that which is" and "that which should be" drifted farther and farther apart after 1965. The force that held them so close together—the realization of the dream, the "beloved community," the "Kingdom of God"—has now disappeared. The ideals remain as such, but their relationship to the values in the soul of the nation, as expressed in the Constitution, for example, is no longer the same.

North and South

During the first phase of the struggle, King could create a tension between the persistence of segregation in the South and its absence in the North and thereby ally the struggle with the authority of the federal government. He used this tension as a strategic tool and as an important rhetorical vehicle; the situation in the South stood between the North and the realization of the "real" America that was outlined in the Constitution. These representations of the North and South pressured the federal government to intervene. If the laws of the nation, including the Constitution, were to be followed, segregation had to be abolished. After 1965, this strategy was no longer possible. Segregation had been abolished. King does not stop speaking of the Constitution, but in the new context, it is used an accusation instead of a promise.[6]

And when the position of the South changes in his rhetoric, so does the position of the North. No longer is the North the foremost place where support can be found or where the power

of the federal government is situated. Instead the North represents another variation of racial oppression and thereby King
also comes to redefine the mission of the movement in his
rhetoric. In response, King's wing of the civil rights movement redefines its mission. The white backlash King speaks of
extensively after 1965 can be explained by these altered positions.[7] The old dichotomy between the North and the South
could no longer be used. This change in King's rhetoric about
the North represents a key change the civil rights movement
discourse.

King was of course not oblivious to the existence of oppression, prejudice, and inequality in the North and he never for-
got that the two parts of the struggle were interconnected.[8]
But the way he talked about these issues vis-à-vis the North
changed after 1965. He no longer spoke of them as southern
problems. After 1965, the problems simply became poverty,
unequal housing, unequal education, and so forth.

Even if the effects of segregation in the North and the South
are ultimately the same—lack of freedom and inequality—the
oppression of the North is based on another and in many ways
more complex structure. In the South, the enemy of equality
was clearly identified; anyone who supported or participated in
segregation. In the North, the enemy was not as clearly visible.[9] The struggle in the North required an examination of
how deeply racism, oppression, and inequality had infected the
American dream. So when King literally changed the arena of
the struggle, the landscape in which the arena was placed was
transformed, given a new meaning, and seen in a new light.

Black and White

The changed assumptions about where the struggle needed
to take place as expressed in King's rhetoric meant that the
meaning and position of the prime agents of this struggle also
changed. Let me use a concrete example: King's last SCLC presidential address (August 1967), where the old title of "Where
Do We Go From Here?" is once again used. This speech con-

tains most aspects of his more radical points of view. Yet it also attempts to outline the opportunities for and responsibilities of African Americans in the new reality of post-1965 America:

> The tendency to ignore the Negro's contribution to American life and to strip him of his personhood is as old as the earliest history books and as contemporary as the morning's newspaper.
>
> To offset this cultural homicide, the Negro must rise up with an affirmation of his own Olympian manhood. Any movement for the Negro's freedom that overlooks this necessity is waiting to be buried. As long as the mind is enslaved, the body can never be free. Psychological freedom, a firm sense of self-esteem, is the most powerful weapon against the long night of physical slavery. No Lincolnian Emancipation Proclamation, no Johnsonian civil rights bill can totally bring this kind of freedom. The Negro will only be free when he reaches down to the inner depths of his own being and signs with the pen and ink of assertive manhood his own emancipation proclamation. And with the spirit straining toward true self-esteem, the Negro must boldly throw off the manacles of self-abnegation and say to himself and the world, "I am somebody. I am a person. I am a man with dignity and honor. I have a rich and noble history, however painful and exploited that history has been. Yes, I was a slave through my foreparents, and now I'm not ashamed of that. I am ashamed of the people who were so sinful to make me a slave." Yes, yes, we must stand up and say, "I'm black, but I'm black and I'm beautiful." This, this self-affirmation is the black man's need, made compelling by the white man's crimes against him.[10]

Here we can recognize the continuing role of "the Negro" in King's rhetoric. Unlike the changes in his attitude toward the North and the South, it is not possible to detect a clean break regarding this theme in his rhetoric. While the legislative changes meant that "the North" and "the South" could no longer mean what they had meant, there was not the same effect regarding the black population's role as the agents of the struggle. Within this theme in King's rhetoric there is a less dramatic and more gradual change. But it is still possible to point to certain features that become more dominant in King's later rhetoric.

What may be explicitly absent in the quote, but is neverthe-

less a definite part of its subtext, is a transformation regarding
the role of "the Negro" in King's rhetoric that is more directly
stated in other speeches (for example, the passage from "Impasse in Race Relations" quoted in the beginning of this chapter). During the early struggle, blacks were often presented as
the moral agents of hope; in the later stages of the struggle, they
are more often presented as the agents of doom. While the moral
agents of hope were tied to the mission of defeating the evil of
segregation that stood against the intentions behind the formation of the United States, the agents of doom are tied to a struggle
that has both a different starting point and a different motive:
They hold up a warning finger in the face of the nation and say
that if you do not change, you will not live. But there is no definite line between these positions. The agents of hope are not
totally absent in the King's later rhetoric, as is clearly visible, for
example, in his last speech, "I've Been to the Mountaintop," but
it is a hope related to another situation and another type of
change.[11] The agents of this change must therefore be understood in another way. They are no longer out to abolish and reveal; now they are out to bring down and build anew.

During the last three years of King's life, he referred more
frequently to individuals from black history and culture, as can
be seen in "Where Do We Go From Here." He tapped into a
new awareness of racial pride among African Americans. In
part he was responding to the more radical challenge of the
Black Power movement and its intense focus on racial identity.
But the change in his rhetoric also reflects a gradual process in
King, whose rhetoric comes to include "black is beautiful," who
speaks of a rich and noble African history. This King no longer
relies exclusively on the Western intellectual tradition; he now
speaks of a unique black intellectual history that must be a
central feature in the consciousness of the black community,
especially of its young.[12]

So even if throughout his career King tries hard to avoid the
position where the dichotomy between the forces of light are
represented by blacks and the forces of darkness are represented

by whites, he comes closer and closer to such a position toward the end of his life. In King's later rhetoric, "black" and "white" function to determine the meaning of the struggle, to determine what it is, while in his earlier rhetoric, the meaning of the terms was always subordinate to the meaning of the struggle. They did not have any definitional meaning of their own. One part of this reversal is the change in identifying the agents of the struggle as the agents of doom rather than as the moral agents of hope, but there is also another part.

The passage from "Where Do We Go From Here?" also illustrates King's use of what he called the positive connotations of Black Power: the realization that the black population is an economic, political, and consuming collective. It is through this collectivity that they can exercise power in American society. Their self-understanding should no longer be focused exclusively on their role as moral agents—now that self-understanding should include their potential role as a political and economic power bloc. This idea is not something that suddenly appears in King's rhetoric after the move to the North, it was as "old" as the strategy behind the bus boycott, but it is much more explicit and central in the definition of the struggle in King's later rhetoric. It is also tied in another way to a different perception of the United States and of society as such.

King's earlier rhetoric had focused on the search for consensus; his later rhetoric acknowledged the centrality of conflict. American society is characterized by a constant struggle for power. Taken to its logical conclusion, this stance meant that for some in the civil rights movement, they would be in direct conflict with the federal government.

The difference between the March on Washington in 1963 and the Poor People's Campaign in 1968 also illustrates this change. The March on Washington was about jobs and freedom, about demanding the ear of the government, about trying to influence the authorities to empower the demonstrators by listening to their demands. The Poor People's Campaign, in contrast, was about coming to Washington and as a group, as a collective, exercising power and through this power *forcing* change. King understands that asking for influence in American society is no longer effective; if African Americans want influence, they will have to take it.

The new position of the federal government structures the "Where Do We Go From Here?" speech as a whole and it can be seen in King's concrete demands: He wants a guaranteed annual income, better housing, and better education. He also analyzes the Watts riot and other riots, and he discusses "Black Power" and other revolutionary sentiments in the black community. He criticizes the capitalist system without *openly* endorsing democratic socialism.

King regards revolution as a utopian impossibility and says that "this is no time for romantic illusions and empty philosophical debates about freedom. This is a time for action."[13] King understands that the enemy of racial equality runs deep in American society and that it cannot be fought with ideals alone. The enemy is no longer the Bull Connors of this world; the enemy is not segregation; the enemy is no longer even the idea of white superiority. The enemy is "the white power structure," which expresses its threats to racial equality with lower wages for African-American workers, ghettoes, unequal education, deep-seated racism, violence, and backlash against integration.

In one sense, the aims are the same in "Where Do We Go From Here?" as they were during the earlier struggle. The goal of the movement is to "bring the Negro into the mainstream of American life as quickly as possible"; this is the simple and at the same time very complex issue of "justice in this country." It is still a question of action, of working in praxis: "The movement must address itself to the question of restructuring the whole of American society." The difference is that the praxis has changed; appealing to the conscience of white America or the federal government is no longer adequate. Now it is necessary to *force* white America, the federal government, and the political system to change.

King's faith in the conscience of white America was an integral part of the southern phase of the struggle. It was a key thought behind the strategy of nonviolence. The premise was that when civil rights activists answered the brutality and cruelty of segregation with passive resistance and love, the individual segregationist could and would be transformed. It would touch upon the Godlike qualities of his or her nature. There was an individual conscience in every white American that could be activated, no matter how pro-segregation this individual was. That was the basic power of nonviolence, and it applied equally to the South and the entire nation.

On several occasions in his late rhetoric, King points out how deeply situated the racist understanding of reality is in the minds of many white Americans and white America as a collective. He notes his disappointment with northern liberals who supported the movement when it was in the South but who became less enthusiastic about his work when it moved into their own backyards.[14] Because they deserted the movement after the victories of the Civil Rights and Voting Rights Acts, he holds the northern liberals responsible for the white backlash:

> When the Negroes could use public facilities, register and vote in some areas of the South, find token educational advancement, again in token form find new areas of employment, it brought to the Negro a sense of achievement, but it brought to the whites a sense of completion. When the Negroes assertively moved on to ascend the second rung of the ladder, a firm resistance from the white community developed. This resistance characterized the second phase, which we are now experiencing. In some quarters it was a courteous rejection, in others it was a stinging white backlash. In all quarters unmistakably, it was outright resistance.[15]

In this rhetoric, white America cannot be reached through appeals to its conscience any longer. Now that the struggle is about integrating northern neighborhoods, changing the structure of the economy, and understanding the connection between the racism of American society and the Vietnam War, it is their resistance to change that defines white Americans. And they are extremely reluctant to acknowledge their part in the racism that courses through the veins of the American social body.

The white backlash that "declared that true equality could never be a reality in the United States" disillusioned King, but it also presented a discursive problem.[16] From the time of the Montgomery bus boycott he had repeatedly stated that the struggle was not about black and white, that the morality of the issue went way beyond skin color, and that integration and brotherhood were the only desirable as well as feasible solutions.

In general King does not move beyond these basic positions, but his gradually transformed perception of both black and white America takes his rhetoric to a place where his characterization of the struggle gives his new comprehensions a central place. The resistance of white America means that the concept of "the white man" comes to hold the position of the enemy. The rules of the old and new discourse seem to clash when King tries to solve this dilemma in the following way:

> In using the term "white man" I am seeking to in general terms describe the Negro's adversary. It is not meant to encompass all white people. There are millions who have morally risen above prevailing prejudices. They are willing to share power and to accept structural alterations of society even at the cost of traditional privilege. To deny their existence as some ultranationalists do is to deny an evident truth. More than that, it drives away allies who can strengthen our struggle. Their support not only serves to enhance our power, but in breaking from the attitudes of the larger society it splits and weakens our opposition. To develop a sense of black consciousness and peoplehood does not require that we scorn the white race as a whole. It is not the race per se that we fight but the policies and ideology that the leaders of that race have formulated to perpetuate oppression.[17]

"White" here becomes a political and economic notion that represents that which stands as a wall between equality and the poor from all ethnic groups (even, for example, white Appalachians). This represents a third change in King's conceptualization of the notion of white America. King now sees white America as the structure that maintains inequality, oppression, and economic exploitation. It is a term for a country and government that has shown itself in Vietnam to be the "greatest purveyor of violence in the world."[18] The moral conscience of white America has proved to be inadequate. "White" represents the evil triplets of racism, materialism, and militarism. But when King portrays the new situation in this way, does it also mean that he also portrays nonviolence as the means of transformation as inadequate in the new situation?

The Methods of the Struggle

The action strategies of the movement also underwent a process of radicalization. In the 1950s, buses were boycotted in Montgomery in order to put pressure on the local white authorities and to get the attention of the federal government. In the late 1960s, the clearly stated purpose of the coming Poor People's Campaign was to use massive civil disobedience activities to stop the federal government from functioning.

Although civil disobedience had been used as a tactic of the civil rights movement since the early 1960s in the South, when the movement spread to the North it was necessary for the movement to find new ways to attack the system of oppression. The goal of the movement was to take actions that pointed out the need for change; the theory was that such actions would create so much tension that change would be unavoidable. It was one thing to take such actions in the South, where the overt brutality of segregation was newsworthy and undeniably clear. It was another thing to plan such actions in a northern city such as Chicago, where African Americans needed access to fair housing, equal education, and equal employment opportunities. The goal of the Poor People's Campaign—to change the economic structure of the nation—could not be accomplished through local boycotts or skirmishes with local law authorities.

King never wavered from the conviction that absolute nonviolence was the only way to go, from a moral as well as a strategic perspective, but he realized that the methods had to be adjusted to the demands that were being made and the context in which they were being made:

> I am still convinced that a solution of nonviolence remains possible. However, nonviolence must be adapted to urban conditions and urban moods. The effectiveness of street marches in cities is limited because of the normal turbulence of city life absorbs them as mere transitory drama quite common in the ordinary movement of the masses. In the South, a march was a social earthquake; in the North, it is a faint, brief exclamation of protest.
>
> Nonviolent protest must now mature to a new level to correspond to heightened black impatience and stiffened white resistance. This higher level is mass civil disobedience. There must be more than a statement to the larger society; there must be a force that interrupts its functioning at some point.[19]

The expansion of the method King prescribes can be tied to a shift of positions in two senses. The first shift is that from the South to the North; to be heard in the "turbulence" of the northern city life, you must make greater commotion. The second shift is the new position of King and the movement as a result of the changes in federal law. The method would have to be different when *facing* the federal authorities instead of trying to incorporate them into the demands. But the method is not a change in kind; it is only a change in degree. The context in which direct action was to be executed and the position from which it would be launched transforms it into something larger in scope and more disruptive in effect.

Rhetorical Transformation

THE COMMON DISCOURSE I

From the beginning, King's rhetorical project was one of inclusion. It attached itself to the center of an American self-understanding that went beyond the concrete realities of black and white existence. The language he used to interpret the world, and thereby to present and legitimize the movement, was based on and used an already established pattern of understanding. King used existing discursive frames.

But he used the ground he stood on not just as a base; he built a public discourse on it so smoothly that its structure could not be differentiated from its base. King spoke in many different contexts that required him to tailor his rhetoric; black, white, southern, northern, religious, secular, fund-raising, marches, campaigns, and so on. His task was to make one out of the many.

One of the high points (possibly *the* high point) of this discourse creation, this turning of the many into one, was the "I Have a Dream" speech. In one of its classic passages, King intricately weaves threads from disparate discourses, but through his use of their relatedness to a basic American self-understanding he manages to form a specific civil rights movement discourse that still has an almost universal applicability:

> I say to you my friends, so even though we must face the difficulties of today and tomorrow, I still have a dream. It is a dream deeply rooted in the American dream.
>
> I have a dream that one day this nation will rise up and live out the true meaning of its creed: "We hold these truths to be self-evident, that all men are created equal."
>
> I have a dream that one day on the red hills of Georgia, sons of former slaves and former slaveowners will be able to sit down together at the table of brotherhood.
>
> I have a dream that one day even the state of Mississippi, a state sweltering with the heat of injustice, sweltering with the heat of oppression, will be transformed into an oasis of freedom and justice.
>
> I have a dream that my four little children will one day live in a nation where they will not be judged by the color of their skin but by the content of their character. I have a dream today.
>
> I have a dream that one day down in Alabama, with its vicious racists, with its governor having his lips dripping with the words of "interposition" and "nullification," one day right there in Alabama little black boys and little black girls will be able to join hands with little white boys and white girls as sisters and brothers. I have a dream today.
>
> I have a dream that one day every valley shall be exalted, and every hill and mountain shall be made low, the rough places shall be made plain, and the crooked places shall be made straight, and the glory of the Lord shall be revealed, and all flesh shall see it together.[20]

The passage is built up by the use of structural opposites. One by one he sums up the goals of the movement.

King opposes positive and negative realities in the passage. The positive keywords and phrases are "equal," "brotherhood," "freedom," "justice," "judged by content of character," and "be able to join hands." In opposition to these values and goals, King speaks of "slavery," "injustice," "oppression," "judged by color of skin," "racists," "interposition and nullification."

All of these keywords have central positions in the civil rights movement discourse as expressed in King's rhetoric. They reappear in one or another combination over and over again in King's speeches, sermons, and books. But this repetitiveness serves a distinct purpose. It hammers home what the struggle is really about. And the strategy of using short slogans to define larger concepts is very effective. It grabs the attention of listeners and readers; it associates the message-deliverer with an uncontestable truth. Take for example the three first positive keywords and rearrange their internal order: *Liberté, égalité, fraternité* will forever be associated with the French Revolution.

These terms also came to define the civil rights movement. The intimate relationship between the movement and the moral righteousness of the terms created a hard shell beneath which the more realpolitik nucleus of the demands in an ideological sense could be safely situated: End segregation! Restructure the South! Real equality between blacks and whites! When he defines the struggle through these keywords King signifies from a level above that of everyday contemporary reality. The ladder of signification means that there is always a final instance of righteousness and justification that also must be refuted if an argument below it in the signifying order is refuted.

King's rhetoric is inviting and encompassing. The values that through the ladder of signification come to define the struggle have the quality of being generally desirable. Freedom, equality, brotherhood, justice are all used to define the struggle as a struggle that has universal moral authority. These values do not have a specific racial content, nor do they in themselves have a concrete political or even ideological content besides being tied to a general American tradition. By ascribing to values and terms central not only for an American self-understanding, but also for Christianity, he places the struggle at this center. Viewed this way, the civil rights movement discourse, as it is formulated in King's words, becomes familiar to Americans. Ideologically, it is known and reassuring.

The construction of the discourse can also be detected in the outline of the speech. In each of its different sections King addresses a specific premise of American beliefs. King relates each of these premises to the most fundamental ways Americans understand themselves and then connects that premise with the civil rights movement. The first and last section stand out in this respect and both should be understood as rungs on the ladder of signification King constructs in this speech.

In the first section of the speech, King creates the frame for the identity and destiny of the United States of America; the dream is about how "this nation will rise up and live out the true meaning of its creed." That premise determines (most of) the rest of the passage. He then paints five verbal pictures to fill the frame. Once he has established the idealistic rung of the ladder of signification (the inherent ideals of the United States, the self-evident fact that all men are created equal), King can move on to what this rung signifies. First he speaks of actual American history; he mentions slavery and slaveowners. That legacy is still a source of great pain. Slavery, through the structure of the passage, is not only related to the "table of brotherhood" that the dream speaks of but also to the true meaning of the American creed that has been established as the idealistic norm of the dream. Herein lies one of the passage's central dichotomies.

Thereafter, King speaks of the situation of the 1960s. Contemporary Mississippi swelters with the heat of injustice and oppression. It is the struggle against these forces that the speech, the march, and the movement are about. But for the dream to become the central metaphor of this speech, march, and movement, it must also be put against the creed of the nation. In these lines we can also detect a temporal scheme that goes beyond the basic time frame of the speech in general: the present reality and the coming reality of the dream.[21] Here we move from the founding fathers, pass through slavery, and arrive at the contemporary reality of oppression in Mississippi. This time line is fully developed in the next two sections, which both are positively associated with children, who represent the new, that which is being born and developed through the civil rights movement.

These two passages also represent two more rungs on the ladder of signification. We have met the nation, history, and the civil rights movement; now we meet first the family (King speaks of his own children) and, finally, the individual. Although King does not individualize the children holding hands, they are posited against particular governors and racists. And these governors and racists must answer not only to the dream of the black and white children but also to the ideals of the nation—the idealistic frame of the dream.

Then, in the last section of the speech, King introduces the ultimate signification. King becomes Jeremiah. The words of the Bible ultimately define the other rungs on the ladder. If secular righteousness is not enough, then the sacred righteousness of the Bible comes in as the guarantee that the struggle is just. When one discusses or even tries to understand concrete reality in relation to civil rights, one must place oneself in relation to the higher levels through which this lived experience is named and ordered.

This passage from "I Have a Dream" illustrates how the pre-1965 civil rights movement discourse worked and how it was adjusted to the struggle against segregation. But where did this leave King and his rhetoric when the legislative changes came in 1964 and 1965 and the struggle was no longer a struggle against legal segregation?

As we enter the summer of 1965 and move forward through the Chicago campaign for fair housing, the emergence of Black Power as a militant arm of the civil rights movement, the Vietnam War, and the planning for the Poor People's Campaign, we will see that even if the old keywords have to share space with a few new ones, most of them are still present, as is the ladder of signification. But still, something is decidedly different.

God, The Constitution, and the United States of America

To find this difference, let us turn to a passage from "A Christmas Sermon on Peace," delivered in December 1967. Here King reveals how the dream he had presented at the foot of the Lincoln Memorial in August 1963 has been shattered by several blows, which began with the church-bombing in Birmingham and escalated to the Vietnam War. "I am personally the victim of deferred dreams, of blasted hopes," he says. But he also steadfastly declares, almost as if he is trying to convince himself, that "I still have a dream, because you know, you can't give up in life. If you lose hope, somehow you lose the vitality that keeps life moving, you lose that quality that helps you to go on in spite of all. And so today I still have a dream."[22]

Let us compare the dream he then goes on to speak of with the dream that was presented in "I Have a Dream." Here too, in the final passages of "A Christmas Sermon on Peace," he discusses the relationship between the identity of the nation, the civil rights struggle, the aims and role of the movement, and how those goals are related to the structures of a universe ruled by the forces of an almighty God:

> I have a dream that one day men will rise up and come to see that they are made to live together as brothers. I still have a dream this morning that one day every Negro in this country, every colored person in the world, will be judged on the basis of the content of his character rather than the color of his skin, and every man will respect the dignity and worth of human personality. I still have a dream that one day the idle industries of Appalachia will be revitalized, and the empty stomachs of Mississippi will be filled, and brotherhood will be more than a few words at the end of a prayer, but rather the first order of business on every legislative agenda. I still have a dream today that one day justice will roll down like water, and righteousness like a mighty stream. I still have a dream that in all of our state houses and city halls men will be elected to

go there who will do justly and love mercy and walk humbly with
their God. I still have a dream today that one day war will come to
an end, that men will beat their swords into plowshares and their
spears into pruning hooks, that nations no longer will rise up
against nations, neither will they study war no more. I still have a
dream today that one day the lamb and the lion will lie down together and every man will sit under his own vine and fig tree and
none shall be afraid. I still have a dream today that one day every
valley shall be exalted and every mountain and hill will be made
low, the rough places will be made smooth and the crooked places
straight, and the glory of the Lord shall be revealed, and all flesh
shall see it together. I still have a dream that with this faith we will
be able to adjourn the councils of despair and bring new light into
the chambers of pessimism. With this faith we will be able to speed
up the day when there will be peace on earth and goodwill toward
men. It will be a glorious day, the morning stars will sing together,
and the sons of God will shout for joy.[23]

This passage may seem to be entirely structured around the
system of signification used in "I Have a Dream," but a closer
look shows that this in not the case. Two general observations
can serve as starting points.

first, there is no openly manifested adversary in this passage, there is no clear statement that "this is what must and
will be changed." Half of the passage's central dichotomy is
silent, but that silence does not mean that it is any less important.

Second, the dream of "I Have a Dream" serves as a mean-
ing-determiner in the dream of this sermon just as the difference between them does. Directly after King has described how
the dream he spoke of at the March on Washington has been
shattered, it may seem as if he reinstates it. And in one way he
does; the dreams are not incompatible in any way. But it is not
the same dream. Even though the utopian place, the kingdom
of God where "one day the lamb and the lion will lie down
together" from which they both derive is the same, the dreams
are dreamed, so to speak, in different situations.

The absence of a manifest dichotomy plays an important
part in the difference of the new dream and it is also related to

how the "I Have a Dream" speech functions in this passage. "I Have a Dream" functions here much in the same way as the Constitution and the promise of the nation did in that speech. The passage from "A Christmas Sermon on Peace" is also built around the discrepancy between "that which is" and "that which ought to be," but "that which is" is no longer explained as a deviation from the ideals engraved in the identity of the nation. It is no longer explained as something that stands opposed to the real America. "That which is" is instead the real America of inequality, and this reality comes to define what the nation is. What stands against the ideals that ultimately emanate from God is no longer segregation; it is America.

The ladder of signification, so prominently used in the passage from "I Have a Dream," is not the same in the dream of "A Christmas Sermon on Peace." The direction and the overall process are the same—meaning is given from "above" in a hierarchical order—but a crucial step is missing in this latter passage. In its place stands the monumental silence of the hidden dichotomy. The ideals of the nation are replaced by the realities of post-1965 America.

Thus the relationship between reality, dream, and utopia is different here. The realities of post-1965 American society are such that it is very difficult for King to use the kind of discourse of inclusion he had used in the early civil rights movement. An internal contradiction is present here *within* the discourse. Earlier, the evils of segregation and racism were something that stood outside and were defined by a ladder of signification where righteousness was developed step by step and set in opposition to all that which worked against this process. Now the reality of structural racism has become a part of the process of signification. Instead of proclaiming "what ought to be" through describing that which is wrong, King defines that which is wrong here by speaking solely of that which ought to be. And in that way the promise of the American tradition and the Constitution has become an accusation of the same things.

A crucial part of this transformation concerns what happens to the idealistic rung in the ladder of signification. In "I Have a

Dream," its function was to create legitimacy to the movement within the context of the American political tradition and ideology. The idealistic rung was explicitly stated so that King could create a dichotomy of what American really was and what racial discrimination was. There is no such explicit use in "A Christmas Sermon on Peace." In a sense, the idealistic rung is an important part of the sermon's subtext that creates the accusation that America is not what it has promised to be. The absence of the American political tradition in this passage is thus an absence full of meaning. When the intermediate rung— the "real" and "true" American values—in the signification structure disappears, it means that America has to answer directly to the power of the almighty God. That is the new logic of the discourse.

The promise of the American political tradition does not disappear from King's rhetoric after 1965. But what happens— and what this passage exemplifies—is that it shifts position; instead of defining what America is, it defines what America is not. Through this change of position the creation of a common discourse becomes a much more complex project since it does not use a dichotomy to define itself. Instead it comes to harbor this dichotomy at its own core. The dream of "A Christmas Sermon on Peace" is not, like the dream of "I Have a Dream," something that defines the dichotomy; it exists in the space between its two poles. It does not celebrate the best in the American dream; it directly accuses American reality.

This radicalization can also be seen in the demands of the passage. Within the framework of the dream, King incorporates all of the issues that were parts of this broadened and more radical quest. The dream is not just a rhetorical device in the speech but it also symbolizes the early civil rights movement. By speaking of the dream he "still has," King tries to establish the coherence between the movement's early goals and its later goals. The quest of the movement is not different as such, but reality has forced it to incorporate other demands. Through the phrase "every colored person in the world" he allies himself with the poor nations of the world and the challenge they will sooner or later pose to the Western world. He speaks of the need for an alliance between all the poor in America and the impending Poor People's Campaign through mentioning of the industries of Appalachia and the empty stomachs in Mississippi.[24] He calls out northern white liberals whose idea of brotherhood is limited to "a few words at the end of a prayer." He criticizes federal and state governments, who are not yet electing people to office who will "do justly and love mercy and walk humbly with their God." Finally, King also alludes to his critique of the Vietnam War when he dreams that "one day war will come to an end."

"A Christmas Sermon on Peace" points in several directions. In one sense it points back to the old dream; King uses the widely acknowledged righteousness of that speech here. But at the same time it also points beyond it: This speech has new dreams that surpass the original dream.

But a deeply structured discursive change is also part of the radicalization process, a change that goes hand in hand with the radical demands of King's last years. The crucial discursive rearrangement is that reality is now directly religiously determined. The idealistic level is no longer used to signify that the movement's quest is about realizing America's true identity. The struggle is no longer about awakening a sleeping conscience; the struggle declares that racism is a structural feature of the nation.

But the more radical demands and the rhetoric in which they were put forth should be understood as a two-way street. King still fights for as an expanded version of his old civil rights movement discourse. His radicalization is more a development than a clean break. But the system of signification also has another meaning in this sermon. His attempts to use inclusive rhetoric contrast with the radicalness of his demands. The clearly outlined dichotomies of the old dream had different effects than the silent dichotomies of the new dream. In the old dream, the wrongs of society were repairable through correct action. In the new dream, King does not deem it politically wise to speak overtly of the wrongs of his society. What he does *not* say in this new dream is its most radical part.

FREEDOM AND EQUALITY

One of the most important features of King's pre-1965 movement discourse was the presence of certain keywords that defined what the struggle was about. Several of these could be seen in the passage from "I Have a Dream": "freedom," "equality," "justice," "truth," "brotherhood." King uses two of these keywords, "freedom" and "equality," in "A Christmas Sermon on Peace," but he uses them in ways that illustrate his process of radicalization. What functions do the words actually come to have in King's rhetoric during the last years and do these functions have any bearing on his discourse creation?

The terms are ever-present in King's rhetoric from Montgomery to Memphis.[25] During the first phase of the civil rights movement, "freedom" both meant and included "equality," but that relationship became much less clear in King's later rhetoric. He invests both terms with new meaning and gives them new functions within his rhetoric.

In consequence, the definition of the civil rights movement's project begins to float. The early discourse cannot encompass a situation in which freedom and equality cannot be understood and implied by each other. The later discourse loses part of the power the discourse had gained by being interconnected with a traditional American historico-political understanding of these terms.

We can illustrate this if we compare the rhetoric of the 1963 March on Washington with the rhetoric of the SCLC's Poor People's Campaign in 1967–1968.

When stating the purpose of the March on Washington in "I Have a Dream," King says:

> In a sense we've come to our nation's capital to cash a check. When the architects of our republic wrote the magnificent words of the Constitution and the Declaration of Independence, they were signing a promissory note to which every American was to fall heir.

This note was the promise that all men, yes, black men as well as white men, would be guaranteed the "unalienable Rights of Life, Liberty, and the pursuit of Happiness." It is obvious today that America has defaulted on the promissory note insofar as her citizens of color are concerned. Instead of honoring this sacred obligation, America has given the Negro people a bad check, a check which has come back marked "insufficient funds."

But we refuse to believe that the bank of justice is bankrupt. We refuse to believe that there are insufficient funds in the great vaults of opportunity of this nation. And so we've come to cash this check, a check that will give us upon demand the riches of freedom and the security of justice.

We have also come to this hallowed spot to remind America of the fierce urgency of now. This is not the time to engage in the luxury of cooling off or to take the tranquilizing drug of gradualism. Now is the time to make real the promises of democracy. Now is the time to rise from the dark and desolate valley of segregation to the sunlit path of racial justice. Now is the time to lift our nation from the quicksands of racial injustice to the solid rock of brotherhood. Now is the time to make justice a reality for all God's children.

It would be fatal for the nation to overlook the urgency of the moment. This sweltering summer of the Negro's legitimate discontent will not pass until there is an invigorating autumn of freedom and equality.[26]

We can see here how intimately freedom and equality are linked with each other: The latter is defined by the meanings of the first and vice versa. If the freedom inherent in the founding documents of the nation is attained, equality will be the result. The two terms depend on each other; one signifies the other.

This is clearly a *civil rights* discourse. The project that is described here is a project that is understood—and a problem that will be solved—within the realms of *racial* equality, a result of becoming free from *racial* discrimination.

Paradoxically, the generality of the terms limits the possible interpretations of the problem. The rhetoric states that the struggle is fought at the level of grand words and ideas; it is about righteousness against evil, truth against falsehood, and justice against injustice. The aim of the struggle is to become free and equal. But King's language in this speech does not offer a more specific definition of freedom and equality. They are coupled together in this scheme, almost signifying only each other: When you are free, you become equal and when you are equal you have been freed. The problems King and the movement want to solve are strictly placed within a civil rights discourse; it is in that arena that the problems are described, are understood, and will be solved. This is a base for the discourse's inclusiveness, its comprehensibility, and easy-to-access righteousness, but it also means that the meaning of the terms "freedom" and "equality" is incorporative rather than penetrating, affirmative rather than challenging.

The rhetoric of "I Have a Dream" and the way it defines "equality" is constructed in a way that John Louis Lucaites and Celeste Michelle Condit have defined as "culturetypal." In their essay "Reconstructing <Equality>: Culturetypal and Counter-Cultural Rhetorics in the Martyred Black Vision," which compares the rhetoric of Martin Luther King and Malcolm X, they define culturetypal rhetoric as rhetoric that "refers to the sacred words of a particular culture which function to preserve and reform social and political traditions." Their analysis goes beyond the sacred words to include "sacred narratives and characterizations." They state that King signified equality "as a formal and identical sameness between two entities, such that each was ultimately indistinguishable with the other" and that it was firmly placed within the bounds of a culturetypal rhetoric that has "culturally authorized characterizations and narratives in place which link and support the community's key values."[27]

But does this definition also apply to the function of "equality" in King's later rhetoric? Although Lucaites and Condit acknowledge that "to talk about King's rhetoric as a monolithic entity is an obvious oversimplification," that "his rhetoric became less hopeful and indeed more militant as he grew older," and that clarifying "these changes in any generalization is not entirely possible," they still conclude that "I Have a Dream" is "truly representative of King's rhetoric."[28] In their article, it is

Malcolm X who represents what they call a "counter-cultural" meaning of the term. This argument is hard to refute, even though the juxtapositioning of King and Malcolm X has proved to be rather problematic in recent years.[29] The definition and meaning of "equality" present in Malcolm's rhetoric was indeed, in Lucaites and Condit's term, "counter-cultural."

But if we reexamine this term, can it not also be said to define the meaning of "equality" in King's later rhetoric? The difference between culturetypal and countercultural rhetoric, according to Lucaites and Condit, is how you use and relate to the "public vocabulary," which they define as "a number of culturally established and sanctioned narratives, characterizations and ideographs" that constitutes a "social group's ideology." Counter-cultural rhetoricians, then, are those who "introduce new—and thus culturally unauthorized—characterizations and narratives to the public vocabulary and who challenge existing characterizations and narratives."[30] As in any dichotomy, the "clearly" defined poles are not always as clear as they seem. In concrete rhetoric, there is more often than not an active space between the poles that allows for a variety of meanings. This space is characteristic of King's later rhetoric.

King speech introducing the Poor People's Campaign, "Nonviolence and Social Change," has similarities with the goals of "I Have a Dream," but it also contains something new. Is it still possible to argue that the "equality" of King's rhetoric is culturetypal in this speech?

> Of course, by now it is obvious that new laws are not enough. The emergency we now face is economic, and it is a desperate and worsening situation. For the 35 million poor in America—not even to mention, just yet, the poor in other nations—there is a kind of strangulation in the air. In our society it is murder, psychologically, to deprive a man of a job or an income. You are in substance saying to that man that he has no right to exist. You are in a real way depriving him of life, liberty, and the pursuit of happiness, denying in his case the very creed of his society. Now, millions of people are being strangled that way. The problem is international in scope. And it is getting worse, as the gap between the poor and the "affluent society" increases.[31]

And farther on:

> The dispossessed of this nation—the poor, both white and Negro—live in a cruelly unjust society. They must organize a revolution against that injustice, not against the lives of the persons who are their fellow citizens, but against the structures through which the society is refusing to take means which have been called for, and which are at hand, to lift the load of poverty.
>
> The only real revolutionary, people say, is a man who has nothing to lose. There are millions of poor people in this country who have very little, or even nothing, to lose. If they can be helped to take action together, they will do so with a freedom and a power that will be a new and unsettling force in our complacent national life. Beginning in the New Year, we will be recruiting three thousand of the poorest citizens from ten different urban and rural areas to initiate and lead a sustained, massive, direct-action movement in Washington.[32]

There are many differences between how King presents the Poor People's Campaign and how he presented the March on Washington in "I Have a Dream." In "I Have a Dream," the people who needed to take action were people of color in America (or even people in America in general), here it is "the 35 million poor in America" (and around the world). In "I Have a Dream," the goals were the "unalienable rights of life, liberty, and the pursuit of happiness," "the riches of freedom and security of justice," and "an invigorating autumn of freedom and equality"; here the goal of life, liberty and the pursuit of happiness remain, but the tone with which it is uttered and what it signifies are another matter. Instead of being related to other grand words and monumental righteousness, they are related here to the very specific goals of providing a job and an income for every man and lifting the burden of poverty from the shoulders of the dispossessed—a revolution against the structures of economic injustice.

The key difference between the two speeches can in fact be seen in the first sentence of the first passage from "Nonviolence and Social Change": "It is by now obvious that laws are not enough." With this King explains the relationship between the two phases of the movement. In one sense it can be seen as a self-criticism—our earlier struggle was too shallow and optimistic—but mainly he says it to legitimize the development and deepening of the movement's goals. Achieving the goal of legal desegregation was not the victorious end of the movement, it was merely a plateau from which it was possible to see much farther into the land of American racism and inequality.

In "Nonviolence and Social Change," "freedom" and "equality" have been separated from each other. The meanings of the two words are still connected, but they are no longer synonymous with the formula "freedom means equality." Instead they signify several different steps on the path to the goal that still is defined as life, liberty, and the pursuit of happiness. The meaning of "freedom" has been fragmented into different parts, which also shows a different emphasis in the meaning of equality.

There is the freedom that the new laws have meant, but that freedom did not establish equality. There is the freedom expressed in the Constitution's promise of life, liberty, and the pursuit of happiness, but that freedom has not yet been achieved. The inequality that persists is first and foremost economic. In "I Have a Dream," King proclaimed that freedom would lead to equality. Now he is saying that equality is an essential precondition for freedom. The freedom of the Constitution cannot become a reality any other way than through the establishment of economic equality. King now argues that legal freedom by itself is not sufficient; freedom requires both social and economic equality.

King's earlier strategy of positioning himself between cultures is no longer sufficient, either. Now he must position himself between discourses and ideologies. The inclusive power of the former position is transformed into a position where King becomes excluded from several comprehensive systems of understanding. Where formerly he could create a specific logic out of his position, the discourse now becomes a victim of the truths of several different logics.

Lucaites and Condit's model of culturetypal and countercultural rhetoric is helpful here. King's rhetoric in "Nonviolence and Social Change" still has some culturetypal features; it refers to the Constitution. More than that, the rhetoric and vocabulary of the "old" civil rights movement has become a public vocabulary in itself. By when he speaks of the movement and compares what it must do now to what it had done, King evokes its "culturetypal" rhetoric and tries to extend that language beyond its limits. For he does go beyond those limits here; there are counter-cultural elements to his rhetoric. As he expands the scope of the struggle, he challenges the signification structure of the civil rights movement discourse. He challenges the established American notion of freedom and equality by *not* equating the two, by *not* giving them a general content within which tacit specifications are made. This creates a "disharmony" within the discourse since it comes to incorporate counter-cultural elements within the frames of culturetypal rhetoric. But it does this at the cost of a broken discourse.

THE COMMON DISCOURSE II

King struggled in his later rhetoric to come to terms with SNCC's increasing militance and the language of Black Power. In his many discussions of the negative and positive sides of Black Power we can detect several elements of his radicalization. At about the same time as "Black Power" entered the national political vocabulary, another phrase made its way into King's rhetoric: "the white power structure." Both expressions can be defined as countercultural expressions. Each in their own way poses a challenge to the discourse of the traditional struggle of the civil rights movement.

King acknowledges this challenge when he discusses Black Power and explains his reluctance to accept it when it first became a public battle cry during SNCC member James Meredith's March against Fear in 1966. The lengthy discussion of the term in *Chaos or Community* pinpoints the discursive problems King faced in his work to create discourse after 1965. He writes:

Immediately, however, I had reservations about its use. I had the deep feeling that it was an unfortunate choice of words for a slogan. Moreover, I saw it bringing about division within the ranks of the marchers. For a day or two there was fierce competition between those who were wedded to the Black Power slogan and those wedded to Freedom Now. Speakers on each side sought desperately to get the crowds to chant their slogan the loudest.

Sensing this widening split in our ranks, I asked Stokely [Carmichael] and Floyd [McKissick] to join me in a frank discussion of the problem. We met the next morning, along with member of each of our staffs, in a small Catholic parish house in Yazoo City. For five long hours I pleaded with the group to abandon the Black Power slogan. It was my contention that a leader has to be concerned about the problems of semantics. Each word, I said, has denotative meaning—its explicit and recognized sense—and a connotative meaning—its suggestive sense. While the concept of legitimate Black Power might be denotatively sound, the slogan "Black Power" carried the wrong connections. I mentioned the implications of violence that the press had already attached to the phrase. And I went on to say that some of the rash statements on the part of a few marchers only reinforced this impression.[33]

King suggested compromises such as "black consciousness" or "black equality." These compromises would not give "the impression that we are talking about black domination rather than black equality."[34] That King points to the connotations of the slogan as the reason behind his objections reveals that he views the creation of slogans to be a discursive as well as a political process. He analyzes the roots and possible meaning of the slogan, its "content," in his book about the state of the civil rights movement and the race question in the United States a year later (*Chaos or Community*).

Because the connotations of "Black Power" challenged some of the culturally authorized notions deeply imbedded in King's discourse, it not only created a conflict within his wing of the civil rights movement, it was also incompatible with the project of creating a common discourse. So regardless of whether the content within the slogan squared with the aims of the movement or not, it was, as King expressed it, "an unfortunate choice of words."

In using the term "white power structure" as a description of American society, King shows less restraint than he had previously. In the 1967 speech "Impasse in Race Relations," one of his most radical moments, he states without hesitation that discrimination, unemployment, ignorance, and poverty are created by the "policy-makers of the white society," that the "white man does not abide by the law in the ghettos," and that "slums are the handiwork of a vicious system of the white society; Negroes live in them, but they do not make them, any more than prisoners makes a prison." Then, as if suddenly becoming aware of the significations just created, he reassures the audience that the term "white man" should be understood as a general term for "the Negro's adversary" although there are whites who have "morally risen above prevailing prejudices" and that some are willing to "share power" and "accept structural alterations of society even at the cost of traditional privilege." In other words, some whites have accepted the moral universe of the early years of the civil rights movement and are willing to extend the boundaries of that universe even if it costs them personally.[35] But despite these qualifiers, King continues to use "white" as a central signifier of the problem. He says:

> To sum up the general causes of riots, we would have to say that the white power structure is still seeking to keep the walls of segregation and inequality substantially intact while Negro determination to break through them has intensified. The white society, unprepared and unwilling to accept radical structural change, is resisting firmly and thus producing chaos because the force for change is vital and aggressive. The irony is that the white society ruefully complains that if there were no chaos great changes would come, yet it creates the circumstances breeding the chaos.[36]

These words are a long way from King's characterization of the struggle during the early days, when he often stated that the struggle should not be understood as a polarization between black and white—it was about injustice versus justice, the forces of light versus the forces of darkness. Here he uses "white" to name the darkness. Thus, he defies the established discourse of inclusion. The ladder of signification is reversed. Now instead of naming evil and oppression from the top of the ladder—the higher authority of Christian ideals—he is naming them from the bottom of the ladder—from within the material reality of economic inequality. Where earlier he had used terms such as "injustice" and "evil" to describe the *deeds* of white people, now he equates those deeds with the term "white" man.

Since the order is reversed, the condemnation becomes much more severe. When a "white power structure" is given the central position of the enemy within the discourse, it is different from when the position is held by "the forces of darkness." It is as impossible to imagine the phrase "white power structure" as the manifest name on that which stood between freedom and the Negro in the rhetoric of "I Have a Dream" as it is to imagine the phrase "Black Power" being the manifest aim of that speech. Neither is a part of an inclusive discourse.

How is it then that "Black Power" initially poses such a problem for King, while "the white power structure" becomes an unproblematic vehicle in his late rhetoric? Why does he object to the use of the slogan "Black Power" even when he agrees with much of its potential content? His own language offers a severe condemnation of "the white man"; he says that racial oppression is the result of a "white power structure," he calls his own government "the greatest purveyor of violence in the world," and confesses that he believes that "true equality could never be a reality in the United States."[37]

I believe that during King's last three years the structure he had created with his earlier rhetoric was beginning to crumble; it no longer was adequate to address the economic and material realities that framed the civil rights movement of the late 1960s. But he knew that his earlier rhetoric was built around a powerful system of signification; its language had become part of the language of American culture. During this period of transition for the movement, King attempted to bring as much of the older structure into the new context as he could. It was not as if he had not spoken of the issues of the new movement during his early years. He had spoken extensively of economic injustice, the problems of the northern ghettos, and the reluctance of white America to bring about a truly equal society long before 1965 and 1966.

The difference is that those kinds of problems had then been defined within the logic of the pre-1965 civil rights movement discourse. Within this logic they were directly tied to the struggle against segregation; they were subordinate parts of a civil rights struggle, identified and situated within that struggle. But this is no longer possible after 1965, when the problems of racial inequality have to be reidentified and redefined. The language King had used could no longer describe the new and acute problems King and the movement faced; that language was already becoming part of the history and tradition of the movement. King was faced with the dilemma of trying to marry language whose structure had been built on the core values of mainstream society to language that openly proclaimed that mainstream society was the central problem of the movement. He had to reconcile the culturetypical rhetoric he had created and with the counter-cultural language that his more radical standpoints demanded. The civil rights movement had become much more complex, and the project of creating a common discourse had become equally complex.

This can be seen in the ways that King positions the terms "Black Power" and "white power structure" within his discourse. On the one hand, he continues the process of creating a common discourse by using established meanings and metaphors. There are not two Kings, one culturetypal and the other counter-cultural. King naturally views his goals as coherent, albeit expanding. To the very end, King tries to present his goals as whole and as defined within the rubrics he set out in the initial struggle against segregation.[38] As a slogan, "Black Power" poses a problem for him in this sense; he immediately understands that it steps outside the discursive frames he established. It places the movement in a position where it no longer has an unquestionable claim to moral authority.

On the other hand, King's unified discourse of the early years begins to disintegrate when it confronts a reality which cannot be entirely fit inside its rubrics after 1965. He had created his

discourse around the evils of segregation and the righteousness of the struggle. It was relatively easy to find a language
for cosmic battles between good and evil, to draw upon the ideals of the founding documents of the nation and the wisdom of
the great thinkers of history. But when the dream of the early
years was partially realized in the legal changes of the mid-1960s
and the people still were not free, the system of signification of
the former discourse was no longer satisfactory. Although some
parts of the earlier language continued to be relevant, other words
and expressions became empty. Their specific relationship to a
particular situation in the South makes them incompatible with
the deeply entrenched and complex problems in the North and
across the nation.

Understanding King's Radicalization

How fundamental then was King's ideological radicalization?
Was this process really about ideology at all? Was it not foremost rather about new strategy rather than about new ideas?

In one sense, this argument can be made.[39] It is difficult to
identify a definite pre-1965 and post-1965 King. But is it possible to differentiate between "strategy" and "ideas" in this
manner? If so, where does that leave "ideology"? A strict line
of demarcation between strategy and ideas presupposes a problematic view of how ideas are produced and manifested; it tends
to view ideas as floating above or outside a concrete context. I
believe that it is their very interaction that is of importance.
Ideas do not float above or outside a concrete context; they exist within that context. The judicial, the political, and the social
cannot be divorced from ideas; the world of ideas is not a separate sphere of reality. Ideological truths and values are more
than just the precondition for speaking about particular ideas
in a particular way. They are also created by a particular way of
speaking. Ideas are never "pure"; something happens when they
are uttered.

But still, in King's radicalization process, some things changed
and some did not. For example, it is hard to find convincing

evidence that King's fundamental assumptions regarding God, reality, man, and history changed in any extensive manner. There are some slight shifts, but God is still love and justice, reality is still a moral order threatened by evil irrationality, man is still a dual nature of spirit and matter, and all three concepts of history (neutral, force/zeitgeist, and typological) are present in King's rhetoric until the very end.

But does this mean that no transformation takes place? Or does it rather mean that a process of transformation must be viewed as exactly that—a process? An ideological change does not have to be complete, and the line between ideological conviction and reaction to context does not have to be absolutely clear. A process of transformation is always gradual. King's entire career as a public speaker lasted only twelve years. If we limit King's radicalization process to the post-1965 period, it lasted for only three years.

Change in strategy is also a process. After 1965, the strategy of King's civil rights movement was to engage in large-scale civil disobedience, make alliances among the poor people of the nation regardless of race or ethnicity, and call upon blacks to use political and economic power to achieve movement goals. But what is the "new" in this strategy? King had proposed several of these measures earlier.

One thing was new: The relationship of the movement to the federal government changed when the subject of the struggle changed from segregation to the more nebulous concepts of racial inequality and poverty, but the basic strategy of forcing, almost blackmailing, authorities to act through boycotts and nonviolent activities was present throughout King's career. The Montgomery bus boycott used the strategy of economic withdrawal, as did the Birmingham campaign. Right up to passage of the Civil Rights Act and Voting Rights Act, the basic strategy was in fact the same: dramatize the issue in order to force the federal government to act and at the same time put economic pressure on the local white segregationist community. King maintained that this dual strategy should continue after 1965. Demonstrations and boycotts should still dramatize injustice and blacks should still exercise their power as a collective, both politically and economically, to force through the needed changes. The difference lay in the scope of the actions, the position from where they were launched, and the view of the society that provided the context for those actions.

King now saw society as an arena in which various groups struggled for power, an arena where equality could never be guaranteed by laws and idealistic values, and an arena where the source of power was strength in numbers. King's new understanding of society brings new language such as "the white power structure" to King's vocabulary and shows how harsh realities forced him to think of society in a new way. Once his thought process changed, his rhetoric had to change as well. This was a process of constant interplay, in which the different parts of the process are impossible to separate from each other.

After 1965, King realized that segregation was the tip of the iceberg of oppression. However, his "new" position at the end of his life was not a complete departure from his pre-1965 position. King tried to retain as much as possible of the signification structure of the old civil rights movement as he could, and he continued to use as many of those ideas as he could. But cracks were beginning to show in the rhetorical structure he was creating. The old discourse could not encompass the new ideological components that became necessary for the understanding of the society in which the struggle was being waged. At the end of his life, King had come to understand that nothing less than fundamental structural change was necessary if his dream of liberation and freedom was to be realized.

Epilogue

Several King scholars during recent years have deplored the fact that the King who lives on today is not the one who demanded economic democracy, who bitterly opposed his own government, and whose final call for justice meant much more than the easy-to-accept words of integration, love, and brotherhood.[1] King has even been used by conservatives in their opposition to affirmative action. As absurd as it may seem and is, the potential that his words could be used in this way rests to a large degree on his discursive rhetoric itself. The rhetoric he used during the first phase of the civil rights movement was universal and inclusive; it was made to include many shades of meaning within the frame of righteousness.

The pre-1965 civil rights movement discourse is an open, shared, and what I have called *common* discourse. It is constructed to be as inviting as possible for as many as possible. It is mainly non-offensive, if the proponents of segregation are excluded; in the sense that it is about recognition and affirmation.

The discourse works the same way today. The vague generality means that King's rhetoric can still be filled with meaning from different sources. It can still confirm a particular identity of traditional American ideology and self-understanding, and, and this is crucial in this context, its system of signification (concepts, terms, and sources of naming power) has become tied in with this identity. King has been incorporated as a significant signifier of guaranteed righteousness just like the signifiers he himself strove to incorporate: Christianity, American political history, Western intellectualism, and so forth.

This may explain why King's legacy seems to have been frozen at the time of the "I Have a Dream" speech. Just as King used an established righteousness in that speech, the speech itself has been established as a signifier of righteousness. It is possible to use it in a wide range of circumstances.

The later King is not available to use in that manner since his transformation meant a gradual disintegration of the civil rights movement discourse. The later King could not and cannot be filled with different kinds of meaning in the same way. His later rhetoric poses a grave challenge and makes an accusation, and that is much harder to handle and use than an affirmation.

Ideally, King's legacy should be about continuing this challenge rather than establishing and fossilizing the affirmation. It should be about developing the accusation rather than celebrating a frozen memory. But sadly, as Vincent Harding has pointed out, dead men make such convenient heroes.[2]

NOTES

INTRODUCTION

1. "I Have a Dream," Washington, D.C., August 28, 1963, in Clayborne Carson and Kris Shepard, eds., *A Call to Conscience: The Landmark Speeches of Dr. Martin Luther King, Jr.* (New York: Intellectual Properties Management in association with Warner Books, 2001), 87. Hereafter, the date and location of speeches and sermons will be presented in the first footnote in which the respective speech or sermon appears; thereafter I will refer only to the title. Speeches and sermons that have the same title will be presented with the location and date throughout the notes. In quotations from speeches and sermons, I have, for the sake of clarity and readability, omitted all audience responses.

2. See Taylor Branch's books *Parting the Waters: America in the King Years, 1954–63* (New York: Simon and Schuster, 1989); and *Pillar of Fire: America in the King Years, 1963–65* (New York: Simon and Schuster, 1998). The forthcoming final volume of the trilogy, covering the period 1965 to 1968, will be called *At Canaan's Edge.*

3. Ella Baker, quoted in David J. Garrow, *Bearing the Cross: Martin Luther King, Jr. and The Southern Christian Leadership Conference* (London: Vintage, 1993), 625.

4. The terms "African American," "black," and "Negro" are all used in this study. "African American" and "black" are used rather interchangeably (depending on the context), while in order to avoid anachronisms I sometimes use "Negro" in discussions of passages in which King used that term.

5. Garrow, *Bearing the Cross*, 479.

6. Martin Luther King, Jr., *Stride toward Freedom: The Montgomery Story* (New York: Harper, 1958); *Strength to Love* (New York: Harper and Row, 1963); *Where Do We Go From Here: Chaos or Community?* (New York: Harper and Row, 1967); and *The Trumpet of Conscience* (New York: Harper and Row, 1968).

7. James Melvin Washington, ed., *A Testament of Hope: The Essential Writings and Speeches of Martin Luther King, Jr.* (San Francisco: HarperSanFrancisco, 1991); and *I Have a Dream: Writings and Speeches That Changed the World* (San Francisco: HarperSanFrancisco, 1992).

8. Clayborne Carson, ed., *The Papers of Martin Luther King, Jr.*, vol. 1, *Called to Serve: January 1929–June 1951* (Berkeley: University of

California Press, 1991); vol. 2, *Rediscovering Precious Values: July 1951–November 1955* (Berkeley: University of California Press, 1994); vol. 3, *Birth of a New Age: December 1955–December 1956* (Berkeley: University of California Press, 1997); and vol. 4, *Symbol of the Movement: January 1957–December 1958* (Berkeley: University of California Press, 2000). Hereafter referred to by the title *Papers* and the volume number.

9. Clayborne Carson and Peter Holloran, eds., *A Knock at Midnight: Inspiration From the Great Sermons of Martin Luther King, Jr.* (New York: Intellectual Properties Management in association with Warner Books, 1998). Carson has also edited *The Autobiography of Martin Luther King, Jr.* (New York: Intellectual Properties Management in association with Warner Books, 1998), which contains both published and previously unpublished material.

10. Martin Luther King, Jr. Papers, Special Collections Department, Mugar Library, Boston University, Boston, Massachusetts (hereafter King Papers, Boston University) and The Martin Luther King, Jr. Papers, King Library and Archives, The Martin Luther King, Jr. Center for Nonviolent Social Change, Atlanta, Georgia (hereafter King Library and Archives). The box location of items in question will be provided only for the Boston material, since the Atlanta archive was in the middle of a cataloguing and rebuilding effort when I conducted my research there (1997), which unfortunately has the consequence that such direct references are impossible in this study.

11. See "Introduction" (1–14) in Lewis Baldwin, *There Is a Balm in Gilead: The Cultural Roots of Martin Luther King, Jr.* (Minneapolis: University of Minnesota Press, 1991) for a good discussion of these viewpoints.

12. For typical examples, see Hanes Walton, Jr., *The Political Philosophy of Martin Luther King, Jr.* (Westport, Conn.: Greenwood Press, 1971); Kenneth L. Smith and Ira G. Zepp, *Search for the Beloved Community: The Thinking of Martin Luther King, Jr.* (Valley Forge, Pa.: Judson Press, 1998); Ervin Smith, *The Ethics of Martin Luther King, Jr.* (New York: E. Mellen Press, 1981); and John J. Ansbro, *Martin Luther King, Jr.: The Making of a Mind* (Maryknoll, N.Y.: Orbis, 1982). Noel Leo Erskine's more recent *King among the Theologians* (Cleveland, Ohio: Pilgrim Press, 1994) may also be added to this list.

13. For typical examples, see Baldwin, *There Is a Balm in Gilead* and *To Make the Wounded Whole: The Cultural Legacy of Martin Luther King, Jr.* (Minneapolis: University of Minnesota Press, 1992); Keith D. Miller, *Voice of Deliverance: The Language of Martin Luther King, Jr. and Its Sources* (New York: Free Press, 1992); Richard Lischer, *The Preacher King: Martin Luther King, Jr. and the Word That Moved America* (New York: Oxford University Press, 1995); and Eric Michael Dyson, *I May Not Get There with You: The True Martin Luther King, Jr.* (New York: Free Press, 2000). There is no shortage of positions between these two poles or attempts to synthesize them in different ways. See, for example, Clayborne Carson's introductions to the paper volumes and

his essay "Martin Luther King, Jr. and the African-American Social Gospel" in Timothy E. Fulop and Albert J. Raboteau, eds., *African-American Religion: Interpretive Essays in History and Culture* (New York: Routledge, 1997), 341–362. This attempt to synthesize the two ways of understanding King can also, to a certain extent, be found in James H. Cone's comparison of King and Malcolm X in *Martin & Malcolm & America: A Dream or a Nightmare* (London: Fount, 1993). In *Revolution of Conscience: Martin Luther King, Jr. and the Philosophy of Nonviolence* (New York: Guilford Press, 1997), Greg Moses portrays another problem. He places King in a distinctively African-American tradition, but his work suffers from the attempt to construct a coherent philosophical system out of King's writings. The best example of a philosophical treatment of King and the civil rights movement as a whole is Richard H. King's *Civil Rights and the Idea of Freedom* (New York: Oxford University Press, 1992).

14. In this study, "signification" is used in the general discourse analytical sense, which should not be confused with the sense it is used by, for example, Henry Louis Gates, Jr. (even if a kinship exists). In my analysis, "signification" is used to capture how meaning is created, transferred, and endowed in King's rhetoric. It is closely connected with the act of definition and the attempt to stabilize the meaning-structure of the civil rights movement discourse.

1. A Discourse of Faith

1. Carson and Holloran, *A Knock at Midnight*, 3.

2. After much thought, I have decided to use the same language King did to speak of humanity. King's language was formulated before second-wave feminism changed the way we use language. I found the silent accusation of gender-inclusive language in my own text too jarring and have chosen to discuss King's ideas using his own language. It is unfortunate that King was not able to extend his inclusive language to include the many women who worked in countless civil rights campaigns, who were in fact the foot soldiers of the movement.

3. These sentences of course only show a small tip of an iceberg of several thousands years of philosophical arguments, discussions, and traditions that include a myriad of different complexities. As an introduction, see, for example, "Idealism" and "Materialism," in Paul Edwards, *The Encyclopedia of Philosophy* (New York: Macmillan, 1967), 4: 110–118 and 5: 179–188.

4. See other versions of this speech delivered in similar circumstances: "The Role of the Church in Facing the Nation's Chief Moral Dilemma," April 25, 1957, made to the Conference on Christian Faith and Human Relations in Nashville, Tennessee, in *Papers*, 4: 184–191; and "America's Chief Moral Dilemma," July 6, 1965, made to the General Synod, United Church of Christ in Chicago, Illinois, unpublished, King Library and Archives.

5. "The Church on the Frontier of Racial Tension," April 19, 1961, Southern Baptist Theological Seminary, Louisville, Kentucky, unpublished, King Library and Archives, 2.

6. Ibid., 3.

7. Ibid., 9.

8. All three extracts contain standard themes that can be found throughout King's rhetoric. The materialistic explanation in particular recurred almost word for word on several occasions. See, for example, "An Address before the National Press Club," July 19, 1962, Washington, D.C., in Washington, *A Testament of Hope*, 101.

9. See "The Power of Nonviolence," June 4, 1957, Berkeley, California, in Washington, *A Testament of Hope*, 13–14 for a typical example of this formulation that frequently reappears in King's rhetoric.

10. See, for example, *Chaos or Community*, 186.

11. This is how King regularly describes the course of events in Montgomery. It can be seen in *Stride toward Freedom* and in several speeches and articles that describe the boycott. For an example see "The Montgomery Story," June 27, 1956, San Francisco, California, in *Papers*, 3: 299–310.

12. The sermon "What Is Man?" in King, *Strength to Love*, 87–92, is a typical example of this line of reasoning. For another, very similar, version, see "What Is Man?" January 12, 1958, Chicago, Illinois, King Papers, Boston University, Box 2, Folder I-2.

13. King explicitly discusses the origin of the first human societies/ communities in "The Ethical Demands for Integration," December 27, 1962, Nashville, Tennessee, in Washington, *A Testament of Hope*, 122.

14. Typology was traditionally a way of interpreting the Bible by which characters and narratives of the Old Testament were seen as types that became fulfilled in Christ and the Church of the New Testament. This practice was developed in the black preaching tradition. The truths of Bible were not confined to a text between the covers of a book. The narratives and characters of the Bible moved through history, which thereby came to be understood as a sacred history. The reality of the Bible was lived and understood every day as persistently recurring experiences: The exodus was as much a reality in the American South as it was for the Israelites in Egypt. The Bible and its narratives were, like a dramatic play, always being reenacted. For discussions see Miller, *Voice of Deliverance*, 8–24; Lischer, *The Preacher King*, 205–212; and Northrop Frye, *The Great Code: The Bible and Literature* (San Diego: Harcourt Brace Jovanovich, 1983), 78–101 and 105–138. For an example of how all three conceptions of history can coexist in King's rhetoric, see "Letter from Birmingham Jail" in *Why We Can't Wait*. First King writes that he "must constantly respond to the Macedonian call for help" (77, typological), then he criticizes the "tragic misconception of time, . . . the strangely irrational notion that there is something in the very flow of time that will inevitably cure all ills. Actually time itself is neutral; it

can be used either destructively or constructively" (86, neutral), and finally he states that "Oppressed people cannot remain oppressed forever.
The yearning for freedom eventually manifests itself, and that is what
has happened to the American Negro. Something within has reminded
him of his birthright of freedom, and something without has reminded
him that it can be gained. Consciously or unconsciously, he has been
caught up by the *Zeitgeist*" (87, inherent force).

15. For a typical example of how King formulates this, see "Our God
Is Able" in King, *Strength to Love*, 105.

16. An example of King's view of the role of the pastor and his relationship with the congregation can be seen in "Recommendations to the
Dexter Avenue Baptist Church for the Fiscal Year 1954–1955," in *Papers*, 2: 287.

17. An early example is "Autobiography of Religious Development,"
which King wrote in 1950 when attending Crozer. See *Papers*, 1: 359–
363. The graduate school exams and essays in volume 2 of the *Papers*
show King's more mature handling of theological complexities and are
not as directly related to himself and his own background. The writings
nevertheless constitute a development that is interesting to follow. See
also Carson, "Introduction," in *Papers*, 1: 1–57 and Carson, "Introduction," in *Papers*, 2: 1–37.

18. Ernesto Laclau and Chantal Mouffe, *Hegemony and Socialist
Strategy: Towards a Radical Democratic Politics* (London: Verso, 1998).
The Lacanian term is *points de capiton*.

19. Ibid., 112.

20. For typical examples of how King discussed and defined "agape"
during the early movement years, see "The Power of Nonviolence," 13;
or "Facing the Challenge of a New Age," December 3, 1956, Montgomery, Alabama, in *Papers*, 3: 458–459. For King's earlier understanding of
the notion in relationship to the thinking of Anders Nygren and Reinhold
Niebuhr, see *Papers*, 2: 124–128 and 139–151. He also discussed it in his
dissertation, "A Comparison of the Conceptions of God in the Thinking
of Paul Tillich and Henry Nelson Wieman," in *Papers*, 2: 440–442. For
other sources of King's use of "agape," see Carson, "Introduction," in
Papers, 2: 9 note 34.

21. "MIA Mass Meeting at Holt Street Baptist Church," December 5,
1955, Montgomery, Alabama, 73–74. King refers to Hosea 11:1 and, probably, Psalm 46:10.

22. See also Moses's discussion of King's concept of justice in *Revolution of Conscience*, 186–187.

23. For a discussion of how this became the dominant theme in King's
later rhetoric, see Lischer, *The Preacher King*, 172–184.

24. "Our God Is Able," 104–105.

25. "Love, Law and Civil Disobedience," November 16, 1961, Atlanta,
Georgia, in Washington, *A Testament of Hope*, 49. The most famous
version of this set piece is probably the one in "Letter from Birmingham

Jail," 82–84, where King directly refers to the roots of the idea in the theology of St. Augustine and Thomas Aquinas.

26. "What Is Man?" in King, *Strength to Love*, 90. For one of the many variations of this theme, and one where King uses several interesting formulations, see "Loving Your Enemies," November 17, 1957, Montgomery, Alabama, in *Papers*, 4: 315–324, especially 318. For the written version of this often-preached sermon, see King, *Strength to Love*, 34–41.

27. "The American Dream," July 4, 1965, Atlanta, Georgia, in Carson and Holloran, *A Knock at Midnight*, 88.

28. One such moment was King's so-called kitchen experience in Montgomery. See King, *Stride toward Freedom*, 134–135. Branch calls this King's "first transcendent religious experience" (*Parting the Waters*, 162). For other discussions of this experience, see David J. Garrow, "Martin Luther King, Jr., and the Spirit of Leadership," in Peter J. Albert and Albert Hoffman, eds., *We Shall Overcome: Martin Luther King, Jr., and the Black Freedom Struggle* (New York: Da Capo Press, 1993), 11–34; and James H. Cone, "Martin Luther King: The Source of His Courage to Face Death," *Concilium* 183 (March 1983): 74–79.

29. See Miller, *Voice of Deliverance*, 62 for comments on how King used the amalgamation of his Baptist background and his theological studies in his rhetoric.

30. See the speech "Facing the Challenge of a New Age," January 1, 1957, Atlanta, Georgia, in *Papers*, 4: 73–89 for a typical example of how the creative ability of humanity is a structural feature of King's rhetoric. See especially pages 73–83.

31. For a typical example of how King builds and develops a sermon around the notion of Jesus as an ethical example, see "Answer to a Perplexing Question," March 3, 1963, Atlanta, Georgia, unpublished, King Library and Archives. For a written, and quite different, version of this sermon, see King, *Strength to Love*, 118–126.

32. "Loving Your Enemies," November 17, 1957, Montgomery, Alabama, 316.

33. "Drum Major Instinct," February 4, 1968, Atlanta, Georgia, in Carson and Holloran, *A Knock at Midnight*, 183–184.

34. For a discussion of the centrality of hope in the black religious tradition and its presence in the faith and messages of King, see Baldwin, *To Make the Wounded Whole*, 59–69; and Baldwin, *There Is a Balm in Gilead*, 229–272.

35. See Miller, *Voice of Deliverance*, 173–175; Lischer, *The Preacher King*, 187–191; and Branch, *Parting the Waters*, 550.

36. The collections of sermons in both *Strength to Love* and in Carson and Holloran, *A Knock at Midnight* show the general pattern of the use of parables. For a longer version of the example used here, see the sermon "Lazarus and Dives," March 10, 1963, Atlanta, Georgia, unpublished, King Library and Archives.

37. "Remaining Awake Through a Great Revolution," March 31, 1968, Washington, D.C., in Carson and Holloran, *A Knock at Midnight*, 215.

38. Ibid., 216.

39. It is worth remembering that in *Civil Rights and the Idea of Freedom*, Richard King suggests that King could be viewed as what Foucault calls an "author-function" (111), in which there is always a host of voices and instances speaking through the pen of a writer or the mouth of a speaker. The use and function of Jesus as storyteller in King's rhetoric is an example of this. See Michel Foucault, "What Is an Author?" in *Language, Counter-Memory, Practice: Selected Essays and Interviews*, ed. Donald F. Bouchard (Ithaca, N.Y.: Cornell University Press, 1977), 113–138.

40. See Eugene Genovese, *Roll, Jordan, Roll: The World the Slaves Made* (New York: Vintage Books, 1976), 445–479; Henry H. Mitchell, *Black Preaching: The Rediscovery of a Powerful Art* (Nashville, Tenn.: Abingdon Press, 1990), 56–75; and James H. Cone, *God of the Oppressed* (Maryknoll, N.Y.: Orbis, 1997), 49–56.

41. It is possible, however, to be slightly misled by the sermons in *Strength to Love* since the altar calls at the end of the sermons are omitted (as they have to be since the sermons are written and not spoken in a church). This gives them a strong Social Gospel thrust in which it can seem that salvation is reached primarily through collective social activity in the movement and not in the individual act of accepting the flesh and blood of Christ. Although the first aspect was important in King's faith, it was never, in reality, independent of the latter.

42. Jesus as Christ the Savior is naturally a recurring theme in King's sermons. A typical example can be found in "Is The Universe Friendly?" December 12, 1965, Atlanta, Georgia, unpublished, King Library and Archives.

43. Both Hans A. Baer and Merrill Sillinger, *African-American Religion in the Twentieth Century: Variations of Protest and Accommodation* (Knoxville: University of Tennessee Press, 1992); and Fulop and Raboteau, *African-American Religion* provide a wide range of illustrations of the role of the church in African-American religion. For an enlightening introduction to the subject, see Baer and Sillinger, ix–xxiii.

44. "Guidelines for a Constructive Church," June 5, 1966, Atlanta, Georgia, in Carson and Holloran, *A Knock at Midnight*, 105–115. The role and responsibility of the church are consistent themes throughout King's career, but some of the more interesting examples are King's "Recommendations to the Dexter Avenue Baptist Church for the Fiscal Year 1954–1955," where King expresses some of his basic assumptions of what a church is and ought to be; the discussion of the church in King, *Stride toward Freedom*, 205–211; the discussion in "Letter from Birmingham Jail" (especially 89–93); the sermon "A Knock at Midnight," both in the version printed in King, *Strength to Love*, 42–50, and the preached versions as for example New York, August 9, 1964, unpublished, King Li-

brary and Archives; and the speech "The Role of the Church in Facing the Nation's Chief Moral Dilemma."

45. "The Church on the Frontier of Racial Tension," 3.

46. Ibid.

47. Ibid., 5.

48. Ibid.

49. Ibid., 6.

50. Ibid., 7.

51. Ibid., 3–4.

52. Ibid., 4.

53. Ibid., 5.

54. Ibid., 6.

55. Here I use the term "false consciousness" in a traditional and general Marxist understanding of the term; that is, having imposed on one and accepting a false truth that both justifies and makes further oppression natural. The false consciousness hinders the oppressed from correctly understanding their situation.

56. "The Church on the Frontier of Racial Tension," 6.

57. Ibid.

58. Ibid., 6–7.

59. For other (although very similar) versions of this critique see, for example, "An Address before the National Press Club," 101; "Paul's Letter to American Christians," November 4, 1956, Montgomery, Alabama, 417 (and the written version in *Strength to Love*, 129–130); or "Some Things We Must Do," December 5, 1957, Montgomery, Alabama, in *Papers*, 4: 332.

60. "The Church on the Frontier of Racial Tension," 7–8.

61. Ibid.

62. Ibid., 8–9.

63. Ibid., 9.

64. "Guidelines for a Constructive Church," 110–112.

65. Isaiah 61:2.

66. "Guidelines For a Constructive Church," 112.

67. All quotes ibid., 112–114.

68. Ibid., 114.

69. For discussions of this term, see Smith and Zepp, *Search for the Beloved Community*, especially 119–140; Walton, *The Political Philosophy of Martin Luther King, Jr.*, 65–77; Smith, *The Ethics of Martin Luther King, Jr.*, 191–195; Ansbro, *The Making of a Mind*, 187–193; Cone, *Martin & Malcolm & America*, 214; and Bradford T. Stull, *Amid the Fall, Dreaming of Eden: Du Bois, King, Malcolm X, and Emancipatory Composition* (Carbondale: Southern Illinois University Press, 1999), 136–137 note 5.

70. "Facing the Challenge of a New Age," December 3, 1956, Montgomery, Alabama, 458.

71. "Nonviolence: The Only Road to Freedom," in Washington, *A*

Testament of Hope, 58 (originally published in *Ebony* 21 [October 1966]: 27–30).

72. Ibid., 58.

73. This is based on the theories of French philosopher Paul Ricoeur. See George H. Taylor, ed., *Lectures on Ideology and Utopia* (New York: Columbia University Press, 1986), especially 16.

74. See Lischer, *The Preacher King,* 234–236 for a short discussion of the role of the "Kingdom of God" in King's rhetoric.

75. "I Have a Dream," 85–86. (See Isaiah 40:4–5.)

76. "I Have a Dream," 87.

77. In *The Political Philosophy of Martin Luther King, Jr.,* Hanes Walton, Jr. even goes as far as to view "the beloved community" as a modern descendant of a tradition originating with St. Augustine's State of God. See 69–74.

78. *Chaos or Community,* 186.

2. Western Intellectualism and American Ideals

1. Cornel West clarifies his position as a Christian with the phrase "I subscribe to a discourse where God is a significant signifying term." See the discussion that follows his essay "Marxist Theory and the Specificity of Afro-American Oppression," in Lawrence Grossberg and Cary Nelson, eds., *Marxism and the Interpretation of Culture* (Urbana: University of Illinois Press, 1988), 32. The sentence is not only witty in context, it is also interesting and illuminating in respect to the analysis of this chapter and the study as a whole.

2. The first version of "Pilgrimage to Nonviolence" appears in King, *Stride toward Freedom,* 90–107; the second originally appeared in *Christian Century* 77 (April 1960): 439–441, reprinted in Washington, *A Testament of Hope,* 35–40; and the third appeared in King, *Strength to Love,* 135–145.

3. The difference between the versions is mainly a question of length; the later versions are much shorter than the questions in the first version. In the *Christian Century* version many things are omitted, notably the discussion of Marx, and the main addition is a discussion of existentialism, a discussion that remains in the last version, which is almost identical to the 1960 article.

4. Both quotes from King, *Stride toward Freedom,* 90.

5. King attended Morehouse College from 1944 to 1948. For one of the few remaining documents of his work from this period, see the essay he wrote for a sociology course entitled "Ritual" in *Papers,* 1: 127–142. For different appraisals of the academic records of his Morehouse years, see ibid., 151–157.

6. King, *Stride toward Freedom,* 91.

7. King attended Crozer Theological Seminary from 1948 to 1951

and graduated with a Bachelor of Divinity degree. For a full list of the courses King took during these years, see Carson, "Introduction" in *Papers*, 1: 48. For many examples of his academic work during the Crozer years, see *Papers*, 1: 161–441.

8. King, *Stride toward Freedom*, 91–92.

9. Ibid., 92.

10. These philosophers, however, appear infrequently in the documents from his Crozer years. The only course King took during this period that was directly related to a specific philosopher was a course on Kant in 1950–1951.

11. King, *Stride toward Freedom*, 92 For examples of how King came in contact with Marx and Marxism during his education, see Clayborne Carson, "Introduction" in *Papers*, 1: 41 and 51. For an example of his early (1952) understanding of the theory, see "Examination Answers, History of Recent Philosophy" in *Papers*, 2: 152–155.

12. For a typical example, see "How Should a Christian View Communism," in King, *Strength to Love*, 93–100.

13. King, *Stride toward Freedom*, 93.

14. For Gandhi, see King, *Stride toward Freedom*, 96–97; for Niebuhr, see 97–99; for Hegel, see 100–101; and for the general discussion of nonviolence, see 101–107.

15. For a discussion of early Gandhiism in America, how King came in contact with it, and how he used these sources, see Miller, *Voice of Deliverance*, 86–100. See also Sudarshan Kapur, *Raising Up a Prophet: The African-American Encounter with Gandhi* (Boston: Beacon Press, 1992).

16. For a discussion of how Rustin, with the help of others, "brought" Gandhi more explicitly into the Montgomery boycott, see Carson, "Introduction," in *Papers*, 3: 16–22; and Garrow, *Bearing the Cross*, 66–73. But it was not, as Carson shows, totally absent before Rustin entered the scene ("Introduction," 17).

17. See Carson, "Introduction," in *Papers*, 3: 17–22.

18. King, *Stride toward Freedom*, 97.

19. This accusation has seldom been highlighted in the King scholarship, but in a review of the book in the journal *Fellowship* in March 1959, reviewer Richard Goldhurst draws out this line of argument in full. See "Gandhi and Christ in Montgomery," *Fellowship*, March 1, 1959, 28–29. King Papers, Boston University, Box 81, Folder V-55.

20. King, *Stride toward Freedom*, 99.

21. Ibid.

22. Ibid., 100. King completed his coursework at Boston University from 1951 to 1953 and passed his qualifying examinations early in 1954. For a list of the courses King took see Carson, "Introduction" *Papers*, 2: 18. Personalism is a religious philosophy that is primarily interested in the individual's relationship to God and the individuality and personality of God himself.

23. King encountered Hegel in various courses during his stay at Boston University. In 1952, he took a year-long course on Hegel's thought. King failed a German language examination test early in the semester (he passed it later) and had difficulties with Hegel's philosophy. His seminar papers were largely based on secondary sources. See Carson, "Introduction" in *Papers*, 2: 16. For an example of King's writings on Hegel, see "An Exposition of the First Triad of Categories of the Hegelian Logic—Being, Non-being, Becoming," in *Papers*, 2: 196–201. That King had problems with Hegelian philosophy is also illustrated in his "Qualification Examination Answers, History of Philosophy" (February 23, 1954). He had to answer six out of seven questions, and the one he left out was the one regarding Hegel. See *Papers*, 2: 242–247.

24. King, *Stride toward Freedom*, 100–101.

25. Ibid., 101.

26. See Miller, *Voice of Deliverance*, 63–66 for a discussion of this question.

27. See the versions of "Pilgrimage to Nonviolence" in Washington, *A Testament of Hope*, 36; and, with some minor modifications, King, *Strength to Love*, 136–137.

28. *Papers*, 2: 339–544. King chose his topic in 1953 and began working more systematically on the dissertation early in 1954. He received his doctorate on June 5, 1955. He was working as a full-time pastor at Dexter Avenue Baptist Church from May 1954 while he completed his dissertation. This situation, where his research relied on handwritten notecards from his initial studies in Boston, has been used as an explanation for the erroneous use of sources in the dissertation. Without acknowledging that he had done so, King relied heavily on secondary sources, for example, another dissertation on Tillich's thought written at Boston University three years before. This was not, however, noted by his advisor Harold DeWolf in "first Reader's Report," in *Papers*, 2: 333–334, or S. Paul Schilling in "Second Reader's Report," in *Papers*, 2: 334–335. For discussions of this, see Carson, "Introduction," in *Papers*, 2: 25–26, and the several essays and discussions in "Becoming Martin Luther King, Jr.: Plagiarism and Originality—A Round Table," *The Journal of American History* 78 (June 1991): 11–123. See also Dyson, *I May Not Get There with You*, 145–154.

29. "Rediscovering Lost Values," February 28, 1954, Detroit, Michigan, in *Papers*, 2: 253; "Remaining Awake Through a Great Revolution," 223.

30. Thomas Carlyle (1795–1881) was a Scottish writer. King probably paraphrases a passage from Carlyle's most famous work *The French Revolution* (1837); see *Papers*, 2: 253 note 3. William Cullen Bryant (1794–1878) was an American writer and publicist who, among other things, led a campaign against slavery in the New York paper *The Evening Post*. The line is from "The Battlefield" (1839), stanza 9. James Russell Lowell (1819–1891) was an American writer and publicist who later be-

came professor of French and Spanish at Harvard University. The quote is from "The Present Crisis" (1844), stanza 8, an antislavery poem written at the time of the annexation of Texas.

31. When King quotes Shakespeare it is in most cases from *Macbeth* or *Othello*; when he uses Donne it is almost always the passage starting with "No man is an Iland, intire of its selfe" from "Devotions upon Emergent Occasions." His use of Tolstoy is more varied but often focuses on the accounts of his conversion. Other writers that King quotes or paraphrases include Tennyson, Hugo, Emerson, Chesterton, Longfellow, and Dante.

32. This specific example, which reappeared in many other texts almost word for word, is from the sermon "Love in Action," in King, *Strength to Love*, 30.

33. By "the definitional power of neutrality" I mean that as a neutral, you can define things "objectively." You do not define as a part of a social or political struggle; you define from the position where you know what "truth" is. That is the position King strives for here, a position where he can stand above the concrete situation and define it according to the logic of intellectual truths. Through this position what he says is not "political" or "the views of a segregated Negro"; it is the truth shaped through centuries of collective human intellectual achievement. That is the definitional power of neutrality.

34. Martin Buber (1878–1965) first developed his dialogical principle in *Ich und Du* (1923). Its fundamental idea is that the "I" is different depending on whether it is part of a dialogue with a "Thou" or only regards or reflects upon an "It." Every "I" is threatened with becoming an "It" and every dialogue is threatened with being transformed into a reflection of an object. Other philosophers that King uses include Heraclitus, Cicero, Spencer, Condorcet, Schopenhauer, Spinoza, and Dewey.

35. "America's Chief Moral Dilemma," 5–6. For other examples of King's use of Buber, see "Paul's Letter to American Christians," November 4, 1956, Montgomery, Alabama, 418 (or the written version in *Strength to Love*, 130–131); or "The Ethical Demands of Integration," 119.

36. The written sermons in *Strength to Love* are filled with examples of discussions of contemporary theological debates, but it is also common in other sermons, speeches, and writings.

37. "MIA Mass Meeting at Holt Street Baptist Church," December 5, 1955, 73.

38. For typical examples, see "Paul's Letter to American Christians," November 4, 1956, Montgomery, Alabama, 415–416; "Answer to a Perplexing Question," March 3, 1963, Atlanta, Georgia, unpublished, King Library and Archives, especially 3–5; and "Answer to a Perplexing Question," in King, *Strength to Love*, 119–121.

39. See, for example, "The American Dream," June 6, 1961, Lincoln

University, Pennsylvania, in Washington, *A Testament of Hope*, 211; and *Chaos or Community*, 69–74.

40. See, for example, "MIA Mass Meeting at Holt Street Baptist Church," November 14, 1956, in *Papers*, 3: 431; "Some Things We Must Do," 333–334; and *Chaos or Community*, 84–88, 92, and 106–110.

41. The behaviorist he refers to most often is John B. Watson. For an early and typical example, see "MIA Mass Meeting at Holt Street Baptist Church," November 14, 1956, 431. King's sources of legitimization in the field of psychology underwent some changes. In "Drum Major Instinct," he briefly discusses Freud and Adler; see 171.

42. "MIA Mass Meeting at Holt Street Baptist Church," December 5, 1955, 71.

43. King's sermons at Dexter Avenue Baptist Church and Ebenezer Baptist Church offer examples of his use of philosophy and other disciplines. However, both these churches drew their membership from the professional (upper) middle class whereas Holt Street Baptist Church, where Ralph Abernathy was pastor, traditionally had a poorer and uneducated membership. These differences may have some importance in some respects, but not in this case, since the audience both inside and outside the church was not tied to a specific church. For the background of the Montgomery churches, see Branch, *Parting the Waters*, 1–21. See also Wally G. Vaughn and Richard W. Willis, eds., *Reflections on Our Pastor: Dr. Martin Luther King, Jr. at Dexter Avenue Baptist Church 1954–1960* (Dover, Mass.: Majority Press, 1999) for the Dexter Avenue congregation's (early) perceptions of him.

44. "America's Chief Moral Dilemma," 2.

45. The reference to contemporary theological debate is the sentence "Shall I be a humanist or a theist?" (8). Dr. Harry Emerson Fosdick (1878–1969) was a liberal Baptist preacher who became famous for his challenges to fundamentalism in the 1920s. He later became pastor of the nondenominational and powerful Riverside Church in New York City. He was also a professor of practical theology and was one of the most forceful and eloquent spokesmen for liberal Protestantism for four decades. King often incorporated parts of Fosdick's sermons into his own. Miller offers many examples in *Voice of Deliverance*. Whittaker Chambers (1904–1961) was a former Soviet agent (1930s) who became a national figure in 1948 when he accused a former official of the State Department, Alger Hiss, of passing classified material to him when Chambers was an agent. The conviction of Hiss precipitated Senator Joseph McCarthy's activities. Chambers became a fierce anti-Communist, fearing that any kind of secular liberalism would eventually lead to Stalinism. His autobiography *Witness* (New York: Random House, 1952) became a bestseller. See also Hilton Kramer, *The Twilight of the Intellectuals: Culture and Politics in the Era of the Cold War* (Chicago: I. R. Dee, 1999), 3–31.

46. The post-1965 sermons in Carson and Holloran, *A Knock at Midnight* confirm that the reference practice still exists in his later rhetoric,

as do the speeches and sermon in *The Trumpet of Conscience.*

47. "A Testament of Hope," in Washington, *A Testament of Hope,* 313–328 (originally published in *Playboy,* January 1969, 175ff.).

48. "A Testament of Hope," 328.

49. Ibid.

50. The minutemen are a special case. They fought in the early battles of the American Revolution and were therefore not dissenters within the American system because the nation was yet to be founded at the time. But still they represent a serious challenge to an existing and established system, even if in their case it was the rule of the British.

51. See Lischer, *The Preacher King,* 4–5 for a brief discussion.

52. "Antidotes for Fear," in King, *Strength to Love,* 110–111.

53. "Birmingham Negroes' Plea for Freedom," October 22, 1963, Birmingham, Alabama, unpublished, King Library and Archives, 2.

54. King, of course, knew that every word he uttered was being monitored by (at least) the local police. How and to what extent this affected King's formulations in this specific case is difficult to say. See Kenneth O'Reilly, *Racial Matters: The FBI's Secret File on Black America, 1960–1972* (New York: Free Press, 1991), 110–111 and 380 note 98.

55. "Some Things We Must Do," 338. The paraphrased poem is Douglas Malloch, "Be the Best of Whatever You Are" (1926). King used the passage in many speeches and sermons. See, for example, "Facing the Challenge of a New Age," January 1, 1957, Atlanta, Georgia, 79 (where King credits his Morehouse professor Benjamin Mays for the phrases). It was often also included in King's flagship sermon "Three Dimensions of a Complete Life"; see, for example, April 9, 1967, Chicago, Illinois, in Carson and Holloran, *A Knock at Midnight,* 125–126.

56. "Is the Universe Friendly?" 6.

3. The Problem of Race

1. King, *Stride toward Freedom,* 224.

2. Ibid.

3. *Chaos or Community,* 134.

4. "How Should A Christian View Communism?," 97. The passage, with slight variations, reappears throughout King's work and refers to Acts 3:28.

5. "I Have a Dream," 83.

6. Robert Cox recognizes the importance of this turning point in the speech in "The Fulfillment of Time: King's 'I Have a Dream' Speech (August 28, 1963)," in Michael C. Leff and Fred J. Kauffeld, eds., *Texts in Context: Dialogues on Significant Episodes in American Political Rhetoric* (Davis, Calif.: Hermagoras Press, 1989), 195–199. See also Robert Hariman's response "Time and Reconstitution of Gradualism in King's Address: A Response to Cox," 213–214.

7. "Paul's Letter to American Christians," November 4, 1956, Montgomery, Alabama, 415.

8. Ibid., 418.

9. Ibid., 416. The quote is from Romans 12:2. In the written version in *Strength to Love*, King/Paul defines the addressees of the letter as "the salt of the earth," "the light of the world," and the "vitally active leaven in the lump of the nation." See page 129.

10. "Paul's Letter to American Christians," November 4, 1956, Dexter Avenue Baptist Church, 418.

11. For a discussion of the relationship between racial and religious identity among African Americans, see C. Eric Lincoln, "Black Religion and Racial Identity," in Herbert W. Harris, Howard C. Blue, and Ezra E. H. Griffith, eds., *Racial and Ethnic Identity: Psychological Development and Creative Expression* (New York: Routledge, 1995), 209–221.

12. Michael Omi and Henry Winant, *Racial Formation in the United States from the 1960s to the 1990s* (New York: Routledge, 1994).

13. Ibid., 15.

14. See ibid., 15–19 for a description and discussion of assimilationism and cultural pluralism. See also Christopher Lasch, *The True and Only Heaven: Progress and Its Critics* (New York: Norton, 1991), 353–355; and Walter A. Jackson, *Gunnar Myrdal and America's Conscience: Social Engineering and Racial Liberalism, 1938–1987* (Chapel Hill: University of North Carolina Press, 1990).

15. In the introduction to the 1970 edition of their book, Glazer and Moynihan offer some interesting comments about their conclusions in the 1963 edition (*Beyond the Melting Pot: The Negroes, Puerto Ricans, Jews, Italians, and Irish of New York City* [Cambridge, Mass.: MIT Press, 1970), vii–xcv, see especially xiii–xxiv.

16. The racial formation of the South practiced through the institution of segregation is important here. The bedrock of the social and political reality of the region represented the opposite of the understanding of race as a mere marker of ethnic affinity.

17. It is also questionable whether the mosaic of the cultural pluralist view included the color black. It was more a mosaic formed from the different "shades" of white—Irish, Italian, Jewish, and so forth. See Omi and Winant, *Racial Formation in the United States*, 16 and 20–22.

18. The chapter "The Days To Come" in *Why We Can't Wait*, 126–152 is a typical example of this kind of argumentation. The emphasis on the mainly political character of integration became stronger during King's last years. See Garrow, *Bearing the Cross*, 608 for an interesting example.

19. "The Time for Freedom Has Come," in *A Testament of Hope*, 160–166 (originally in *New York Times Magazine*, September 10, 1961, 25ff.), 163.

20. Ibid., 160.

21. Ibid.

22. *Chaos or Community*, 30–31.

23. Garrow, *Bearing the Cross*, 479.

24. Clayborne Carson provides a good summary of the contemporary meanings and understandings of the phrase "Black Power" in *In Struggle: SNCC and the Black Awakening of the 1960s* (Cambridge, Mass.: Harvard University Press, 1995), 209–228. The phrase was not new; Richard Wright had used it in a book title in the 1950s and activists and politicians such as Paul Robeson, Jesse Gray, and Adam Clayton Powell, among others, had all used it. In the SNCC version, it grew out of the slogan "Black Power for Black People" that was used by activists in Alabama. Stokely Carmichael and Charles V. Hamilton later developed the concept in the book *Black Power: The Politics of Liberation in America* (New York: Random House, 1967).

25. See *Chaos or Community*, 44–63 for a discussion.

26. That "race" has a meaning and quality in itself must not be confused with essentialism. "Race" is still a construct in history and society, but because of U.S. history and society it is a construct that is difficult to contain within, or reduce to, something else. This is also Omi and Winant's argument in their critique of ethnicity, class, and nation-based understandings of "race." See *Racial Formation in the United States*, especially 48–50.

27. See, for example, King, *Stride toward Freedom*, 18–21 and 90.

28. See, for example, "Acceptance Address for the Nobel Peace Prize," December 10, 1964, Oslo, Norway, in Carson and Shepard, *A Call to Conscience*, 105–109.

29. "Letter From Birmingham Jail," 81–82.

30. Ibid., 93.

31. See Lischer, *The Preacher King*, 183–191.

32. *Chaos or Community*, 102–103.

33. "Letter from Birmingham Jail" was initially written in April 1963 as an open letter to eight white clergymen who in another open letter had criticized the movement for demanding too much and for using nonviolent resistance a few months earlier. See E. Culpepper Clark, "The American Dilemma in King's 'Letter From Birmingham Jail,'" in John Louis Lucaites and Carolyn Calloway-Thomas, eds., *Martin Luther King, Jr. and The Sermonic Power of Public Discourse* (Tuscaloosa: University of Alabama Press, 1993), 33–49 for an interesting discussion and analysis of the letter.

34. *Chaos or Community*, 103.

35. See "Impasse in Race Relations," in *Trumpet of Conscience*, 3–17 for a typical example of this argument.

36. "Our Struggle," in Washington, *A Testament of Hope*, 75–76. Originally published in *Liberation* 1 (April 1956): 3–6.

37. "Where Do We Go from Here?" August 16, 1967, Atlanta, Georgia, in Carson and Shepard, *A Call to Conscience*, 184.

38. That the accomplishments of the civil rights movement up until 1965 were not enough also reveals the impossibility of the ethnicity paradigm. To Omi and Winant, the late 1960s represent this crisis of the paradigm. See *Racial Formation in the United States*, 95–112.

4. THIRD WORLD, COLD WAR, AND VIETNAM

1. The only other study I have seen where King's use of international situations and places is extensively discussed is Stull's *Amid the Fall, Dreaming of Eden*. There "The Orient" and "Africa" are understood and analyzed as "commonplaces" in King's rhetoric, playing a crucial part in his "emancipatory composition." Stull presents his purpose and his theoretical foundations on 1–20 and analyzes "The Orient" and "Africa" in King's (as well as DuBois's and Malcolm X's) rhetoric on 48–73 and 74–98, respectively.

2. The trip (financed by the American Baptist Convention) was also meant to include a visit to the Soviet Union. It had been postponed due to health reasons (King was stabbed by a deranged woman during a book signing in Harlem on September 20, 1958) and "the urgency of the racial conflict in the South." See King Papers, Boston University, Box 1, Folder V.

3. "Sermon on Gandhi" is a typical example, but this is a recurring theme in King's rhetoric. March 22, 1959, Montgomery, Alabama, unpublished, King Library and Archives,

4. "My Trip to the Land of Gandhi," in Washington, *A Testament of Hope*, 23–30 (originally published in *Ebony*, July 1959, 88–90 and 92).

5. "My Trip to the Land of Gandhi," 23.

6. It is not especially remarkable that King's text includes the view of the Orient as a counterpart to Western civilization. He writes himself into the discourse of Orientalism that Edward Said has described and is, as a Westerner and an American writing in the end of the 1950s, stuck in this historical and contextual position's relationship to the Orient as the Other. See Edward W. Said, *Orientalism* (New York: Pantheon Books, 1978). Stull follows this analysis a bit further; see *Amid the Fall, Dreaming of Eden*, 48–49, 52–53, 64–65, and 83–84.

7. "My Trip to the Land of Gandhi," 23.

8. Ibid., 24.

9. Ibid.

10. Ibid.

11. Ibid., 25–26.

12. Ibid., 25.

13. Ibid., 25–26.

14. Ibid., 26.

15. Ibid., 27.

16. Ibid., 28.

17. Ibid., 29.

18. Ibid., 28–29.

19. Ibid., 29.

20. Ibid., 30.

21. For the influence of African decolonization on SNCC, see Carson, *In Struggle*, 16, 134–136, and 276–277.

22. For Malcolm X's view of colonialism and imperialism and the fight

against it, see George Breitman, ed., *Malcolm X Speaks* (New York: Grove Weidenfeld, 1965), 160; and *In Struggle*, 135–136 and 192.

23. See, for example, "The Time for Freedom Has Come" or "Speech Regarding the Influence of African Movements on U.S. Students," May 1962, unknown location, unpublished, King Library and Archives.

24. See the speeches "Facing the Challenge of a New Age," December 3, 1956, Montgomery, Alabama, 453–454; and "The Rising Tide of Racial Consciousness," in Washington, *A Testament of Hope*, 146 (originally published in *YMCA Magazine*, December 1960, 4–6). See also Carson, "Introduction," in *Papers*, 3: 22–23.

25. "The Birth of a New Nation," April 7, 1957, Montgomery, Alabama, in *Papers*, 4: 155–167.

26. Ibid., 155.
27. Ibid., 155–156.
28. Ibid., 156.
29. Ibid.
30. Ibid., 157.
31. Ibid., 156–157.
32. Ibid.
33. Ibid.
34. Ibid., 157.
35. Ibid.
36. Ibid., 158.
37. Ibid.
38. Ibid., 159.
39. Ibid.
40. Ibid., 159–160.
41. Ibid., 160.
42. Ibid., 161.
43. Ibid., 161–162.
44. Ibid., 163.
45. Ibid.
46. Ibid., 164.

47. For an example of the "positive view," see August Meier and Elliot Rudwick, *From Plantation to Ghetto* (New York: Hill and Wang, 1976). For an example of the "negative" view, see Manning Marable, *Race, Reform and Rebellion: The Second Reconstruction in Black America 1945–1990* (Jackson: University Press of Mississippi, 1991).

48. See Marable, *Race, Reform and Rebellion*, 27–32.
49. "The Montgomery Story," 300–301.
50. Ibid., 301.
51. Ibid., 305.
52. Ibid., 308.
53. Ibid.

54. King offered similar types of guarantees at the very first mass meeting of the Montgomery bus boycott. See "MIA Mass Meeting at Holt Street Baptist Church," December 5, 1955, Montgomery, Alabama, 72–73.

55. This part of the sermon may be related to the earlier discussion of the celebration on the evening of independence. King mentions there that the Duchess of Kent in relationship to Ghana is no more than an official visitor like himself and that she even danced with Nkrumah at the reception. This scene indicates another ideological effect of King's discourse that shows its compatibility with middle-class interests: Nkrumah's dance with the Duchess of Kent (representing the British Queen) is a telling metaphor for the upward social mobility black middle-class individuals sought. It is not the society that changes; it is the individual's position in and relationship to it that does. See "The Birth of a New Nation," 160 and 162.

56. Ibid., 165–166.

57. See David V. Levy, *The Debate over Vietnam* (Baltimore: Johns Hopkins University Press, 1993).

58. Ibid., 111.

59. Ibid., 112.

60. Ibid.

61. Frederick J. Anyczak, "When 'Silence Is Betrayal': An Ethical Criticism of the Revolution of Values in the Speech at Riverside Church," in Lucaites and Thomas, *The Sermonic Power of Public Discourse*, 130.

62. The civil rights movement's (and the SCLC's) internal discussion of the war is a prominent theme in Garrow, *Bearing the Cross*, from page 394 onward. See also Andrew Young, *An Easy Burden: The Civil Rights Movement and the Transformation of America* (New York: HarperCollins, 1996), 422–435.

63. The first time King spoke critically of the war was in a speech at Howard University on March 2, 1965, when he said that "the war in Vietnam is accomplishing nothing." Quoted in Garrow, *Bearing the Cross*, 394. See also Dyson, *I May Not Get There with You*, 54.

64. "Beyond Vietnam," April 4, 1967, New York City; Carson and Shepard, *A Call to Conscience*, 139–164. (The speech has sometimes been referred to as "A Time to Break Silence.") For other discussions of the speech, see Anyczak, "When 'Silence Is Betrayal'"; and Vincent Harding, *Martin Luther King: The Inconvenient Hero* (Maryknoll, N.Y.: Orbis, 1996), 69–81.

65. "Beyond Vietnam," 140.

66. Ibid., 141.

67. Ibid.

68. Ibid., 142.

69. Ibid., 145.

70. Ibid., 148.

71. Ibid., 154.
72. Ibid., 158.

5. RADICALIZATION

1. King, *Stride toward Freedom*, 224. For another example of this passage, see "MIA Mass Meeting at Holt Street Baptist Church," December 5, 1955, Montgomery, Alabama, 74.
2. The speeches in *The Trumpet of Conscience* were broadcast during November and December 1967 over the Canadian Broadcasting Corporation as the seventh annual series of Massey Lectures.
3. "Impasse in Race Relations," 17.
4. "When Peace Becomes Obnoxious," March 18, 1956, Montgomery, Alabama, in *Papers*, 3: 208; and the article "The 'New Negro' of the South: Behind the Montgomery Story," ibid., 286 (originally published in *Socialist Call*, 24 June 1956, 16–19), respectively.
5. "I Have a Dream," 81. Dyson stresses the importance of this passage and discusses how and why it to a large degree has been forgotten in *I May Not Get There with You*, 14–19.
6. See, for example, "Nonviolence and Social Change," in *The Trumpet of Conscience*, 55.
7. King's most extensive discussion of white backlash is in the chapter "Racism and the White Backlash" in *Chaos or Community*, 67–101. For a short and direct formulation, see "Impasse in Race Relations," 9–10.
8. See, for example, "The Montgomery Story," 308; or "Introduction," in *Why We Can't Wait*, ix–xi.
9. See the article "Next Stop: The North," in Washington, *A Testament of Hope*, 189–194 (originally published in *Saturday Review*, 13 November 1965, 33–35 and 105) for an example of King's and the SCLC's initial view of the difference between the problems and campaigns in the North and South. For a later example that illustrates the complexity of locating the root of the northern problem, see *Chaos or Community*, 113–119.
10. "Where Do We Go From Here?" 184–185.
11. See "I've Been to the Mountaintop," April 2, 1968, Memphis, Tennessee, in Carson and Shepard, *A Call to Conscience*, 207–223, 219.
12. See Cone, *Martin and Malcolm and America*, 230; and *Chaos or Community*, 126–127.
13. "Where Do We Go from Here?" 191.
14. For the deeply situated racism, see, for example, "Impasse in Race Relations," 6; and "A Testament of Hope," 316. For King's view that the majority of white Americans are racists, see Cone, *Martin, Malcolm and America*, 233; and Dyson, *I May Not Get There with You*, 39–40. For King's disappointment with the liberals, see, for example, "Impasse in Race Relations," 10; and *Chaos or Community*, 88–96.

15. "Impasse in Race Relations," 6.

16. Ibid., 10.

17. Ibid., 8–9. This can be compared to what Malcolm X writes in his autobiography: "'White man' as commonly used, means complexion only secondary; primarily it describes attitudes and actions. In America, 'white man' meant specific attitudes and actions toward the black man." *The Autobiography of Malcolm X* (with Alex Haley) (New York: Grove Press, 1965), 447.

18. "Conscience and the Vietnam War," in *The Trumpet of Conscience*, 24.

19. "Impasse in Race Relations," 14–15.

20. "I Have a Dream," 85–86.

21. For discussions of temporality and time in "I Have a Dream," see Cox, "The Fulfillment of Time"; and Hariman, "Time and Reconstitution of Gradualism in King's Address."

22. "A Christmas Sermon on Peace," in *The Trumpet of Conscience*, 76.

23. Ibid., 77–78.

24. These were geographical areas that King commonly used in the rhetoric surrounding the Poor People's Campaign. See, for example, "Remaining Awake Through a Great Revolution," 214–219.

25. For discussions of this topic, see Richard H. King, "Martin Luther King, Jr., and the Meaning of Freedom: A Political Interpretation," in Albert and Hoffman, *We Shall Overcome*, 130–152; and *Civil Rights and the Idea of Freedom*, 87–107.

26. "I Have a Dream," 82–83. For a discussion of the check metaphor, see Cox, "The Fulfillment of Time," 192–194; and Hariman, "Time and Reconstitution of Gradualism in King's Address," 210–211.

27. John Louis Lucaites and Celeste Michelle Condit, "Reconstructing <Equality>: Culturetypal and Counter-Cultural Rhetorics in the Martyred Black Vision," *Communication Monographs* 57 (March 1990): 21 notes 6, 7, 14. For another discussion of King's "equality," see Moses, *Revolution of Conscience*, 25–36.

28. Ibid., 21 note 7. This is yet another example of how King's rhetoric and ideas have been frozen in the positions of "I Have a Dream."

29. See primarily Cone, *Martin and Malcolm and America*, especially 244–314.

30. Lucaites and Condit, "Reconstructing <Equality>," 8.

31. "Nonviolence and Social Change," 55.

32. Ibid., 59–60.

33. *Chaos or Community*, 29–30.

34. Ibid., 31.

35. All quotes from "Impasse in Race Relations," 8.

36. Ibid., 9.

37. "Conscience and the Vietnam War," 24, and "Impasse in Race Relations," 10, respectively.

38. For a typical example, see "I've Been to the Mountaintop," 280–282.

39. Louis R. Harlan argues that King's radicalization consisted of new strategy but no new ideas in "Thoughts on the Leadership of Martin Luther King, Jr.," in Albert and Hoffman, *We Shall Overcome*, 59–68.

EPILOGUE

1. This has been argued most convincingly and eloquently by Harding in *The Inconvenient Hero* and Dyson in *I May Not Get There with You*.

2. The phrase originally comes from the poem "Now That He Is Safely Dead" by Carl Wendel Himes, Jr. See Harding, *The Inconvenient Hero*, 1–22 and 143 note 1.

Bibliography

Archival Collections

Martin Luther King, Jr. Papers, King Library and Archives, The Martin Luther King, Jr. Center for Nonviolent Social Change, Atlanta, Georgia

Martin Luther King, Jr. Papers, Special Collections Department, Mugar Library, Boston University, Boston, Massachusetts

Books, Articles, and Documents

Albert, Peter J., and Ronald Hoffman, eds. *We Shall Overcome: Martin Luther King, Jr. and the Black Freedom Struggle.* 1990; reprint, New York: Da Capo Press, 1993.

Ansbro, John J. *Martin Luther King, Jr.: The Making of a Mind.* Maryknoll, N.Y.: Orbis, 1982.

Anyczak, Frederick J. "When 'Silence Is Betrayal': An Ethical Criticism of the Revolution of Values in the Speech at Riverside Church." In Lucaites and Thomas, eds., *The Sermonic Power of Public Discourse,* 127–146.

Baer, Hans A., and Merrill Singer. *African-American Religion in the Twentieth Century: Varieties of Protest and Accommodation.* Knoxville: University of Tennessee Press, 1992.

Baldwin, Lewis L. *There Is a Balm in Gilead: The Cultural Roots of Martin Luther King, Jr.* Minneapolis: University of Minnesota Press, 1991.

———. *To Make the Wounded Whole: The Cultural Legacy of Martin Luther King, Jr.* Minneapolis: University of Minnesota Press, 1992.

"Becoming Martin Luther King, Jr.: Plagiarism and Originality—A Round Table." *The Journal of American History* 78, no. 1 (June 1991): 11–123.

Branch, Taylor. *Parting the Waters: America in the King Years, 1954–63.* 1988; reprint, New York: Simon and Schuster, 1991.

———. *Pillar of Fire: America in the King Years, 1963–65.* New York: Simon and Schuster, 1998.

Breitman, George, ed. *Malcolm X Speaks.* 1965; reprint, New York: Grove Weidenfeld, 1990.

Buber, Martin. *Ich und Du.* 1923; reprint, Heidelberg: L. Schneider, 1983.

Carmichael, Stokely, and Charles V. Hamilton. *Black Power: The Politics of Liberation in America*. New York: Random House, 1967.

Carson, Clayborne. *In Struggle: SNCC and the Black Awakening of the 1960s*. 1981; reprint, Cambridge, Mass.: Harvard University Press, 1995.

———. "Martin Luther King, Jr. and the African-American Social Gospel." In Fulop and Raboteau, eds., *African-American Religion*, 341–362.

Carson, Clayborne, ed. *The Papers of Martin Luther King, Jr.* Volume I: *Called to Serve, January 1929–June 1951*. Berkeley: University of California Press, 1992.

———. *The Papers of Martin Luther King, Jr.* Volume II: *Rediscovering Precious Values, July 1951–November 1955*. Berkeley: University of California Press, 1994.

———. *The Papers of Martin Luther King, Jr.* Volume III: *Birth of a New Age, December 1955–December 1956*. Berkeley: University of California Press, 1997.

———. *The Papers of Martin Luther King, Jr.* Volume IV: *Symbol of the Movement: January 1957–December 1958*. Berkeley: University of California Press, 2000.

———. *The Autobiography of Martin Luther King, Jr.* New York: Intellectual Properties Management in association with Warner Books, 1998.

Carson, Clayborne, and Peter Holloran, eds. *A Knock at Midnight: Inspiration from the Great Sermons of Reverend Martin Luther King, Jr.* New York: Intellectual Properties Management in association with Warner Books, 1998.

Carson, Clayborne, and Kris Shepard, eds. *A Call to Conscience: The Landmark Speeches of Martin Luther King, Jr.* New York: Intellectual Properties Management in association with Warner Books, 2001.

Chambers, Whittaker. *Witness*. New York: Random House, 1952.

Cone, James H. *God of the Oppressed*. 1975; reprint, Maryknoll, N.Y.: Orbis, 1997.

———. *Martin and Malcolm and America: A Dream or a Nightmare*. 1991; reprint, London: Fount, 1993.

Clark, E. Culpepper. "The American Dilemma in King's 'Letter from Birmingham Jail.'" In Lucaites and Thomas, eds., *The Sermonic Power of Public Discourse*, 33–49.

Cone, James H. "Martin Luther King: The Source for His Courage to Face Death." *Concilium* 183 (March 1983): 74–79.

Cox, Robert. "The Fulfillment of Time: King's 'I Have a Dream' Speech (August 28, 1963)." In Leff and Kauffeld, eds., *Texts in Context*, 181–204.

DeWolf, Harold. "first Reader's Report." 1955. In *Papers*, 2: 333–334.

Dyson, Eric Michael. *I May Not Get There with You: The True Martin Luther King, Jr.* New York: Free Press, 2000.

Edwards, Paul. *The Encyclopedia of Philosophy.* New York: Macmillan, 1967.

Erskine, Noel Leo. *King among the Theologians.* Cleveland, Ohio: Pilgrim Press, 1994.

Foucault, Michel. *Language, Counter-Memory, Practice: Selected Essays and Interviews.* Edited by Donald F. Bouchard. Ithaca, N.Y.: Cornell University Press, 1977.

———. "What Is an Author?" In Foucault, *Language, Counter-Memory, Practice,* 113–138.

Frye, Northrop. *The Great Code: The Bible and Literature.* 1981; reprint, San Diego: Harcourt Brace Jovanovich, 1983.

Fulop, Timothy E., and Albert J. Raboteau, eds. *African-American Religion: Interpretive Essays in History and Culture.* New York: Routledge, 1997.

Garrow, David J. *Bearing the Cross: Martin Luther King, Jr. and the Southern Christian Leadership Conference.* 1986; reprint, London: Vintage, 1993.

———. "Martin Luther King, Jr. and the Spirit of Leadership." In Albert and Hoffman, eds., *We Shall Overcome,* 11–34.

Genovese, Eugene D. *Roll, Jordan, Roll: The World the Slaves Made.* 1974; reprint, New York: Vintage Books, 1976.

Glazer, Nathan, and Daniel Moynihan. *Beyond the Melting Pot: The Negroes, Puerto Ricans, Jews, Italians, and Irish of New York City.* 1963; reprint, Cambridge, Mass.: MIT Press, 1970.

Goldhurst, Richard. "Gandhi and Christ in Montgomery." *Fellowship,* 1 March 1959, 28–29. King Papers, Boston University, Box 81, Folder V-55.

Grossberg, Lawrence, and Cary Nelson, eds. *Marxism and the Interpretation of Culture.* Urbana: University of Illinois Press, 1988.

Harding, Vincent. *Martin Luther King: The Inconvenient Hero.* Maryknoll, N.Y.: Orbis, 1996.

Hariman, Robert. "Time and Reconstitution of Gradualism in King's Address: A Response to Cox." In Leff and Kauffeld, *Texts in Context,* 205–217.

Harlan, Louis R. "Thoughts on the Leadership of Martin Luther King, Jr." In Albert and Hoffman, eds., *We Shall Overcome,* 59–68.

Harris, Herbert W., Howard C. Blue, and Ezra E. H. Griffith, eds. *Racial and Ethnic Identity: Psychological Development and Creative Expression.* New York: Routledge, 1995.

Jackson, Walter A. *Gunnar Myrdal and America's Conscience: Social Engineering and Racial Liberalism, 1938–1987.* Chapel Hill: University of North Carolina Press, 1990.

Kapur, Sudarshan. *Raising Up a Prophet: The African-American Encounter with Gandhi.* Boston: Beacon Press, 1992.

King, Martin Luther, Jr. *Strength to Love.* New York: Harper and Row, 1963.

———. *Stride toward Freedom: The Montgomery Story.* New York: Harper, 1958.

———. *The Trumpet of Conscience.* New York: Harper and Row, 1968.

———. *Where Do We Go from Here: Chaos or Community?* New York: Harper and Row, 1967.

———. *Why We Can't Wait.* New York: Harper and Row, 1964.

King, Richard H. *Civil Rights and the Idea of Freedom.* New York: Oxford University Press, 1992.

———. "Martin Luther King, Jr. and the Meaning of Freedom." In Albert and Hoffman, *We Shall Overcome,* 130–152.

Kramer, Hilton. *The Twilight of the Intellectuals: Culture and Politics in the Era of the Cold War.* Chicago: I. R. Dee, 1999.

Laclau, Ernesto, and Chantal Mouffe. *Hegemony and Socialist Strategy: Towards a Radical Democratic Politics.* 1985; reprint, London: Verso, 1998.

Lasch, Christopher. *The True and Only Heaven: Progress and Its Critics.* New York: Norton, 1991.

Leff, Michael C., and Fred J. Kauffeld. *Texts in Context: Dialogues on Significant Episodes in American Political Rhetoric.* Davis, Calif.: Hermagoras Press, 1989.

Levy, David W. *The Debate over Vietnam.* 1991; reprint, Baltimore: Johns Hopkins University Press, 1993.

Lincoln, C. Eric. "Black Religion and Racial Identity." In Harris, Blue, and Griffith, eds., *Racial and Ethnic Identity,* 209–221.

Lischer, Richard. *The Preacher King: Martin Luther King, Jr. and the Word That Moved America.* New York: Oxford University Press, 1995.

Lucaites, John Louis, and Carolyn Calloway-Thomas, eds. *Martin Luther King, Jr., and the Sermonic Power of Public Discourse.* Tuscaloosa: University of Alabama Press, 1993.

Lucaites, John Louis, and Celeste Michelle Condit. "Reconstructing <Equality>: Culturetypal and Counter-Cultural Rhetorics in the Martyred Black Vision." *Communication Monographs* 57 (March 1990): 2–24.

Malcolm X. *The Autobiography of Malcolm X.* With Alex Haley. New York: Grove Press, 1965.

Marable, Manning. *Race, Reform and Rebellion: The Second Reconstruction in Black America, 1945–1990.* 1983; reprint, Jackson: University Press of Mississippi, 1991.

Meier, August, and Elliott Rudwick. *From Plantation to Ghetto.* 1966; reprint, New York: Hill and Wang, 1976.

Miller, Keith D. *Voice of Deliverance: The Language of Martin Luther King, Jr. and Its Sources.* New York: Free Press, 1992.

Mitchell, Henry H. *Black Preaching: The Recovery of a Powerful Art.* Nashville, Tenn.: Abingdon Press, 1990.

Moses, Greg. *Revolution of Conscience: Martin Luther King, Jr. and the*

Philosophy of Nonviolence. New York: Guilford Press, 1997.

Omi, Michael, and Henry Winant. *Racial Formation in the United States from the 1960s to the 1990s.* 1986; reprint, New York: Routledge, 1994.

O'Reilly, Kenneth. *Racial Matters: The FBI's Secret File on Black America, 1960–1972.* 1989; reprint, New York: Free Press, 1991.

Ricoeur, Paul. *Lectures on Ideology and Utopia.* Edited by George H. Taylor. New York: Columbia University Press, 1986.

Said, Edward. *Orientalism.* New York: Pantheon Books, 1978.

Schilling, S. Paul. "Second Reader's Report." 1955. In *Papers*, 2: 334–335.

Smith, Ervin. *The Ethics of Martin Luther King, Jr.* New York: E. Mellen Press, 1981.

Smith, Kenneth L., and Ira G. Zepp. *Search for the Beloved Community: The Thinking of Martin Luther King, Jr.* 1974; reprint, Valley Forge, Pa.: Judson Press, 1998.

Stull, Bradford T. *Amid the Fall, Dreaming of Eden: Du Bois, King, Malcolm X, and Emancipatory Composition.* Carbondale, Ill.: Southern Illinois University Press, 1999.

Vaughn, Wally G., and Richard W. Wills, eds. *Reflections on Our Pastor: Dr. Martin Luther King, Jr. at Dexter Avenue Baptist Church, 1955–1960.* Dover, Mass.: Majority Press, 1999.

Walton, Hanes, Jr. *The Political Philosophy of Martin Luther King, Jr.* Westport, Conn.: Greenwood Press, 1971.

Washington, James Melvin, ed. *A Testament of Hope: The Essential Writings and Speeches of Martin Luther King, Jr.* 1986; reprint, San Francisco: HarperSanFrancisco, 1991.

———. *I Have a Dream: Writings and Speeches That Changed the World.* San Francisco: HarperSanFrancisco, 1992.

West, Cornel. "Marxist Theory and the Specificity of Afro-American Oppression." In Grossberg and Nelson, eds., *Marxism and the Interpretation of Culture*, 17–29.

Young, Andrew. *An Easy Burden: The Civil Rights Movement and the Transformation of America.* New York: HarperCollins, 1996.

SERMONS AND SPEECHES
BY MARTIN LUTHER KING, JR.

"Acceptance Speech for Nobel Peace Prize." December 10, 1964. Oslo, Norway. In *A Call to Conscience*, 105–109.

"An Address before the National Press Club." July 19, 1962. Washington, D.C. In *A Testament of Hope*, 99–105.

"America's Chief Moral Dilemma." July 6, 1965. Chicago, Illinois. Unpublished. King Library and Archives.

"The American Dream." June 6, 1961. Lincoln University, Pennsylvania. In *A Testament of Hope*, 208–216.

"The American Dream." July 4, 1965. Atlanta, Georgia. In *A Knock at Midnight*, 85–100.

"Answer to a Perplexing Question." March 3, 1963. Atlanta, Georgia. Unpublished. King Library and Archives.

"Beyond Vietnam." April 4, 1967. New York. In *A Call to Conscience*, 139–164.

"Birmingham Negroes' Plea for Freedom." October 22, 1963. Birmingham, Alabama. Unpublished. King Library and Archives.

"The Birth of a New Nation." April 7, 1957. Montgomery, Alabama. In *Papers*, 4: 155–167.

"A Christmas Sermon on Peace." December 24, 1967. Atlanta, Georgia/Canadian Broadcasting Corporation. In *The Trumpet of Conscience*, 65–78.

"The Church on the Frontier of Racial Tension." April 19, 1961. Louisville, Kentucky. Unpublished. King Library and Archives.

"Conscience and the Vietnam War." November–December 1967. Canadian Broadcasting Corporation. In *The Trumpet of Conscience*, 21–34.

"Drum Major Instinct." February 4, 1968. Atlanta, Georgia. In *A Knock at Midnight*, 196–186.

"The Ethical Demands for Integration." December 27, 1962. Nashville, Tennessee. In *A Testament of Hope*, 115–125.

"Facing the Challenge of a New Age." December 3, 1956. Montgomery, Alabama. In *Papers*, 3: 451–463.

"Facing the Challenge of a New Age." January 1, 1957. Atlanta, Georgia. In *Papers*, 4: 73–89.

"Guidelines for a Constructive Church." June 5, 1966. Atlanta, Georgia. In *A Knock at Midnight*, 105–115.

"I Have a Dream." August 28, 1963. Washington, D.C. In *A Call to Conscience*, 81–87.

"Impasse in Race Relations." November–December 1967. Canadian Broadcasting Corporation. In *The Trumpet of Conscience*, 3–17.

"Is the Universe Friendly?" December 12, 1965. Atlanta, Georgia. Unpublished. King Library and Archives.

"I've Been to the Mountaintop." April 2, 1968. Memphis, Tennessee. In *A Call to Conscience*, 207–223.

"A Knock at Midnight." August 9, 1964. New York. Unpublished. King Library and Archives.

"Lazarus and Dives." March 10, 1963. Atlanta, Georgia. Unpublished. King Library and Archives.

"Love, Law and Civil Disobedience." November 16, 1961. Atlanta, Georgia. In *A Testament of Hope*, 43–53.

"Loving Your Enemies." November 17, 1957. Montgomery, Alabama. In *Papers*, 4: 315–324.

"MIA Mass Meeting at Holt Street Baptist Church." December 5, 1955. Montgomery, Alabama. In *Papers*, 3: 71–79.

"MIA Mass Meeting at Holt Street Baptist Church." November 14, 1956. In *Papers*, 3: 424–433.

"The Montgomery Story." June 27, 1956. San Francisco, California. In *Papers*, 3: 299–310.

"Nonviolence and Social Change." November–December 1967. Canadian Broadcasting Corporation. In *The Trumpet of Conscience*, 51–64.

"Paul's Letter to American Christians." November 4, 1956. Montgomery, Alabama. In *Papers*, 3: 414–420.

"The Power of Nonviolence." June 4, 1957. Berkeley, California. In *A Testament of Hope*, 12–15.

"Rediscovering Lost Values." February 28, 1954. Detroit, Michigan. In *Papers*, 2: 248–256.

"Remaining Awake Through a Great Revolution." March 31, 1968. Washington, D.C. In *A Knock at Midnight*, 205–224.

"The Role of the Church in Facing the Nation's Chief Moral Dilemma." April 25, 1957. Nashville, Tennessee. In *Papers*, 4: 184–191.

"Sermon on Gandhi." March 22, 1959. Montgomery, Alabama. Unpublished. King Library and Archives.

"Some Things We Must Do." December 5, 1957. Montgomery, Alabama. In *Papers*, 4: 328–343.

"Speech Regarding the Influence of African Movements on U.S. Students." May 1962. Location unknown. Unpublished. King Library and Archives.

"Three Dimensions of a Complete Life." April 9, 1967. Chicago, Illinois. In *A Knock at Midnight*, 121–140.

"What Is Man?" January 12, 1958. Chicago, Illinois. Unpublished. King Papers, Boston University, Box 2, Folder I-2.

"When Peace Becomes Obnoxious." March 18, 1956. Montgomery, Alabama. *Papers*, 3: 207–208.

"Where Do We Go from Here?" August 16, 1967. Atlanta, Georgia. In *A Call to Conscience*, 171–199.

Articles, Essays, Written Sermons, and Various Documents by Martin Luther King, Jr.

"Answer to a Perplexing Question." 1963. In *Strength to Love*, 118–126.

"Antidotes for Fear." 1963. In *Strength to Love*, 108–117.

"Autobiography of Religious Development." 1950. In *Papers*, 1: 359–363.

"A Comparison of the Concepts of God in the Thinking of Paul Tillich and Henry Nelson Wieman." 1955. In *Papers*, 2: 339–544.

"Examination Answers, History of Recent Philosophy." 1952. In *Papers*, 2: 152–155.

"An Exposition of the First Triad of Categories in the Hegelian Logic—Being, Non-Being, Becoming." 1953. In *Papers*, 2: 196–201.

"How Should a Christian View Communism?" 1963. In *Strength to Love,*
    93–100.

"A Knock at Midnight." 1963. In *Strength to Love,* 42–50.

"Letter from Birmingham Jail." 1963. In *Why We Can't Wait,* 76–95.

"Love in Action." 1963. In *Strength to Love,* 25–33.

"Loving Your Enemies." 1963. In *Strength to Love,* 34–41.

"My Trip to the Land of Gandhi." In *A Testament of Hope,* 23–30 (origi-
    nally in *Ebony,* July 1959, 84–86, 88–90, and 92.)

"The New Negro of the South." In *Papers,* 3: 280–286 (originally in
    Socialist Call 24 [June 1956]: 16–19).

"Next Stop: The North." In *A Testament of Hope,* 189–194 (originally
    in *Saturday Review,* 13 November 1965, 33–35 and 105).

"Nonviolence: The Only Road to Freedom." In *A Testament of Hope,*
    54–61 (originally in *Ebony* 21 [October 1966]: 27–30).

"Our God Is Able." 1963. In *Strength to Love,* 101–107.

"Our Struggle." In *A Testament of Hope,* 75–81 (originally in *Libera-
    tion* 1 [April 1956]: 3–6).

"Paul's Letter to American Christians." 1963. In *Strength to Love,* 127–
    134.

"Pilgrimage to Nonviolence." 1958. In *Stride toward Freedom,* 90–107.

"Pilgrimage to Nonviolence." In *A Testament of Hope,* 35–40 (origi-
    nally in *Christian Century* 77 [27 April 1960]: 510).

"Pilgrimage to Nonviolence." 1963. In *Strength to Love,* 135–145.

"Qualification Examination Answers, History of Philosophy." 1954. In
    Papers, 2: 242–247.

"Recommendations to the Dexter Avenue Baptist Church for the Fiscal
    Year 1954–1955." 1954. In *Papers,* 2: 287–294.

"The Rising Tide of Racial Consciousness." In *A Testament of Hope,*
    145–151 (originally in *YMCA Magazine,* December 1960, 4–6).

"Ritual." 1946–1948. In *Papers,* 1: 127–142.

"A Testament of Hope." In *A Testament of Hope,* 313–328 (originally in
    Playboy 16 [January 1969]: 175ff.).

"The Time for Freedom Has Come." In *A Testament of Hope,* 160–166
    (originally in *New York Times Magazine,* 10 September 1961,
    25ff.).

"What Is Man?" 1963. In *Strength to Love,* 87–92.

INDEX

*Fredrik Sunnemark received his Ph.D. in the
History of Ideas from Gothenburg University, Sweden,
and is now Senior Lecturer in Cultural Studies at
University Trollhättan-Uddevalla, Sweden.*